THE EMERGENCE OF THE FEDERAL
CONCEPT IN CANADA, 1839–1845

CANADIAN STUDIES IN HISTORY AND GOVERNMENT

A series of studies edited by Goldwin French, sponsored by the Social Science Research Council of Canada, and published with financial assistance from the Canada Council.

The Emergence
of the Federal Concept
in Canada

1839-1845

WILLIAM ORMSBY

Brock University

UNIVERSITY OF TORONTO PRESS

PREFACE

THE IDEAS PRESENTED in this study grew out of continuing informal discussions over a number of years with my former colleagues at the Public Archives of Canada and with scholars whose research brought them to Ottawa. It is impossible to mention all of them by name but I should like to record my gratitude to them. The assistance and kindness of Dr. G. W. Spragge, formerly Archivist of Ontario, and Miss Edith Firth, custodian of manuscripts at the Toronto Public Library, greatly facilitated my research at their institutions.

When this work was being written in its original form for presentation as a master's thesis at Carleton University, the direction, criticism, and advice of Dean D. M. L. Farr was most helpful and was sincerely appreciated. I am indebted to Professor S. R. Mealing of Carleton University, Professor J. S. Moir of Scarborough College and the University of Toronto, and Professor S. F. Wise, formerly of Queen's University and now Director of the Canadian Armed Forces Historical Section, for valuable suggestions which led me to increase the depth and expand the scope of the study. I wish to thank Miss Ann Liddell of the University of Toronto Press for her careful editorial work which has improved my prose and saved me a number of errors and inconsistencies.

I am happy to acknowledge a grant in aid of publication made by the Social Science Research Council from funds provided by the Canada Council. Finally, I should like to pay a special tribute to my wife for her unfailing assistance at every stage of the work. It is most fitting that this book should be dedicated to her.

W.O.

FOR ELIZABETH

CONTENTS

THE EMERGENCE OF THE FEDERAL
CONCEPT IN CANADA, 1839–1845

INTRODUCTION

IT HAS BECOME TRADITIONAL to regard the 1840's as the "responsible government" decade in Canadian history. While this emphasis on constitutional development is no doubt warranted, it has tended to obscure the fact that it was during these same years that the federal implications of the Canadian situation began to be recognized. The continued existence of two distinct cultures within the Province of Canada demanded the development of some guarantee for the peculiar interests and values of each group. In short, the survival of French Canada, despite the deliberate attempt to overwhelm it in a union of the two Canadas, demanded the emergence of a federal concept.

After the American Revolution the Imperial government was confronted with the problem of two races dwelling, though not yet warring, in the bosom of a single state. In an effort to avoid friction, the old province of Quebec was divided along roughly racial lines to form the provinces of Upper and Lower Canada. As a solution for a potential ethnological and social problem the division had much to recommend it, but it created more problems than it solved. It ignored the basic economic unity of the commercial empire of the St. Lawrence, and it also ignored the problem of the English-speaking minority left in Lower Canada. The division left the new province of Upper Canada without an ocean port and paved the way for perpetual disagreement with the lower province over the division of customs revenue. Equally important was the fact that Upper Canada had not sufficient economic strength to finance the development of canals which were necessary for a realization of its full potential. Economic and geographic factors strongly suggested a re-union of the two provinces and the attempted union of 1822 was primarily a response to these forces.

If there were economic and geographic arguments for unity, the ethnological and cultural factors in favour of separation remained, and it was the latter which triumphed to defeat the projected union in 1822. A two-way pull for and against union had created a deadlock, but there were two possible solutions. Either a federal arrangement could be worked out to satisfy the economic demands for unity, or the assimilation of French Canada could make possible a complete legislative union. Although the Imperial government undoubtedly hoped that assimilation would gradually take place, there was no serious thought of deliberate anglicization until the rebellions occurred. It is quite possible that but for the rebellions some form of federal union would have been effected before 1850. Indeed, the arrangement for the division of customs revenue under the Canada Trade Act may be regarded as an elementary form of federalism.

The Lower Canadian rebellions convinced Lord Durham that, if the connection with the mother country was to be maintained, the province would have to be made thoroughly British in character, and he recommended a legislative union with Upper Canada as the means to achieve that end. His conviction that there was no future for French Canada as a separate cultural entity led him to assume that the objective of total assimilation could be attained by a gradual process once the union had taken place and favourable circumstances had been created. Convinced that assimilation would be to the ultimate advantage of French Canada, Durham completely underestimated the strength and vitality of the culture he sought to eradicate. He had no concept of the French Canadian's deep personal pride in his family and his race, or of his strong attachment to his own way of life symbolized by the language, laws, and religion he had inherited.

When the Imperial government accepted Durham's recommendation in favour of union, it also adopted the false premise on which it was based. It was not expected that French Canada would welcome the union, or that assimilation would take place overnight, but no serious resistance to the process was anticipated.

The primary justification for a legislative rather than a federal union was the double assumption that the assimilation of French Canada was possible and that it was essential for the maintenance of the British connection. Within five years of the union's inception, however, the British government was forced to abandon the unrealistic objective of assimilation and to recognize the fact of French Canada's survival as a separate entity.

A corollary of *la survivance* was the emergence of a federal concept—a recognition that each section of the province was in fact a separate cultural unit with peculiar values and interests of its own. The concept first began to emerge with the entry of LaFontaine into Bagot's Executive Council as the recognized leader of French Canada, but its full significance did not become apparent until the policy of deliberate assimilation was abandoned under Metcalfe. Although the union was designed as an instrument of assimilation, it contained several features which lent themselves to the expression of dualism and which then gave the government of the province a quasi-federal character. Equal representation, hyphenated ministries, the balancing of Executive Council appointments between French and English, and the rotation of the capital between Toronto and Quebec after 1849 all contributed to the growth of the federal concept.

English-speaking historians who have written on the union period have tended to concentrate on the theme of responsible government and either to ignore the question of French-Canadian survival or to treat it as a minor factor in their colony-to-nation thesis. As leaders of the nationalist school of French-Canadian historians, Guy Frégault, Maurice Séguin, and Michel Brunet have claimed, within recent years, that French-Canadian society was deprived of its mercantile bourgeoisie at the conquest and thus, although total assimilation did not take place, the culture of French Canada was capable of only a wretched half-survival. For them, French Canada did not achieve an ultimate victory in the union, responsible government was of little consequence, and *la survivance* is more myth than reality. Many other French-Canadian historians have interpreted *la survivance* as a positive achievement, but it is seen as being necessarily dependent upon the alliance of Baldwin and LaFontaine and the attainment of responsible government.

In the present work an attempt is made to present a new interpretation. It is suggested that the two questions—responsible government and assimilation—may be profitably considered as two parallel themes which merge only occasionally. Certainly the two questions were regarded as distinct and separate by the Imperial government and the governors whom they sent to Canada. It is suggested that with this new perspective it may be more readily recognized that the emergence of a federal concept owed less to the force of the responsible government movement than has been generally assumed. The primary contention of this study is that assimilation was an impossible objective for the union, and that this fact was brought home to Lord Stanley and his colleagues in the Imperial Government by the combined effect of equal representation and Lord John Russell's dictum that the Executive must be in harmony with the Assembly. The abandonment of the policy of assimilation was due to the recognized necessity of adhering to these two principles rather than to the full theory of collective responsibility as expounded by Baldwin and LaFontaine.

CHAPTER ONE

THE ROOTS OF UNION

WHEN LORD DURHAM RECOMMENDED a legislative union of Upper and Lower Canada in 1839, he was not suggesting a new solution for Canadian problems. The idea of such a union had long been predominant in the minds of Canadian merchants who thought in terms of the commercial unity of the St. Lawrence River system, and it had been considered on several occasions by the British government. Once, in 1822, a union bill had even been introduced in the House of Commons, but with results which only discouraged any further attempts. Legislative union implied a positive policy for the rapid assimilation of French Canada, and such a measure was certain to encounter vigorous opposition in Parliament unless it could be shown that union was essential on political grounds and not merely desirable for economic reasons. A brief review of the development of the union concept and a more detailed examination of the process by which Lord Durham came to endorse a legislative union will help to place his recommendation in the proper perspective.

The division of the old province of Quebec in 1791 was an attempt to provide a solution for the problem created by the presence of two distinct cultures within a single geographic unit. A perfect solution may have been impossible—certainly the arrangement of 1791 had prominent defects. A boundary line drawn to separate the two cultures unavoidably deprived Upper Canada of an ocean port. It might have been assumed that the partition was based upon a recognition that the two cultures would continue to exist side by side. Yet William Pitt, speaking in the House of Commons, sanguinely predicted that the division would result in the assimilation of French-Canadian culture. Upper Canada, he anticipated, would provide such a splendid example of the superiority of English laws and institutions that Lower Canada would eagerly renounce the old laws and customs to emulate her progressive neighbour.

Pitt's prediction is indicative of a fundamental error made by many British statesmen including Lord Durham. So confident were they of the superiority of British government and British culture that they could not conceive of French Canada's deliberately resisting the forces of natural assimilation implicit in the arrival of English-speaking settlers. When the French Canadians revealed a tendency to use their numerical superiority in the Lower Canadian Assembly to protect their way of life, the British reaction was one of astonishment which soon dissolved into more bitter feelings.

In 1791 a version of the British constitution, with adjustments designed to strengthen the executive branch of government, was given to Lower Canada. The experiment was doomed to fail, for the underlying harmony of interests that was generally recognized as essential to the working of the British constitution was lacking in Lower Canada. The Constitutional Act was based on the false assumption that, although two distinct cultural entities inhabited the province, there would be little conflict between their particular interests. In actual practice, the French refused to accept the fact that the conquest had taken place, and the British proved reluctant to recognize that the French held different cultural values. It was natural that French Canada should resent and oppose any measure designed to accelerate the development and settlement of the province. Such measures could only be regarded as anglicization in disguise. Extensive immigration would result in the submergence of French-Canadian culture. While one can understand the attitude of French Canada, it is also possible to appreciate the point of view adopted by the English-speaking population of Lower Canada. It seemed unreasonable that French Canadians should expect to bar the door to progress, to arrest the development of the country's resources, and to discourage British immigration. From the beginning, Lower Canada contained the basic elements of a storm that would eventually overturn the constitutional arrangement of 1791.

In 1810, after clashing with the Assembly, Sir James Craig considered it necessary to recommend the abolition of "the representative part of government" in Lower Canada. His long despatch of May 1, 1810, discussed the attitude of French Canada in general, and the deficiencies of the Assembly in particular, in an attempt to show that there was a complete lack of any harmony of interests in the province. Craig noted that the re-union of Upper and Lower Canada was generally favoured as a solution by the English-speaking population of the latter province, but he feared such a union would produce "a heterogeneous mixture of opposite principles and different interests from which no good could be expected." He preferred to keep Upper Canada as "a foreign and distinct population" which could be used against French Canada should the need arise.

If the British Government should consider the abolition of the Lower Canadian Assembly inexpedient, Craig expressed some hope that an alternative solution might be found by establishing the Eastern Townships as new counties and thus increasing English-speaking representation. Such a measure, he proposed, should be coupled with an increase in the qualification for members sufficient to prevent the control of the Assembly remaining in the hands of "six petty shopkeepers, a Blacksmith, a Miller, and 15 ignorant peasants . . ., a Doctor or Apothecary, [and] twelve Canadian Avocats, and Notaries. . . ." He also urged that the authority of the Crown over the Roman Catholic Bishop and its right of nomination to appointments in the Church should be strongly asserted.'

Craig's recommendations were discussed at length by the Imperial Government, but they were unwilling to consider seriously any modification of the Lower Canadian constitution. Lord Liverpool assured Craig that he and his colleagues were "fully convinced of the evils which have arisen from the Act of 1791, and of the absurdity of giving what is falsely called the British constitution to a people whose education, habits and prejudices render them incapable of receiving it," but, he added, the evil had been done and it would not be easy to retrace steps that had been taken. The immediate objective must be "to make the best use we can of the instrument which has been put into our hands, but above all we must avoid tampering with it." If Parliament was to be called upon to repeal or alter the Lower Canadian constitution, it could only be when the Government could produce "a case far stronger, and very different in its nature, than that which we could bring at present under their consideration."[2]

The horrible example of the American Revolution made the Government extremely reluctant to bring colonial constitutional questions before Parliament. They were equally determined to keep the question of the Roman Catholic Church out of politics, and thus could not look with favour on Craig's proposal that the royal supremacy should be asserted over the Church in Lower Canada. No government would have been likely to have adopted a thorough revision of colonial policy, such as Craig advocated, at a crucial point in the war with France—for the weak Perceval Ministry, fraught with internal friction, it was entirely out of the question.

Craig's secretary, Herman Witsius Ryland, had gone to England to urge action on the Governor's recommendations. On August 17, 1810, he reported, "I plainly perceive that this Ministry is weak, very weak, that they are sensible of the utility and even necessity of the measures you have proposed, and at the same time are afraid to bring them forward lest they should be taken advantage of in Parliament by the opposition."[3] Ryland had come out to Canada in 1793 as Lord Dorchester's secretary and had continued to serve as civil secretary for each successive governor. He soon identified himself with the English-speaking minority and sought to promote the complete anglicization of Lower Canada. It was a bitter disappointment for him to discover that, despite Craig's recommendations and his own arguments, no positive steps were to be taken towards the attainment of his objective.

It was not until 1822 that the Imperial Government ventured to bring in a bill to unite Upper and Lower Canada. A more propitious moment could scarcely have been chosen. In Lower Canada the contest for control of the purse had developed into a bitter conflict between the Governor and the Assembly, and, at the same time, Upper Canada was clamouring for a fair share of the customs revenue collected at Montreal. From the imperial point of view union appeared to be a logical solution for both problems.

The initiative for the attempted union of 1822 came from Edward Ellice who, the year before, had played a prominent part in arranging the amalgamation of the Hudson's Bay and the North West Companies. Acting on advice received from business associates in Lower Canada, Ellice persuaded the Colonial Under-Secretary, Wilmot Horton, that a legislative union of the two Canadas could be carried in the House of Commons without difficulty. Charles Marshall and John Caldwell, two members of the Lower Canadian Executive Council who were in England at the time, were called upon to assist in the preparation of a plan for union, and John Beverley Robinson was added as a fifth member of this informal committee. Robinson had come to England to press Upper Canada's claims for a larger share of the customs revenue collected at Montreal. He was a natural choice for such a mission. The son of a half-pay officer in the Queen's Rangers, he had received his education from John Strachan who henceforth took an active personal interest in his advancement. After serving in the War of 1812, he was appointed Solicitor General. In 1822, although he was still only thirty-one, Robinson had been Attorney General for four years and was regarded by his fellow Tories as one of the most perceptive of their number. It was with considerable reluctance that he agreed to advise on a measure which, instinctively, he felt might be against the best interests of both his party and his province.'

Despite their combined efforts, the five men did not succeed in obtaining the union they had projected. Failure was due in the first instance to unexpected opposition led by Sir James Mackintosh, a vigorous champion of more extensive self-government for the colonies since his election to the House of Commons in 1813, and secondly to the outcry raised in the Canadas. The Imperial Government was still hesitant about coming to grips with colonial problems and had only agreed to take up the measure upon the positive understanding that it would receive virtually unanimous support in Parliament. When the case proved otherwise, and strong opposition developed in the Canadas, the idea of union was deferred.' In 1828, after an adverse report by a Select Committee of Parliament, it appeared to have been abandoned entirely.'

Although the union movement of the 1820's was abortive, it did serve to outline the issues involved and to clarify men's thoughts upon the subject. A bill was introduced that not only indicated the objectives of the unionists, but also provided a centre of focus for the criticism of their opponents. The union bill of 1822, which Robinson considered to be "as favourable as I could succeed in obtaining,'" provided for a legislative union only. The executive in each province was to remain unchanged. The assemblies and legislative councils were to be combined to form a united legislature which would continue until July 1, 1825, unless dissolved earlier by the governor. The Upper Canadian provision for increased representation, passed in 1820, was to remain in force until both provinces had sixty members in the assembly. After this stage was reached, a two-thirds majority in both houses would be required for any alteration in the basis of representation. The duration of Parliament was extended from four to five years. Two provisions, advocated by Chief Justice Jonathan Sewell of Lower Canada as early as 1810, were also incorporated in the bill: a property qualification of £500 was established for election to the assembly, and the governor's sanction was required for all appointments of Roman Catholic clergy. In an attempt to provide spokesmen for the executive in the assembly, the bill authorized the governor to appoint two members of the executive council to participate in the assembly debates. The forced assimilation of French Canadians was contemplated in a clause which decreed that all written proceedings were to be in English and that after a period of fifteen years English was also to be the language of debate.

For French Canadians the union bill spelled out the threat to their national existence which they had feared was implicit in all immigration and development projects. With Papineau at their head, they quickly and vigorously proclaimed their opposition to the measure. Although John Beverley Robinson agreed that the terms were exceedingly favourable to Upper Canada, he feared that, under constant and violent attack from Lower Canada, they would be modified until the position of the upper province would be equated with that of the Eastern Townships. A united legislature with a majority of Lower Canadians would regard the representatives of Upper Canada as "Yankeys or Indian Traders.'" Moreover, he predicted that such a union would place the democratic, republican element in the ascendancy: "90 obstinate people instead of 40 or 50—all be it remembered caring as little for the feelings & convenience of the Executive, & as independent of their control as if they came from Kentucky" could present a genuine problem.' In a larger assembly "the influence of a near acquaintance, family connexions and private friendships" would be drastically reduced. Robinson's opinion was soon reinforced by the opposition of John Macaulay, the Reverend Dr. Strachan, and nearly all the leading Tories of Upper Canada. To Robinson's objections Strachan added the protest that the projected union would place the Church of England at the mercy of a legislature dominated by Roman Catholics and sectaries.[10] Both Strachan and Robinson advocated a union of all the British North American colonies as a much more satisfactory alternative.

Although petitions in favour of union came from such widely divergent points in Upper Canada as Kingston and Niagara, Upper Canadian support for the measure was neither very strong nor very clearly defined. The Canada Trade Act of 1822 appeared to present a solution to the problem of dividing the customs revenue: one-fifth of the revenue collected at Quebec was allocated to Upper Canada and provision was made for a readjustment of the proportion every three years. While the trade clauses were part of the union bill many Upper Canadians, including Robinson, had been prepared to swallow the pill in order to have the sugar coating. But when the Trade Act was passed alone, there seemed to be no need to take the bitter medicine. The strongest and most influential support for the union came from the mercantile element centred in Montreal. In 1791 Adam Lymburner, as the representative of this group, had argued against the division of the old province of Quebec before the bar of the House of Commons. Economically and geographically the merchants had a strong argument. There was no denying the geographic unity of the Canadas, and the dream of a commercial empire of the St. Lawrence was certainly a stirring vision. But Lymburner's mission failed because policy was being determined by what were thought to be the political, sociological, and cultural factors involved. By the 1820's English settlement in the Eastern Townships and the recalcitrant attitude of the French-Canadian members of the Assembly enabled the merchants to introduce new elements into their argument. A petition from the Eastern Townships declared that Great Britain was faced with the decision "either by uniting the Provinces to hold out inducements to the French to become English, or by continuing the separation to hold out inducements to the English in Lower Canada to become French."[11] Undoubtedly the merchants' case was much stronger in 1822 than it had been in 1791, but it was not strong enough to induce an uncertain Government to proceed without the unanimous support of Parliament and the acquiescence of the colonists concerned.

II

After 1828, as it became clear that the Canada Trade Act was not a perfect solution to the customs problem, many Upper Canadian Tories began to think in terms of the annexation of Montreal Island. Coupled with the desire to acquire Montreal was a recurring fear that the project of union would be revived as the ideal solution for the increasing political difficulties in Lower Canada. In the autumn of 1836 Lieutenant-Governor Sir Francis Bond Head, a staunch ally of the Tories, advised the Colonial Secretary, Lord Glenelg: "My humble but deliberate Opinion of this Project [union] is, that it would produce the Effect of separating both the Canadas from the Parent State, on the homely Principle that if tainted and fresh Meat be attached together both are corrupted."[12] He was afraid that in a united assembly the supporters of British institutions would find themselves overpowered, not by the "good Sense and Wealth of the Country, . . . but by the Votes of designing Individuals, misrepresenting a well-meaning inoffensive People." There was, Head insisted, no "moral affinity" between the inhabitants of the two provinces. Upper Canadians were commercial and enterprising while French Canadians were anti-commercial and quiet. In a rather unconvincing manner he introduced economic and geographic factors to support his anti-union thesis. The interests of the two provinces would be constantly at variance, so different was their climate, soil, and geography. Upper Canada, with a fresh-water frontier shared by the United States, would require railroads and markets which it might be against the interests of Lower Canada to promote. The vast extent of the territory involved would render government difficult, if not impossible, and, in addition, the increased power, importance, and influence which a united province would acquire would lead to separation from the Empire.

Head considered two other solutions for the Lower Canadian problem. Theoretically, it would be possible to overcome the French-Canadian preponderance by a concentrated immigration programme, but he felt that such a policy would be doomed to failure by the severity of the Lower Canadian climate. Instead, he advocated a four-point policy designed to set up distinct cultural areas and to confine French-Canadian influence both politically and geographically. The Ripon Act,[12] which placed the proceeds of the Quebec Revenue Act at the disposal of the Canadian legislatures, should be repealed, Gaspé should be annexed to New Brunswick, and Montreal to Upper Canada. In addition, the north bank of the Ottawa River should be made the boundary between Upper and Lower Canada. Upper Canada would be forever dependent upon Great Britain for protection from the United States, and thus an increase in the province's size and prosperity need not cause any uneasiness.

On December 2, 1836, the possibility that the British Government might consider the union of the Canadas to be an expedient solution for Lower Canadian problems was brought to the attention of members of the Upper Canadian Assembly by one of the bright young men in the Tory party, William Henry Draper. Draper had attracted the favourable attention of Tory leaders while serving in the law office of John Beverley Robinson, and recently, at the age of thirty-five, he had been elected to represent York (Toronto) in Sir Francis Bond Head's "bread and butter" election. Within a few years he would emerge as the leader of the moderate wing of the party, but for the moment he was expressing High Tory sentiments when he gave notice of his intention to introduce a series of resolutions that would serve as the basis for an anti-union address to the King.[14]

The Assembly did not find time to turn to the question of union until late in the session, after the date of prorogation had been announced (and then extended), and many members had already left for their homes. On March 3, 1837, an address was passed, by a vote of fifteen to eleven, expressing apprehension that "a mistaken view of the condition and interests of the people of Upper and Lower Canada, may prompt some persons inconsiderately to press upon Your Majesty's Government the measure of uniting these provinces as a remedy for existing evils."[15] After recognizing the desire of the English-speaking minority in Lower Canada for union, the address concluded with the earnest hope that the King would consider the "political condition of 400,000 of Your Majesty's Subjects" and not "suffer a doubtful experiment to be hazarded, which may be attended with consequences most detrimental to their peace, and injurious to the best interests of themselves and their posterity."

The vote on the address revealed divisions in the ranks of both Tories and Reformers. Eleven Tories voted in favour of the address while four, including Allan MacNab, were opposed to it. Five Reformers opposed the protest against union and three supported it. Of the remaining three members, whose political affiliations are uncertain, one voted for the address and two opposed it.[16] In a rather general way the vote reflected the fears concerning union which Tory leaders had held since 1822 and, perhaps also, an awareness on the part of some Reformers that union would greatly increase their strength if they could form an alliance with the French party in Lower Canada. But there were members in both parties who held reservations and misgivings on either side of the question. Some, such as Allan MacNab, may also have been motivated by economic interests. The vote was probably also influenced by the fact that some members were reluctant to see such an important question decided late in the session by a thin House. Attempts were made both by the prominent Tory, Allan MacNab, and by one of the Reform leaders, John Rolph, to carry amendments postponing a decision because of the lateness of the session. MacNab's amendment was supported by nine Tories and eight Reformers and was defeated by only two votes.[17]

A geographical analysis of the vote on the address shows that support for, and opposition to, the idea of union were fairly evenly distributed across the province. Of the ten members residing east of the Trent River who voted on the question, six supported the anti-union address and four opposed it. Nine members from west of the Trent favoured the address, but seven were opposed to it.

On March 4, 1837, the day after the address was approved by the Assembly, the Legislative Council concurred in it and thus it became a joint address. Divisions are not recorded in the journals of the upper house, but it is entirely unlikely that it was adopted unanimously.

When a new session of the Legislature opened in the early summer of 1837, Lieutenant-Governor Sir Francis Bond Head was pleased to be able to inform the members of the reply received from Lord Glenelg, the Colonial Secretary, in response to the joint address. Apparently the fears expressed during the previous session were groundless, for Lord Glenelg had written that union "has not been contemplated by His Majesty as fit to be recommended for the sanction of Parliament."[18]

In the interval between sessions, the Reformers had aligned themselves almost solidly behind the idea of union and they were anxious to undermine any effect the address might have had either in the Canadas or in Great Britain. A motion was introduced requesting the Lieutenant-Governor to inform the Assembly on what authority he had forwarded the address to England. (Through an oversight the request that he should do so had not been passed.) On June 29 John Rolph, who was soon to become involved in the Upper Canadian rebellion and be forced to flee to the United States, followed up the initial attack by moving, "That the Union of the Provinces of Upper and Lower Canada, upon just principles, would be conducive to the interests of both."[19] The question of union was now placed squarely before the members.

Rolph's motion was defeated twenty-seven to seventeen by what amounted to almost a straight party vote with twenty-one Tories, one Reformer, one Independent, and four whose political affiliations have not been determined voting in the negative. Fifteen Reformers and two Tories supported the motion. On a geographical basis, Rolph was supported by seven members residing east of the Trent River and ten members west of it. Sixteen of the members opposed to union were from constituencies west of the river and eleven resided east of it. William Hamilton Merritt, whose interest in the Welland Canal and improvements to navigation facilities in the St. Lawrence River might have been expected to lead him to support the union, voted, instead, with the Tories as he had done consistently hitherto. For the present, at least, it was clear that the Tories were opposed to union and the Reformers favoured it. Personal, economic, and geographic considerations had not swayed many members from their party allegiance.

As the political situation in Lower Canada continued to deteriorate throughout the winter of 1836–1837, it became increasingly clear to the British Government that some policy decisions would have to be made. For many years an attempt had been made, through a series of concessions, to obtain the grant of a permanent civil list from the Lower Canadian Legislature. By the spring of 1837, there was general agreement that the policy of conciliation must end. Lord Glenelg had proposed a limited federal arrangement for British North America and a possible division of Lower Canada into Canada North and Canada South as a final step before rigorous action was taken against the Assembly in Lower Canada, but his suggestion was rejected in favour of sterner measures.[20] The authority of Parliament would be invoked to take what would not be granted voluntarily. On March 6, 1837, Lord John Russell introduced his well-known Ten Resolutions which authorized the Governor of Lower Canada to defray the cost of civil government from the consolidated revenue without the sanction of the Legislature. As the debate progressed, the Radicals, led by J. A. Roebuck and J. T. Leader, proposed that the Lower Canadian demand for an elective legislative council should be met. Roebuck had spent part of his youth in Lower Canada and had received his education there. He was first elected to the House of Commons in 1832 as a supporter of parliamentary reform, and three years later he undertook to represent the interests of the Lower Canadian Assembly in England as its agent. In this capacity he sought to obtain a favourable hearing for the Assembly's views in the Commons.

Although there was general support in the Cabinet for the policy embodied in the Ten Resolutions, Lord Howick was inclined to waver. As Under-Secretary for the Colonies from 1830 to 1833 in the reform administration of his father, the Second Earl Grey, Lord Howick had acquired an active interest in colonial affairs. He was convinced that continued conciliation, rather than coercion, was the only solution for the problems presented by the Canadas. Ten years hence he was to put this philosophy into practice as he presided over the Colonial Office during the period in which responsible government was introduced in British North America. ". . . The more I consider the subject," Howick wrote to Russell on March 30, 1837, "the stronger is my convictn that we ought to endeavour to come to some arrangement upon the basis proposed by Roebuck so as to avoid the necessity of carrying through our measure in the face of his oppositn."[21] It was not that he apprehended any serious difficulty as a result of Roebuck's opposition, but he firmly believed that "no permanent good can be done in Canada except by effecting an accommodatn with the Assembly." In his opinion there would never be a better opportunity of attaining such an accommodation. He suggested that an attempt should be made to induce Roebuck to propose "such a measure as we can approve." If this policy were successful the Lower Canadian Assembly would find it very difficult to refuse to accept the measure. ". . . Besides," Howick continued, "it is the obvious interest both of Roebuck himself & of those whom he represents that the present differences in Canada shd. not be driven to extremities." Russell refused to make any concessions to Roebuck, and Howick was obliged reluctantly to "submit to what seems to be inevitable."[22]

When Roebuck found that an elective legislative council was out of the question, he came forward with an entirely new set of proposals. He suggested that the Legislative Council should be abolished and that in its stead the Executive Council should be empowered to amend, but not to reject, legislation passed by the Assembly. His avowed purpose was to bring the Executive into direct conflict with the Assembly. In addition, Roebuck advocated a federal union of British North America. To the federal assembly he proposed to give both judicial and legislative functions. In its judicial capacity the assembly would serve as the tribunal for the impeachment of provincial judges; as a legislative body it would concern itself with matters of dispute between provinces, and with interprovincial communications. Although Roebuck's proposal was shortly to have a considerable influence on policy, its immediate effect was negligible and the Ten Resolutions were passed on April 24 with only the Radicals in opposition.

III

The Canadian rebellions revived all the forces that had been dormant since 1828. While the insurrection in Upper Canada was pictured as a mere uprising of a few disaffected republicans and a handful of misguided supporters, that of Lower Canada was described by the Radical leaders in the House of Commons as a mass uprising of the whole French-Canadian population. It was the culmination of French-Canadian nationalism with an independent republic as its objective. Such was also the interpretation presented by the mercantile element of Lower Canada, probably with conviction, but certainly also with an awareness that such an impression could be turned to advantage. In 1823, Louis Joseph Papineau's contemptuous repudiation of the suggestion that French Canada was disloyal had been accepted by the Imperial Government at face value. By 1838 Papineau was a fugitive rebel. After the rebellion, there was little attempt to distinguish between passive sympathy with Papineau and his followers, and active insurrection. It mattered not that only a very small fraction of the French-Canadian population had even the remotest connection with the affair. The general opinion held by officials, both in the Canadas and in England, was that expressed by a Committee of the Upper Canadian Assembly: "There can be no reason now for feeling any delicacy or hesitation in speaking of visible and admitted facts, however ungracious or impolitic it might be to do so, under different circumstances. The Canadians of French descent in Lower Canada, are not loyal. The inhabitants of all the other North American Colonies, are loyal: as are also those of British descent in Lower Canada. . . ."[23] Here was an excellent base upon which pro-unionists could build.

The crisis presented by the necessity of formulating a Canadian policy after the rebellions threatened to overturn the weak Whig Ministry. On December 31, 1837, Lord Melbourne, the Prime Minister, informed Russell, "We must either take such measures as are necessary and adequate for the occasion, or if we cannot take them, we must resign the Government to those who have a better chance of being able to do so."[24] Within the Cabinet, opinions were divided on the policy which should be adopted. A majority were for the repeal of Lord Ripon's Act and the temporary suspension of the constitution in Lower Canada. Lord Howick, who had only reluctantly agreed to a policy of no concessions when the Ten Resolutions were being debated, again presented the main stumbling block. He insisted that coercive measures should be kept to an absolute minimum and should be coupled with evidence of a desire for reconciliation. A majority of the Cabinet felt that the time for conciliation had passed, but it was realized that Howick's resignation at the moment would, quite probably, be fatal to the Government. To Russell, Melbourne assigned the difficult task of formulating a policy which would not only reconcile divergent opinions in the Cabinet, but which would also retrieve Radical support in the House of Commons.

Russell had been working out a policy even before he received Melbourne's letter of December 31. As a basic step, he believed that either *habeas corpus* or the Constitutional Act should be suspended in Lower Canada. Personally, he preferred suspension of *habeas corpus* because suspension of the constitution would give the Governor dictatorial powers. But he was prepared to adopt the other alternative provided either Lord Durham or Sir James Kempt could be persuaded to accept the appointment as Governor. On January 1, 1838, Howick informed Russell that, although he was now in favour of suspending the constitution, he did not consider it very material which plan was adopted. He thought that what Russell proposed "in the way of coercion is quite strong enough," but he strongly objected to the proposal to repeal the Ripon Act which he had co-sponsored with Lord Ripon.[25] Russell's policy he criticized as weak because it "contains nothing directed to remove the causes of Canadian agitation." Russell proposed that the Governor should assemble a convention of representatives from Upper and Lower Canada to tender advice on desirable constitutional changes. Such advice was to be transmitted to England and would serve as a basis for future imperial legislation. To Howick this proposal represented a desirable step in the direction of conciliation, but it did not go far enough. He endorsed a proposal of James Stephen, the Permanent Under-Secretary for the Colonies, which bore some similarity to the suggestions advanced by Roebuck the previous spring. Stephen recommended that the resolution of the last session of Parliament, calling for a convention of representatives from all the British North American provinces, should be accepted as a basis for action. Such a policy, he suggested, "would place the Brit. North American Provinces, rather in a Federation than in a Colonial relation to Gt. Britain. . . ."[26]

Because "the unfortunate differences between those of French & English origin" rendered it impossible to leave the question of the future settlement of the government merely to themselves, Howick proposed to Russell that a convention of delegates from all the North American provinces should be summoned.[27] To such an assembly he wished to entrust the power of amending the constitution, subject to final approval by Parliament. He was confident that the delegates' "strong interest in the settlement of the disputes . . . in the Lower Province, & their common feelings with them as subjects of the same empire" would make them satisfactory arbitrators. Parliament should reserve to itself only the final veto. Lower Canada, Howick suggested, would more willingly accept constitutional amendments which fell short of its expectations if they emanated from the convention. Noting that one of the chief complaints against the Lower Canadian Assembly was its anti-commercial bias, Howick recommended that the general assembly should be given jurisdiction over commerce. This solution would give the advantages of union without being subject to the same objections.

In deference to Howick, Russell made some modifications in his plan.[28] If the Constitutional Act was suspended, it would not be necessary to repeal or suspend Lord Ripon's Act. He refused, however, to recommend that Parliament should give a colonial assembly authority to initiate constitutional amendments. As a primary course of action, he recommended that the Governor should be authorized to summon an advisory council of all who had sat in either House of the Legislature during the past ten years and were clear of any connection with the rebellions. To this body the Governor was to "propose . . . the heads, or basis, of alterations to be proposed in the Constitutional Act of 1791." Should this course of action fail, Russell recommended that the Governor should be empowered to call·an assembly of British North American representatives "to advise concerning any act of Parliament named in the writ of summons which may require alteration or modification."

Russell's modified policy was embodied in a bill entitled, "An Act to Make Temporary Provision for the Government of Lower Canada." On January 16, 1838, the day after Durham had accepted the appointment to Canada, Russell introduced the bill in the House of Commons. When it came up for debate the preamble, which related to the advisory council, was attacked by Sir Robert Peel. Russell hesitated —to give way on this point would mean sacrificing the conciliatory aspects for which Howick had contended. A Cabinet conference was called and on January 26 Melbourne reported to Queen Victoria, "We have settled to leave out the Preamble; Lord Howick has given way. . . .. It will be a triumph to the other party, but I don't much mind that."[29]

IV

In Canada, the merchants had lost little time pressing their case. On December 13, 1837, the Constitutional Society of Montreal described the plight of the English-speaking population of Lower Canada in a petition to the Upper Canadian Legislature: ". . . The rights, the interests and the property, of the Provincial Inhabitants of British origin, have been jeopardized, by the designs of a revolutionary French faction, madly bent upon their destruction. . . . Sedition and rebellion, followed by atrocious murder, robbery, and rapine, have loudly proclaimed themselves in the most populous and prosperous portion of Lower Canada."[30] Re-union, the petition asserted, was the only solution. Re-union would give Upper Canada "advantages which cannot be anticipated from any other measure" including a more equal portion of the general revenue, a free outlet to the sea, and a practical utility for the canals which Upper Canada was building. The Constitutional Society's appeal concluded with a request that the Legislature should give the situation careful consideration and "advice [sic] such measures as will promote . . . the complete Anglification of this Province, and its re-union with Upper Canada."

In Upper Canada, both houses of the Legislature referred the Constitutional Society's petition to Select Committees on the political state of the Canadas. The report of the Assembly's Committee, which was received on February 12, 1838, considered a number of alternatives including a federal union of British North America, reversion to government by governor and council in Lower Canada, colonial representation in the House of Commons, the annexation of the island of Montreal to Upper Canada, and a legislative union of the Canadas.[31] Of these, greater attention was given to the latter two as being the most practicable possibilities. As far as Upper Canada alone was concerned annexation of the island of Montreal offered an ideal solution, but it was recognized that this would amount to a rejection of the appeal contained in the Constitutional Society's petition. The Committee was not attracted by the prospect of a legislative union of the Canadas, but did not wish to overlook the plight of Lower Canadian compatriots who "regard this project with much favour and appear to consider it as the best measure for relieving them from the oppression under which they have long suffered from the conduct of the dominant faction in their House of Assembly. . . ." If a union were to be seriously considered, however, care must be taken that British ascendancy was established in both branches of the legislature; ". . . upon no other terms can the measure be sanctioned by this Province; and this should be most clearly and positively stated to Her Majesty."

The Select Committee had been composed of seven Tories (Boulton, Cartwright, Draper, Gowan, Hagerman, McKay, and Sherwood) and one Reformer (Donald A. McDonell). Its report was indicative of a transformation taking place in the minds of many Tories. It was a transformation that involved both a high sense of loyalty and duty, and some degree of rationalization. As they had shown by their vote in the previous session, the Tories did not want union, but now the rebellions raised the question of whether or not Lower Canada could be retained if it were not made thoroughly British in character as speedily as possible—now it became necessary to consider more seriously the situation of the English-speaking minority in Lower Canada, and now the Tories were more susceptible to the propaganda emanating from the Montreal merchants. Under these circumstances, most Tories were willing to see the union take place so that the anglicizing influence of Upper Canada might be brought to bear fully on the lower province. But, as they foresaw grave dangers, not the least of which was the possibility of an alliance between "republican minded" Upper Canadian Reformers and the French party, they insisted that union must be accompanied by conditions which would insure the predominance of British (i.e. Tory) influence. It is true that the terms they considered necessary would give Upper Canada a disproportionate influence in the union, but in their minds this was not the objective; it was, rather, the only means by which the objective could be attained. As they became converted to the idea of union, they also became more immediately conscious of the economic advantages it would offer.

On February 24, 1838, after studying the Select Committee's report, the Assembly passed a series of resolutions recording its opinions on the causes of the rebellions and other "evils under which these Provinces have suffered."[32] The main source of present problems was considered to be the "injudicious division" of the old province of Quebec in 1791 which had given the French control of "all wealth and all means of acquiring wealth" while allocating to the English portion of the population "a mere wilderness." The result of this division and the "impolitic course" pursued by the British government in relation to the Canadas had been "to foster and maintain the French population, perpetuate their language, establish a strong national feeling, encourage a decided hostility to British interests and institutions, and thus create and maintain a national character of French origin." Upper Canada, meanwhile, finding itself without an ocean port and with maritime customs revenue under the control of a French legislature, had been under severe disabilities, and the state of its economic development was in sharp contrast with the neighbouring state of New York.

As a remedy for the existing situation, an additional resolution pronounced in favour of a legislative union, but only if safeguards were included to allay the strong apprehension that it could prove injurious to the best interests of Upper Canada. A "decided majority" in the united legislature must be allocated to Upper Canada; the principles of the constitution must be maintained inviolate; the casual and territorial revenue and every other branch of the revenue must be placed under the control of the legislature; the seat of government must be in Upper Canada; the English language must prevail in the legislature and in the law courts; and, finally, feudal tenure must be abolished and registry offices established in Lower Canada.

In the divisions on the resolutions and a related address to the Queen, and on the various amendments proposed when these were under consideration, four Reformers and two Tories (Bockus and McLean) steadfastly supported the union with or without conditions favourable to Upper Canada. An additional fifteen Tories, including Christopher Hagerman, and three members of uncertain political affiliation endorsed the union, but only on the terms specified in the resolutions. Eight members, five Tories and three Reformers, wished the Queen to determine the best solution unfettered by any indication of a preference for union, but four of the five Tories felt that, should she decide upon union, the terms specified must be part of the arrangement. Two Reformers and one Tory (John Cook, John McIntosh, and William Benjamin Robinson, a younger brother of Chief Justice John Beverley Robinson) were opposed to a union under any circumstances. Sixteen Tories and seven Reformers either were absent or abstained from voting on the subject, and four members did not vote in a sufficient number of divisions, or with sufficient consistency, to permit classification.

The response of the Legislative Council to the Constitutional Association's petition was similar to that of the Assembly. As an abstract question the members of the Select Committee were opposed to re-union of the provinces, but they agreed that if this were the only means by which the British population in Lower Canada could be secured in the enjoyment of British institutions, "the only question for consideration would be, the terms of the measure, and the fittest time for proposing it."[33] The Committee had an abiding fear that a union of Upper and Lower Canada alone would be "unsafe" for the former. They were convinced, however, that, if this measure were considered by the imperial authorities, ample time would be afforded for suggestions relating to terms.

When an address to the Queen, based on the Select Committee's report, was passed by the Council, William Morris, a Perth merchant, insisted on having his dissent formally recorded in the journals. Morris protested that although the Select Committee's report considered three possible solutions, it failed to "give that countenance to the most feasible [a union of the Canadas] . . . which its simplicity and superiority over the others demand. . . ." [34] Possibly other members of Council whose interests were not centred in Toronto may also have favoured the union. At any rate, William Dickson, James Crooks, and John Hamilton, who were ready to support the union a year later, were present when the question was under consideration.

In England, the merchants were also busy. Robert Gillespie, the senior English partner in the Montreal firm of merchants Gillespie, Moffatt and Company, declared in a letter which was forwarded to Durham, "I do trust that it may now fully appear to you and to Government that the Inhabitants of French origin in the Canadas have long meditated revolt. . . . Legislative powers must be conferred on those in the province who have & will support British connection and settlement. . . ." [35] In addition to advocating the union himself, Gillespie sought to influence Durham by sending him extracts from the letters of his numerous Canadian correspondents. ". . . The measure," stated one such epistle, "is now . . . forced upon the Upper Province: it must either agree to it or its connexion with Great Britain must be cut off or greatly impeded by the intervention of a Mass of rebel Frenchmen in this province." [36] Another excerpt from a letter written by Dr. Strachan, for more than twenty years a senior spokesman for Upper Canadian High Toryism, stated, "One thing must never be lost sight of whether the measure be a Union of the Two provinces, or a federal Union of all the B.N. American Colonies, and that is, a representation possessing British principles and feeling must be insured." [37] It is doubtful if Gillespie would have included Strachan among his selected readings had he been more fully aware of the cleric's anti-union sentiments. The day after Gillespie had forwarded his letter to Durham, Strachan informed Simon McGillivray that he was reluctant to deprecate the union of the two Canadas, "but it would do evil & destroy both Provinces." [38] A general union, he suggested, would be much better.

Gillespie was not alone in his efforts. George Moffatt, William Badgley, and Andrew Stuart had come over to London on behalf of Montreal mercantile interests for the express purpose of expediting the union. They restated the grievances of the English population in Lower Canada and reasserted their faith in the union as a panacea. ". . . The evils engendered by the distinctiveness of national origin, and the prejudices of opposite and antagonistic races . . .," they warned Durham, "will remain to wither . . . remedial measures unless they shall be accompanied by the Union of the Canadas." [39] Moffatt and Badgley were also busy presenting petitions to Parliament and lobbying among the members to obtain support for union.

V

Before his departure for Canada, Durham must have grown weary of the continuous pressure exerted by the merchants. His own interest in industrial development and his faith in the nineteenth century concept of progress predisposed him to accept the merchants' interpretation of the basic nature of the conflict in Lower Canada; he could agree that the province must be made thoroughly British in character—that French Canada must be assimilated—but he rejected a legislative union of the Canadas as the means to attain that end. He had formed a favourable impression of the old alternative, British North American union. [40] Roebuck had sketched out a plan for such a union during the debate on the Ten Resolutions and Durham now sought his co-operation in preparing for the mission to Canada. Roebuck curtly rejected the suggestion that he should take up residence on the American border so as to be available for frequent consultation, but he did agree to commit his ideas on British North American union to paper. He insisted upon retaining possession of the original copy of his proposals, but Durham was permitted to have a copy made before he sailed." Here was a policy which Durham quickly perceived would, if successfully executed, greatly enhance his reputation, and it possessed an element of the spectacular that appealed to his imagination. Instead of a union of the Canadas, he would prepare the way for a union of the British North American colonies which would serve as a counterweight to the United States. The "unanimous loyalty" of the maritime provinces would be brought in to counteract American sentiment in Upper Canada. It was, in addition, a project that had found favour with Peel, Howick, and Ellice." A federal union such as Roebuck advocated might also ease the way through a transitional period while French Canada was being anglicized.

Roebuck's plan differed in many respects from the suggestions put forward by Robinson and Strachan fifteen years earlier, of which Durham, apparently, was unaware. The provincial legislative councils were to be abolished and none was to be established for the new central government. Instead, the executive council was to perform the legislative functions of an upper house as Roebuck had described previously in debate." He suggested that the salary of the governor and the executive councillors should be established by the legislature for a period of six years at a time. Under the terms of his plan the executive council was to consist of only five members. Provincial legislatures were to be elected triennially by ballot and were to exercise complete control over provincial revenue. The federal assembly was to be elected by the provincial legislatures on a representation basis of five members for each province plus an additional member for every 50,000 of the population. The powers assigned to the central government were to be explicitly stated and the residual powers were to be left to the provinces. Montreal was suggested as the seat of government. Roebuck also advocated the establishment of a supreme court with jurisdiction over federal-provincial relations and the impeachment of judges. Some form of municipal government would be necessary to complete the plan. If, in the crisis of the moment, the larger union was not feasible, Roebuck suggested that a federal union of Upper and Lower Canada should be implemented at once with provision for the other provinces to join later.

Durham seized upon Roebuck's plan as an acceptable basis for discussion in Canada. With this end in view he had a concise summary prepared and, at the same time, incorporated a few minor alterations of his own." All provincial officials were to be subject to impeachment before the federal assembly. The federal government's jurisdiction was specifically defined as extending to militia, customs, Crown lands, currency, bankruptcy, interprovincial communications, the post office, and general trade. Although he was well aware that he would encounter serious opposition from the English-speaking minority of Lower Canada, Lord Durham was confident he could either win it over or carry his policy without its support.

For the most part the English-speaking portion of the Lower Canadian population would prove unwilling to give serious consideration to any solution other than a legislative union of the Canadas. For years they had harboured both real and imaginary grievances against the French majority in the Assembly which they felt had denied them appropriate representation, had refused to provide adequate funds for roads, bridges, navigation facilities, and other local improvements, and had sought to retard immigration. Now that the rebellions had created a golden opportunity to obtain a united legislature under the control of an English-speaking majority they would not be satisfied with less.

The Montreal merchants, who constituted the most vocal and the most influential element of the English minority, had always thought in terms of the economic unity of the St. Lawrence River system and had looked forward to the moment when its political unity could be restored. They believed that their great opportunity had arrived and they did not intend to let it slip through their fingers. The merchants might have been willing to admit that, if successful, Durham's British North American union would give them virtually all they would need to further their economic interests, but they regarded it as a visionary project which would be impracticable for many years yet. Even if it could have been carried out immediately, however, they much preferred the prospect of a United Province of Canada to that of a federal union in which a French province would be governed locally by a French legislature. Moreover, the merchants had built their whole case on the necessity of anglicizing Lower Canada. They may not have believed all of their anti-French propaganda, but they almost certainly were convinced that French Canada could be assimilated by means of the union they advocated. In any case, to have endorsed Durham's federal plan as an acceptable alternative would have been tantamount to admitting that French Canada did not constitute a political menace, and thus would have undermined their entire argument.

Even before Durham sailed for Canada, Moffatt, Badgley, and Stuart, realizing that the counter proposal of British North American union was likely to be brought forward, had recorded their objections to the larger measure. The division of powers implicit in such a scheme, it was asserted, would present insurmountable difficulties. In order to bestow any powers on a federal government an abridgement of either provincial or imperial jurisdiction would be necessary. It would be impossible to transfer any provincial powers to the federal government without creating "great mischiefs and occasioning much dissatisfaction." On the other hand, should imperial powers be relinquished to the federal government, termination of the imperial connection would inevitably follow. Four examples were offered as proof of this contention. If revenue were placed under federal jurisdiction "jealousies without end and inextricable difficulties" would result. Only the Imperial government possessed the unity of power requisite to exercise jurisdiction over postal services. Currency had been satisfactorily regulated by the provinces, but in a federal legislature, it was predicted, the radical influences would be greater while the counteracting influences would be less. Internal communications might seem, at first glance, to be a sphere for federal administration, but the conflict of local interests would be productive of dangerous collisions. In addition, the increased expense involved provided a concrete objection. "The evils now to be remedied," contended the pro-unionists, "are confined to the Provinces of Upper and Lower Canada the measure commensurate with those evils and adequate to their removal will be found only in the Legislative Union of those Provinces."[48]

CHAPTER TWO

LORD DURHAM'S MISSION

LORD DURHAM ARRIVED in Canada at the end of May 1838, confident that he could solve the constitutional problems which had caused the rebellions, and enthusiastic about the prospect of recommending a union of British North America that would counterbalance American influence. In just a little more than five months he returned to England a disappointed and disillusioned man; he had found little support for his confederation project, and his banishment of the leading rebels to Bermuda had been repudiated by the Melbourne Government. When he submitted his Report, it astounded all except his most intimate associates for he recommended a legislative union of the Canadas alone—a project which he had consistently deprecated while he was in Canada. A transformation had clearly taken place in Lord Durham's mind concerning the problems he had studied in North America. He had come to consider the deliberate assimilation of French Canada essential, and he regarded a legislative union as the necessary first step in attaining that objective.

I

Before he left England, Durham had been deluged with representations from Lower Canadian supporters of union, but, apart from the views expressed by the Legislature, he had received little communication from Upper Canadians. After his arrival in Canada, however, he began to receive a variety of suggestions as to the best solution for the many problems facing him. Prominent among these was a letter from George Herkimer Markland, Inspector General of Upper Canada and a member of the Tory Family Compact. Markland's letter stressed the financial plight of Upper Canada. "The public enterprise in developing resources has led to expenditure far beyond the means of the province," Markland reported.[1] A debt of £1,400,000 had been contracted and an annual deficit of £40,000 was anticipated. Considering possible solutions, Markland rejected direct taxation as certain to be "almost universally opposed." Confederation had a grand appearance and one saw it "mentally afar off, as if hereafter some mighty destiny would be connected with its fate." However, at the moment, Markland considered that the lack of both communications and common interests between the various provinces rendered it premature. The annexation of Montreal to Upper Canada offered obvious advantages, but it would result in the transfer of a French-Canadian minority to Upper Canada while leaving an English-speaking minority in Lower Canada. It would also perpetuate the problem of dividing the customs revenue, with Lower Canada the claimant instead of Upper Canada. Moreover, the transfer of Montreal would mean that the whole expense of the completion of the St. Lawrence canals would fall upon Upper Canada which was already financially overburdened. He saw only one solution—the legislative union of Upper and Lower Canada. French Canada would oppose the measure and coercion would have to be employed, but to Markland the problem was "how the greatest good may be arrived at with the least possible aggravation to the French Canadians." For that matter, Upper Canada did not like the prospect of union, except with modifications, but it was prepared to accept it in the interests of the Empire. There was, of course, the danger that French-Canadian members would join with Upper Canadian radicals in the united legislature, but this risk would have to be taken if the public works programme was to be completed.

James FitzGibbon, an Upper Canadian hero of the War of 1812 and a High Tory, wrote on June 26, 1838, supporting the annexation of Montreal.[2] Many Loyalists, he declared, were less opposed to union with the United States than with Lower Canada. William Morris, a moderate Tory who had supported the union in the previous session of the Legislative Council, met briefly with Durham in July and advised him to unite the Canadas, if necessary, but not to risk a general union of British North America.[3] John Marks, a member of the Legislative Assembly for Frontenac with moderate Tory views, supported the smaller union as essential to the prosperity of Upper Canada. The religious rights and personal property of French Canadians should be protected, he declared, but they must be brought to "think, feel, and act like British subjects."[4] William Hamilton Merritt, the St. Catharines promoter of the Welland Canal, had opposed the union of the Canadas before the rebellion, but had supported it, on terms favourable to Upper Canada, during the last session of the Assembly. On October 4, he wrote to Durham approving such a project, but he declared that a legislative union of all the British North American provinces would be better.[5]

In the summer of 1838, most Upper Canadians who had given any serious thought to the matter were in favour of a union for both economic and political reasons. Many, however, felt that unless the conditions outlined in the Assembly's resolutions were included in the terms of union it would not only fail to achieve its objective, but would also be fatal to Upper Canadian interests. A few High Tories, such as the Reverend John Strachan, John Macaulay, Christopher Hagerman, and John Beverley Robinson, did not believe that the Assembly's terms could be obtained, or that they would be effective even if they were. They saw the union as a serious threat to both Crown and Church, the quintessence of Tory values, and therefore they opposed it outright. The Reformers had voted almost solidly for union in February and there was no reason why they should have changed their opinion.

Unlike William Hamilton Merritt, most Upper Canadians had not given any consideration to the possibility of a British North American union. Strachan and John Beverley Robinson had suggested it in the 1820's, and at one time William Lyon Mackenzie had contemplated it vaguely, but most inhabitants of the province would have agreed with Markland that it could only be considered "mentally afar off."

Although there was little apparent enthusiasm for the larger union, Durham hoped to win many converts to his project. During the month of June, Charles Buller, Durham's secretary, was busy sounding out Montreal businessmen as a preliminary to a more detailed exposition of the plan. After some discussion with

Samuel Gerrard, Peter McGill, and George Moffatt, he advised, "Give them the registry offices,—the abolition of feudal tenures, especially in this Island,—-& some measures of internal improvement of communications, & I am convinced that you will be able to do what you like with the British party, up to the question of the Constitution. But your policy is a good one, to keep this off for awhile."* Sir John Harvey, Lieutenant-Governor of New Brunswick, paid Durham a short visit in the first week of July. During his stay the confederation project was discussed briefly, and Durham found his remarks on the subject encouraging. When Harvey left, he carried with him a copy of the summary for further study and discussion with his Government in New Brunswick.

After Harvey's departure Durham was ready to meet the Montreal merchants. They had always insisted upon a union of the Canadas, but Adam Thom, who had frequently supported their objectives in the *Montreal Herald* while bitterly criticizing French Canada, held other views. It was to Thom that Durham made his first direct approach. On July 8, Thom replied to Durham's letter stating that the proposal to make Lower Canada a "truly British Province" aroused his high hopes but, he added, "I candidly confess to your Lordship, that I do not see any urgent necessity for the union, whether federal or legislative, either of two provinces or of them all."* He was confident Durham's policy would settle all the questions of local interest without a union. Adam Thom was a man with whom Durham was willing to spend some time. If he could be brought to support the general union, his influence might possibly win over many of the merchants. In the meantime, Durham presented the plan for a general federation to a group of Montreal businessmen called together by Peter McGill. George Moffatt, who was present at the meeting, wrote to Sir John Colborne, the Lieutenant-Governor of Upper Canada, that, although he was convinced of Durham's good intentions, he was by no means a convert to the larger union.* The present problems related to the Canadas alone and interference with the maritime provinces was entirely unnecessary. Moffatt and his associates were convinced that no matter which union was decided upon, it would have a much better chance of success if there were no local assemblies. At all costs they wished to avoid a Lower Canadian Assembly in which the French Canadians would have an automatic majority.

During his short visit to Upper Canada, Durham continued to use his modified summary of Roebuck's plan as a basis for constitutional discussion, but failed to find any response equal to his own enthusiasm for the general union. Commenting on his interview with Durham, Robert Baldwin wrote, "I thought I discerned . . . a strong bias in favour of a measure which in my own mind I am convinced can end in nothing but disappointment."* Baldwin had always contended that by conceding responsible government to the colonies the British government could maintain the Empire intact. The establishment of a general legislative body for all the British North American colonies as outlined in the summary he condemned as "worse than useless" unless it was intended as a preparatory step to making them independent—an objective which he would deplore. It would be interesting to know Baldwin's views on the union of the Canadas; a year later, Sir George Arthur, Lieutenant-Governor of Upper Canada, asserted that, at this time, both Baldwin and his father were opposed to it. This was quite possibly so even though most of the Reformers favoured the idea. In any case, Baldwin did not feel strongly enough on the subject to mention it in his letter to Durham. Even after Durham's Report endorsed responsible government, it was Hincks, not Baldwin, who took the initiative in laying the groundwork for an alliance with the French-Canadian leader, Louis Hippolyte LaFontaine.

When Durham left Toronto on July 19, John Beverley Robinson accompanied him on board the steamer *Cobourg* as far as Prescott. It was probably during this journey that Durham discussed his proposed federal union with the Chief Justice. Robinson pencilled numerous criticisms of the plan in the margins of Durham's own copy of the summary.[10] Although he had been an advocate of the larger union in 1823, Robinson now held different views. Nova Scotia and New Brunswick, he felt, would not join the union if they were given any option. The result would be a union of the Canadas alone and this he steadfastly opposed. He strongly criticized the proposed abolition of the Legislative Council. Several provisions of the plan he condemned as infringements of the royal prerogative. He suggested a larger general assembly and direct, instead of indirect, elections. The question of the division of powers, Robinson declared, required long and careful consideration. The plan as it stood contained many defects in this respect, and the provisions relating to the judiciary called forth a whole series of objections from the Chief Justice.

To Sir George Arthur, Robinson wrote on July 27 that Durham was losing time "by abstaining from discussing & considering any other than this one project, which I do not think it likely will be carried upon any principle, & which if carried upon the principles proposed, would assuredly be ruinous to these Colonies."[11] Robinson now favoured the annexation of Montreal Island to Upper Canada. The remainder of Lower Canada he would leave to be governed by the Legislative Council with all the powers of the legislature for a period of ten years. During his discussions with Robinson, Durham sensed that the Tory Family Compact might very well take a stand in opposition to his plan, but he also felt that, if Robinson could be won over to the scheme, this danger would be greatly reduced if not completely eliminated. To attain this end he was prepared to make considerable modifications, but first he wished to hear from the maritimes.

Upon his return from Upper Canada, Durham summoned Sir Colin Campbell, Lieutenant-Governor of Nova Scotia, and Sir Charles Fitzroy, his counterpart in Prince Edward Island, for preliminary consultation. "They both entered cordially into His views & he was perfectly satisfied . . . with them."[12] While Campbell and Fitzroy were with Durham, a confidential memorandum arrived from New Brunswick containing Sir John Harvey's comments on the project.[13] Harvey objected to the abolition of the Legislative Council on the grounds that the lieutenant-governor would then be more exposed to direct collision with the Assembly. In the Canadas when a clash, attributed "justly or otherwise to the High Church & High Tory Principles" of the Legislative Council, occurred between the upper and lower Houses, the Assembly might rejoice at the abolition of the Council. But, he protested, these conditions were non-existent in New Brunswick and such a remedy was unnecessary. He reported a "general indisposition" in his province for any connection with French Canadians and a reluctance to surrender the control of any portion of the revenue to a federal legislature. In Harvey's opinion, the union should be confined, initially, to the Canadas with provision for the other provinces to join when they recognized the benefits to be derived. Durham was keenly disappointed. "I was not a little surprised at the receipt of your confidential memorandum," he replied, "the tenor of it being so different to the result which your conversation here had induced me to expect."¹⁴ He had no desire to force any province into the union, "but," he warned, "those who decline entering into it must be prepared for a non-participation in any of the general benefits accruing from it." Before Campbell and Fitzroy left, it was agreed that a conference of delegates from the three maritime provinces would be convened at Quebec in September to discuss the subject of federal union in greater detail.

In his efforts to win over Adam Thom, Durham was making some progress. By the middle of August, Thom was offering friendly advice on what he considered to be defects in the proposed plan. Since his advice corresponded in part with the criticism of Robinson, Durham expressed his willingness to modify the plan, and Thom became a supporter of federal union. On August 25, Durham appointed him to serve on the commission for municipal government. This appointment underlined the fact that Thom had accepted Durham's views, but it was also indicative of a breach that was opening between Durham and the French Canadians.

As a means of overcoming the merchants' opposition to the federal concept, Durham contemplated the creation of a new, predominantly English-speaking province to be composed of the Kingston and Montreal areas together with the Eastern Townships.¹⁵ Under his proposed federal union an English-speaking majority would control the federal assembly and the local legislatures in both Upper Canada and the new central province. The French Canadians would be left in control of a purely French province to the east. It was probably this measure which Durham had in mind when he spoke, in his despatch of August 9, of abstracting "all legislation on British interests from the control of a French majority . . . without violence to Canadian rights, and in strict accordance with the soundest principles of constitutional government." But the same despatch revealed that Durham did not believe French Canada could survive indefinitely as a separate cultural entity. He condemned British policy since the conquest for having encouraged such delusions among French Canadians. "If Lower Canada had been isolated from other colonies, and so well peopled as to leave little room for emigration from Britain, it might have been right at the conquest to engage for the preservation of French institutions, for the existence of a 'Nation Canadienne'; but considering how certain it was that, sooner or later, the British race would predominate in this country, that engagement seems to have been most unwise." The constitutional arrangement that Durham was contemplating was intended to provide for a transitional period while the inevitable assimilation of French Canada was taking place.¹⁶

Durham had personally interviewed Robinson and Thom, but discussions with French-Canadian leaders had been left almost entirely to Charles Buller and Edward Gibbon Wakefield, and they had not been successful. The appointment of Adam Thom caused the French Canadians to withdraw even further. Etienne Taché, who was also appointed to the municipal commission, refused to serve with Thom. With the exception of Le Canadien, which still urged patience, the French-Canadian press turned against Durham.

As the date for the conference with the maritime delegates approached, Lieutenant-Governor Campbell sent Durham a brief sketch of the Nova Scotian representatives and the opinions which they held. In general they favoured the idea of union, but Campbell believed they would prefer two unions, one of the two

Canadas and another of the maritime provinces. He was persuaded that the Atlantic provinces would not willingly enter confederation. For his own part, he considered the larger union to be "the only means of securing the tranquility and strengthening the connexion of these flourishing Provinces with Great Britain."[17] Buller urged Durham to clarify the terms of his project in preparation for the meeting and to incorporate whatever modifications were considered necessary. The explanations that had been given were only half understood and much misunderstood, he asserted. "The people here take it for Roebuck's plan, & neither party likes it. I think your own experience must show that it requires consideration. Time begins to press: & no progress is made in your most important work."[18]

Goaded on by Buller, Durham set to work on the plan. In deference to Robinson's opinions he modified the terms of his project considerably. "It is not my intention," he wrote to the Chief Justice on September 16, "to propose any change in the Provincial Constitutions."[19] The Legislative Council would not be abolished. Members of the general assembly would be elected by the constituent body instead of by the provincial legislatures as previously proposed. In what may have been a direct bid for Robinson's support, Durham now incorporated the suggestion of colonial representation in the Imperial Parliament as part of his plan. "You will see," he added, "that I have not pressed any of the points to which you apprehended objections and that I have sufficiently shown my desire not to force my own opinions against the settled conviction of those, who from their position, have a right to command respect and consideration." Robinson was on the point of departing for England on leave and it is unlikely that Durham's modifications had any influence upon his opinion. Sir George Arthur, however, expressed the "sincerest gratification" upon learning of the changes and assured Durham, on September 26, that he was convinced they would "remove the difficulty contemplated by all those whom I have heard speak upon the subject."[20]

Scarcely had the conference of maritime delegates been convened in September when Durham learned, unofficially, that Parliament had disallowed his ordinances for the transportation of those implicated in the rebellion. After a passionate outburst in front of the delegates, he broke off all further discussion. He was completely exasperated and intended to resign as soon as he received official confirmation of Parliament's action. Yet, he still continued to hold to confederation as the solution for Canadian problems.

On September 27, five days after the departure of the maritime delegates, Adam Thom informed Buller that although the Montreal businessmen remained opposed to confederation as a rival to their favourite scheme, he planned to use the columns of the *Herald* to advocate the larger union.[21] At a public meeting in Montreal on October 1, Thom again spoke out in support of confederation. Lord Durham, he declared, was convinced that a union of the Canadas alone would "cruelly disappoint the anticipation of its advocates."[22] It would only provide the opportunity for an alliance between Upper Canadian republicans and French Canadians. "If Upper Canada alone cannot give you a truly British majority," Thom urged, "infuse an additional quantity of British blood and British feeling to be found in the unbroken masses in Nova Scotia and New Brunswick." The meeting approved of Lord Durham's policy in all other respects, but Thom failed to win its support for confederation. A resolution in favour of a legislative union of the Canadas alone was passed by a large majority.

Durham's despatch to Sir George Arthur, on October 9, indicated that he was still convinced of the "necessity . . . of some government that might regulate all matters of concern. . . ."[23] His proclamation of the same date stated that he had hoped "to merge the petty jealousies of a small community, and the odious animosities of origin, in the higher feelings of a nobler and more comprehensive nationality."[24] The proclamation revealed that Durham still favoured confederation, but it also indicated a transition in his opinion regarding French Canada. His aim, he declared, was "to elevate the Province of Lower Canada to a thoroughly British character." No longer was there any suggestion that this was to be accomplished "without violence to Canadian rights." A few months earlier Durham had envisaged a constitutional arrangement that would have permitted, during a period of transition, the continued existence of two separate cultures in British North America. Now, the cumulative influence of his failure to establish contact with the French-Canadian leaders, the opinions expressed by Adam Thom, and the maritimes' cool reception of the confederation project, together with Durham's reaction to his disavowal by the British Government, were beginning to have their effect. Upon the publication of the proclamation, *Le Canadien* also turned its back on him with the reluctant realization that there was nothing to hope for from Lord Durham. On November 2, the day after his departure for England, *Le Canadien* commented: "Il était envoyé pour pacifier un pays déchiré par des dissentions politiques, envenimées par des distinctions nationales, et au milieu d'éléments aussi inflamables, il jette un brandon enflammé; il se prononce pour la déchéance nationale de tout un peuple!"[25]

Throughout his entire stay in Canada, Durham gave no indication that he was other than opposed to a legislative union of the Canadas. He advised Sir Allan MacNab, "If you are a friend to your country, *oppose it* [the union] *to the death.*"[26] During a long conversation with Sheriff Jarvis of the Home District, he had declared that "no statesman could propose so injurious a project."[27] After the Montreal meeting had endorsed his administration but still passed a pro-union resolution, he referred to it as a "pet Montreal project, beginning and ending in Montreal selfishness."[28] Just a few days before his departure, Durham described the measure in derogatory terms and stated to both Sir George Arthur and Christopher Hagerman that *"it was absurd to suppose that Upper and Lower Canada could ever exist in harmony as one Province."*[29] Although Lord Durham apparently left Canada strongly opposed to the smaller legislative union, his views were to change radically soon after he arrived home.

II

In England, Durham's return was awaited with apprehension. The shaky Melbourne Ministry feared he might endeavour to use his influence to turn them out of office. Others feared the recommendations he might make. In a letter to Lord Melbourne, Edward Ellice cast aspersions on the mission and the recommendations which it would likely produce. "Well has not this meteor finished his career in the blaze I always predicted?" he exclaimed.[30] The Montreal meeting, called to address Durham, had repudiated his confederation project in favour of an absolute union of the Canadas. Ellice still favoured the smaller union, but added that "without time and preparation it might be found both unjust and impracticable."

John Beverley Robinson wrote to Sir George Arthur, on November 23, 1838, that he was prepared to give Durham every assistance provided he could approve of his recommendations. "But," he added, "I confess I never was, & am not now sanguine in my hope that Ld. Durham's mission will have a satisfactory result."[31]

Even after Durham's arrival in England, the suspense continued for he made no attempt to communicate with the Government nor did he give any indication of his opinions regarding the Canadas. By the end of the first week in December, Melbourne was beginning to find the silence unnerving.[32] The Prime Minister did not anticipate that Durham would propose a concrete solution for the Canadian problems, but rather that he would offer only general observations. Both he and Russell had already formed some definite opinions on the subject of Canadian policy. After reading Durham's despatch of August 9, Russell had commented, "What Durham says agrees much with what I wrote you yesterday. But where I think our Government always failed is that they allowed the French no part of the patronage, and nearly all the power. They ought to have little power, but a fair share of patronage."[33] On this point Russell and Melbourne were in complete agreement. As he contemplated the prospect of Durham's recommendations, Melbourne wrote to Russell, "What is true is, that we can never suffer the French to govern or to have much influence in Canada again, and they being the majority in Lower Canada, this will make it difficult to establish anything like a popular government."[34] Regardless of what Durham might recommend, Russell and Melbourne had predetermined that French Canada should be left without political power or influence. If political power was necessary for the preservation of the French-Canadian culture, they, presumably, had decreed its doom.

Although he was anxious to hear from Durham before formulating a Canadian policy, Melbourne could not wait indefinitely. His Government would have to meet Parliament early in 1839 and it was essential that a policy should be drafted beforehand. "Ellice says that there must be no further delay," he informed Russell, "and that if we do not propose a plan he will propose one himself."[35] Perhaps it would be wise for Russell to make overtures to Durham before Parliament met, he suggested. On December 23, Melbourne wrote to Russell again seeking his advice on Canadian policy. "My own opinion," he stated, "is that the only course is to continue the further suspension of the constitution in Lower Canada. . . ."[36] However, this course would present difficulties if a union of Upper and Lower Canada or a federation of British North America was to take place. "In any of these cases," he continued, "you must give its due weight to the French population, according to its numbers. Swamping them, or any devices by which the real power is given to a minority, will not do in these days." Melbourne was beginning to recognize the difficulty of attempting to deprive French Canadians of all political power and influence within the framework of a constitution designed for both Canadas or the whole of British North America.

While Melbourne and Russell were pondering the problem of a Canadian policy, John Beverley Robinson, guided by Sir Francis Bond Head, was visiting prominent members of the Tory opposition and freely offering his opinions. He also paid a visit to Lord Glenelg at the Colonial Office and was received with "much cordiality and confidence." There were numerous plans being proposed for the Canadas, he informed Sir George Arthur. "The Montreal Merchants, the Military, the Governt.—Lord Durham, all have their notions of what *alone* will save the Country—& no doubt they are right in some things—& wrong in others, & will agree only in crying out agt. any plan that does not exactly tally with their opinions."[37] Robinson asserted that he had no ambition to be the originator of a scheme, "though I would not shrink from it," he admitted. Lord Glenelg had given him to understand that he would be sent for as soon as his advice on Canadian matters was required.

During the last week of December, Robinson called on Lord Durham and came away with the impression that he had not yet determined upon even the main features of the measure which he intended to propose. Edward Ellice sent Robinson a copy of a scheme for a federal union of the two Canadas and requested that they should meet to discuss the subject, but the Chief Justice declined. "I was quite sure," he related to Sir George Arthur, "I could not convince Mr. Ellice, & at least as certain that he could not convert me to his views of Colonial Government. . . ."[38] It was most desirable for the colonies that "a firm & wise measure should proceed *from the Government*," but if the Whigs should fail in this respect, Robinson added, "then we must hope for better things in other quarters."

As the Whigs endeavoured to formulate a policy, Lord John Russell wrote to Ellice asking him to commit his ideas to paper. Ellice replied that he would prefer to wait until he had heard Durham's proposals. At the same time, he requested a conference with Durham which might also be attended by Buller and Wakefield.[39] Durham had no objection to such a meeting and agreed to Ellice's request. When the conference took place, Buller continued to press for a union of British North America, but Durham, although he was not yet definite, revealed that his opinions had undergone a change. The day after the meeting, Ellice wrote to Durham remarking that he was disturbed by Buller's insistence on the larger union which, though ultimately the best policy, "no man in his sober senses would advise."[40] Even if such advice were given, it would not be acted upon without previously consulting the legislatures of Nova Scotia, New Brunswick, and Upper Canada. If the Colonial Office was given such a loophole, a settlement would be delayed "ad Graecas Calendas." Ellice continued:

Your way of viewing the subject leads to very different conclusions,—an *immediate* settlement of the Canada question to come into operation at the earliest possible period, as not only politic but absolutely necessary in the temper of many minds [?] in Canada,—but so framed as to be the foundation of the wider scheme if the colonies should think an union of the whole advisable to promote their interests and to secure their connexion with this country. If you decide on the main features of the lesser plan, Wakefield and Thom would work up the details for you.

By the middle of January 1839, Durham had let it be known, through Lord Duncannon, the Home Secretary, that he did not intend to oppose the Government, but only to defend himself. He was hard at work on his Report and it would be ready when Parliament met. Melbourne and his colleagues could breathe a little easier. Not only was Durham not planning to attack them, but according to the reports of Ellice and Howick his recommendations were likely to be such as they could endorse. Durham signed his Report on the last day of January and submitted the proof sheets to the Cabinet the same day. He officially presented it to the Colonial Office on February 4. Parliament met the next day, but before the Government tabled the Report on February 11, a large section of it had already been published in the *London Times*.

Lord Durham made two major recommendations: the concession of responsible government, and a legislative union of the Canadas. Responsible government was proposed as the solution for the constitutional problems in Upper Canada. But, as he was unwilling either to recommend responsible government for Upper Canada alone, or to trust it in the hands of a predominantly French-Canadian assembly, Durham considered some form of legislative union essential. He would have preferred a British North American union, but in the face of maritime reluctance, as revealed in the communications from the maritime lieutenant-governors, Durham realized that this would require time. Regarding immediate action as essential, he recommended a union of the Canadas in which he hoped the maritime provinces would join at a later date.

In Durham's mind, it was the problem of French Canada which created the need for immediate action. To trust the French-Canadian population "with an entire control over this Province would be, in fact, only facilitating a rebellion," he wrote. ". . . In any plan which may be adopted for the future management of Lower Canada, the first object ought to be that of making it an English Province."[1] The present generation of French Canadians would never again yield a loyal submission to the British government, he predicted, and never again would the English population tolerate a predominantly French assembly. Expanding on his theme of "two nations warring in the bosom of a single state," Durham pointed out that with but few exceptions there was no social or public intercourse between the French and English. Jury duty was the only public function which the two races performed together and then the result was the utter obstruction of justice. The Lower Canadian crisis, which he was called upon to solve, Durham believed could be attributed to "the vain endeavour to preserve a French-Canadian nationality in the midst of Anglo-American colonies and states."[2] If it had been desired to retain French institutions and a French population in Lower Canada, no other institutions should have been permitted and no other race should have been encouraged to settle there. Quebec should have been set apart as a purely French province. Now the die was cast and Durham could see only one possible course:

I entertain no doubts as to the national character which must be given to Lower Canada; it must be that of the British Empire; that of the majority of the population of British America; that of the great race which must, in the lapse of no long period of time, be predominant over the whole North American Continent. Without effecting the change so rapidly or so roughly as to shock the feelings and trample on the welfare of the existing generation, it must henceforth be the first and steady purpose of the British Government to establish an English population, with English laws and language, in this Province, and to trust its government to none but a decidedly English legislature.[3]

Lord Durham, as *Le Canadien* had stated, declared for the "national destruction of a whole people." He did so with some reluctance, but he sincerely believed that French Canadians would benefit by assimilation. When he asked himself if the French-Canadian nationality was something that should be preserved for the good of the people, he replied, "I know of no national distinctions marking and continuing a more hopeless inferiority." He condemned French-Canadian culture as decadent, backward, and lacking in vitality. Even if it were desirable that the culture should be preserved, it would be impossible, for future waves of English-speaking immigrants would overwhelm and engulf it. Meanwhile, it was unreasonable that the prosperity of English-speaking inhabitants and the development of the country should be impeded "by the artificial bar which the backward laws and civilization of a part . . . of Lower Canada, would place between them and the ocean."

A strong legislative union, designed to obliterate all distinctions between Upper and Lower Canada, was the means by which Durham proposed that the French-Canadian political threat should be neutralized. On the basis of current population estimates, which gave the combined English-speaking population of Upper and Lower Canada a majority of 100,000 over the French Canadians, he predicted a clear English majority in a united assembly elected on a representation by population basis. Such an assembly was the only instrument by which French Canada could be controlled for the present and ultimately assimilated. "The only power that can be effectual at once in coercing the present disaffection and hereafter obliterating the nationality of the French Canadians," Durham asserted, "is that of a numerical majority of a loyal and English population. . . ." Once French Canadians found themselves in the minority, the immediate political danger would be averted and assimilation could proceed at a more leisurely pace. He did not expect them to give up their national objectives immediately and passively submit to assimilation, but "the hopelessness of success would gradually subdue the existing animosities, and incline the French Canadian population to acquiesce in their new state of political existence."

In a penetrating analysis of the causes of the Lower Canadian rebellion, Durham had clearly shown that the failure of representative government had been due to two factors. Instead of that community of interest so essential to the working of representative government, he had found bitter racial strife; and the constitution itself had led to a clash between the executive and the popular branch of government. The latter he proposed to correct by means of responsible government, but he considered the assimilation of French Canada vital to the creation of a community of interest. Nonetheless, he argued strongly against any attempt to effect the change "so rapidly or so roughly as to shock the feelings and trample on the welfare of the existing generation. . . ." It would require time, of course, but on the basis of the evidence presented by Louisiana, Durham was confident that French-Canadian leaders would recognize the handwriting on the wall—they would realize that the material well-being of French Canada was directly related to the rate of assimilation and would willingly assist in the process. "I should be indeed surprised," he declared, "if the more reflecting part of the French Canadians entertained, at present, any hope of continuing to preserve their nationality." The pace at which assimilation was to proceed should be set by the French Canadians. A considerable length of time would elapse before English was generally adopted as a first language, but "justice and policy alike require, that while the people continue to use the French language, their Government should take no such means to force the English language upon them as would, in fact, deprive the great mass of the community of the protection of the laws."

Durham was opposed to any plan that advocated assimilation by harsh and arbitrary means, first, because he did not believe it was necessary, and secondly, because he felt certain it would arouse adverse criticism in the United States and Great Britain which would encourage French Canada to resist. For the same reasons he objected strongly to equal representation for the two provinces, or to any other attempt to guarantee an English majority in the Assembly by nefarious means:

With respect to every one of those plans which propose to make the English minority an electoral majority by means of new and strange modes of voting or unfair divisions of the country, I shall only say, that if the Canadians are to be deprived of representative government, it would be better to do it in a straightforward way than to attempt to establish a permanent system of government on the basis of what all mankind would regard as mere electoral frauds. It is not in North America that men can be cheated by an unreal semblance of representative government, or persuaded that they are out-voted, when, in fact, they are disfranchised.

Lest it seem that in urging an unhurried assimilation process he was watering down his recommendation, Durham coupled each argument in favour of a gradual process with a positive declaration that the ultimate goal must be full and absolute anglicization. He did not, however, consider what should be done if French Canada revealed an ability and a determination to resist assimilation. To him this was an utter impossibility.

There were three major flaws in Durham's reasoning concerning union and assimilation. In the first place, French Canada did not really constitute a serious political threat, and if it had it would have been ridiculous to maintain that the danger could be counteracted simply by an English-speaking majority in the united assembly. Upper Canadian High Tories, who considered French Canada to be a very definite political menace, urged immediate assimilation by authoritarian means. Ten years of resolute repressive government was John Beverley Robinson's prescription for Lower Canada if assimilation were really to be achieved."

Secondly, Durham argued, on the basis of the Louisiana example, that French Canadians would come to accept assimilation as being in their own best interests and would willingly participate in the process. In other words, he expected French Canadians to judge their way of life by English materialistic standards, to condemn it, and to pronounce in favour of assimilation. In spite of his having penetrated the political quarrel in Lower Canada to its cultural origins, he failed to understand how firmly attached the French Canadians were to their own culture. He failed to see that their families, their farms, their Church, their language, and their customs meant more to them than material progress. He failed, also, to understand their deep national pride in the fact that they were different from *les anglais*. He recognized that the existing social system had given the priest, the notary, and the doctor positions of great pre-eminence in each village, yet he believed that these people would voluntarily assist a social revolution that would very possibly deprive them of those positions. Moreover, in suggesting that there was an analogy between Louisiana and Lower Canada, he ignored the difference in population proportions and the fact that there was no Canadian counterpart to American nationalism which, on his own evidence, was an important factor in Louisiana.

Finally, Durham's whole argument was based on the naïve assumption that the English-speaking members would act as a bloc in the united assembly. It is incredible that he could recommend responsible government and not realize that the prospect of turning out the government, on a vote of no confidence, would greatly increase the tendency towards political alignments. Whether responsible government was granted or not, if the English-speaking members failed to act as a unit, the French-Canadian bloc would hold the balance of power and would be in an excellent position to thwart assimilation. In all probability, Durham considered the arguments in favour of assimilation to be irrefutable and could not conceive of any English-speaking members joining with the French to oppose what was essential both to British interests and to the proper working of representative government.

He was correct in implying that French Canada could not be assimilated without its consent, but he was wrong in thinking that that consent would be forthcoming. The Upper Canadian High Tories showed much greater foresight when they predicted that the union would lead to an alliance between the Reformers and the French party which would be fatal to High Tory interests.

Union was recommended primarily as a solution for the problem of Lower Canada, but Durham saw other virtues in the measure. He would have preferred a union of all British North America, but, for the moment, this was impossible. A union of the Canadas would provide the nucleus for the nation he had hoped to create. He proposed to eradicate colonial parochialism and, at the same time, to reduce the danger of American annexation "by raising up for the North American colonist some nationality of his own, by elevating these small and unimportant communities into a society having some objects of a national importance. . . ."[45] For Upper Canada, the union would provide both an end to the customs problem and financial assistance for the uncompleted canal projects.

Lord Durham's Report contained additional proposals which were closely linked to his two major recommendations. Coupled with his recommendation for responsible government was a proposal to grant the province self-government in matters of purely internal concern. Closely related, also, was the recommendation that money bills should be introduced only by members of the government. He strongly advocated the creation of a system of municipal government. "The utter want of municipal institutions giving the people any control over their local affairs, may indeed be considered as one of the main causes of the failure of representative government and of the bad administration of the country," he reported.[46] Municipal government would serve as a useful training ground for participation in provincial politics and would also provide an anglicizing influence in Lower Canada. The removal of local improvements from the provincial to the municipal sphere, Durham predicted, would produce a salutary reduction in the prevalent practice of log rolling. Durham also recommended the establishment of a supreme court with appellate jurisdiction as a means of improving the judicature. Realizing that the isolation of the maritime provinces from the Canadas was a serious obstacle in the way of confederation, he recommended that provision for the improvement of interprovincial communications should be made as soon as possible.

III

A great change had occurred in Lord Durham's opinions on French Canada and on the project of confederation. He described the transformation in his Report, but accounted for it only by implication. He had believed that a federation, "sanctioned and consolidated by a monarchical Government," would have a tendency gradually to develop into a complete legislative union. Thus, while conciliating the French Canadians by leaving them "the government of their own Province and their own internal legislation," he could, at the same time, "provide for the protection of British interests by the general government, and for the gradual transition of the Provinces into a united and homogeneous community." He had come to the conclusion, however, that the period of "gradual transition" was passed in Lower Canada. "In the present state of feeling among the French population," he reported, "I cannot doubt that any power which they might possess would be used against the policy and the very existence of any form of British government."[47]

Charles Buller has provided a partial explanation of the change in Durham's views. "The urgency of union," he related, "was more forcibly impressed on our minds in the course of our conferences [with the maritime delegations], and still more by subsequent events. And as we discussed the details of a plan so the merits of a federal scheme faded away by degrees, and we became convinced of the propriety of such a complete legislative union of the provinces as was afterwards proposed in Lord Durham's Report."[48] Some years later Buller gave a slightly different explanation. Durham, he stated, left Canada still "disposed rather to wait for the period at which it [British North American union] might be accomplished than to propose in the first instance any less extensive union."[49] But the second insurrection, which broke out in Lower Canada while Durham was on his way home, "compelled him, much against his inclination, to admit that the present peril must be guarded against by an immediate union."

What interpretation have historians placed upon this aspect of Durham's recommendations? Sir Charles Lucas, in his definitive work on the Report, has added nothing to Durham's implicit explanation. Lord Durham, he states, "set himself to consider in the first place, what is the best constitution; and in the second place, what is the best constitution, given a particular set of conditions. He answered the second problem not so much by departing from his model constitution, as by proposing to alter the conditions so as to enable the model constitution to be brought into being."[50] Chester New added a whole new set of valid factors connected with the political situation in Great Britain.[51] When Durham arrived back in England, he had two possible courses open to him. Either he could seek to obtain the leadership of the Radicals and attack Melbourne's Ministry, or he could co-operate with the Whigs and endeavour to secure the adoption of his Report. In choosing the latter course Durham must have realized that Melbourne would not countenance a provincial legislature, even under a federal system, which would be dominated by French Canadians. Durham believed he could probably obtain the support of the Melbourne Government for most of his measures, perhaps even for responsible government. He was already beginning to have some misgivings about the problem of Lower Canada and, in the light of the political factors at home, he was prepared to modify his proposed solution. "The recommendation of legislative union cleared Melbourne's difficulties, and also left the way open for Responsible Government and for an ultimate union of all the provinces into that nation of which Durham dreamed."[52] Donald Creighton, on the other hand, has suggested that Durham's recommendation of union was due primarily to economic motives.[53] "Union," he states, "was the primary and indispensable step; union was first established; and if it was followed by responsible government, it was followed also by local government, large loans, the canal-building programme and the extinction of seigniorial tenure." In short, Durham had been converted to the views of the Montreal merchants.

There is insufficient evidence to construct a completely satisfactory explanation of the transformation in Durham's opinions during the last half of 1838, but a recapitulation of the established facts will serve as a basis for surmise where gaps exist. Durham's first official pronouncement which contained a definitely anti-French bias was the proclamation of October 9. This occurred but shortly after Adam

Thom had publicly supported the confederation project. Undoubtedly Thom's opinions had a great influence upon Durham. The failure to establish a working contact with moderate French leaders such as LaFontaine helped to strengthen Durham's original prejudice in favour of the English minority in Lower Canada. The proclamation of October 9 also represents Durham's response to the disallowance of his ordinances, a reaction which was quite probably another factor in the alteration of his views. Buller has stated that when Durham left Canada he was resolved to wait until the time was ripe for a union of British North America. The second outbreak of rebellion in Lower Canada and the effect which it had on public opinion in Great Britain forced him to reconsider the Lower Canadian aspects of the problem. The political situation in Great Britain at the moment, as New suggested, was undoubtedly a major factor in the transformation of Durham's opinions. It would also appear that Edward Ellice, despite the fact that he favoured a federal union of the Canadas, personally exerted a determining influence upon Durham while he was still undecided. It is strange, but judging from Ellice's letter dated "Tuesday evening" (January 8, 1839?),[54] he apparently did not realize that when Durham spoke of "an immediate settlement of the Canada question" he was contemplating a legislative union. There is, however, little evidence to support the contention that union was recommended primarily as an economic measure. There can be no argument with the claim that economic factors were also carefully considered, but the whole tenor of the Report suggests that union was essential as an immediate solution for political problems in Upper Canada and racial problems in Lower Canada.

CHAPTER THREE

IN THE WAKE OF THE DURHAM REPORT

WHILE THE CANADAS AWAITED news of Lord Durham's recommendations, rumours circulated freely. In February, a report that a federal union and the division of Lower Canada would be recommended attracted the attention of Quebec and Montreal newspapers. When the Lieutenant-Governor of Nova Scotia made public Durham's confederation project, the *Montreal Gazette* declared that it was impossible to imagine a plan "more incoherent, more democratic, more unconstitutional, and more anti-British." "Cela veut dire," replied *Le Canadien* on February 15, 1839, "que ce plan ne serait pas mauvais, pour le peuple en générale, ou au moins qu'il ne vaudrait rien pour l'Oligarchie."

George Moffatt, a leading force amongst the Montreal merchants, did not concern himself with such rumours for his private mercantile channels of communication kept him better informed than the Governor. Moreover, the Upper Canadian Legislature was in session, and Moffatt wished to secure from it a firm endorsation of union before the Durham Report arrived. He was well aware that such a declaration, uninfluenced by whatever recommendations Durham might have made, would be of great weight when policy decisions were being formulated by the British Government. On February 13, as Moffatt passed through Kingston on his way to Toronto, John Macaulay wrote to his uncle that the merchant was winning many converts to his cause, but added that for himself he could see only ruin as the result of adding "50 or 60 fierce Frenchmen to the radical force" in the Assembly of Upper Canada.[1]

The financial plight of Upper Canada with a very large debt, virtually no revenue or credit, and a host of uncompleted public works projects, provided Moffatt with a convincing argument in favour of union. Arthur informed Colborne that Moffatt was strenuously lobbying for union among the members of the Legislature, telling them that "by that measure alone can they be emancipated from their Embarrassments."[2] Although Arthur was sceptical as to "*how* that will bring them the needful . . .," he reported that many members ". . . in the hope of getting a handsome dowry . . . seem disposed to venture upon the connexion."

It was William Hamilton Merritt, now a firm convert to the idea of union, who reintroduced the subject in the Upper Canadian Assembly. On March 14, Merritt carried a motion that the House resolve itself into a committee of the whole on the state of the province, and proceeded to introduce a series of resolutions calling for a union of the Canadas upon grounds which were predominantly economic. In addition, he sought the repeal of the Canada Trade Act and declared that the regulation of customs duties should be vested in the colonial legislatures.[3] Merritt's proposals touched off a vigorous debate which continued intermittently during the next two weeks.

As the debate progressed Christopher Hagerman, Ogle R. Gowan, J. W. Gamble, and William B. Robinson stood out as the leading spokesmen for High Tory opposition to the union. In the divisions, they were supported by fellow Tories G. S. Boulton, Francis Caldwell, Alexander McDonell, Edward Murney, and Henry Ruttan, and two Reformers from Middlesex County, Thomas Parke and Elias Moore. The opposition of the latter may, possibly, have been due to their dislike of the anti-French Upper Canadian conditions, for they voted against these while most of the Tory anti-unionists voted for them.'

As an alternative to a union from which he could not anticipate either "peace or plenty," Hagerman suggested that Canada could become, in the near future, a kingdom like Ireland with representation in the Imperial Parliament.' William Draper, reflecting the moderate Tory view on the question, stated that, while he was unable to support Merritt's resolutions in their present form, he was, nonetheless, in favour of union. "Let us act," he urged, "with a view to improve the people of Lower Canada in their views and feelings." Peace, security, and prosperity would then attend both colonies and they would be firmly attached to British institutions.'

The split which was developing in Tory ranks over the union question was clearly revealed during the second week of the debate when the High Tories endeavoured to forestall further consideration of the question. On March 23, William Benjamin Robinson, who represented Simcoe County, sought to set aside the Assembly's endorsement of union in the previous session by proposing an amendment recommending an additional duty on goods imported into Lower Canada and a modification of the Lower Canadian constitution. The proceeds from the additional duty would be devoted to financing improvements in Upper Canada. Having thus endeavoured to counter the union's financial attraction, Robinson's amendment proceeded to recommend the virtual disfranchisement of the French-Canadian population in Lower Canada. This was to be accomplished by restricting the franchise to those who held land in free and common soccage. By this means, and a requirement that all public business should be transacted in English, it would be possible with the help of British "emigration" to secure within a very few years "to the loyal and well disposed that preponderance in the affairs of the country, which is now by some sought for through the medium of a Union with Upper Canada."'

Robinson's attempt to shelve the union was defeated thirty-nine to seven by the combined vote of moderate Tories, Reformers, and the independent members. Only Hagerman, Boulton, Gamble, Gowan, Alexander McDonell, and Murney voted with Robinson in support of the amendment. Since Robinson had been careful to provide alternative means of attaining the advantages that the moderate Tories thought they saw in the union, why did he fail to recall them to their "true" Tory duty? Two answers suggest themselves. In the first place, they believed that they were in a strong enough position to be able to dictate the terms of union and, if this were true, they not only saw no danger in the measure, but regarded it as a more efficacious means of dealing with the French-Canadian problem. Secondly, they were becoming increasingly aware that a union would be beneficial to private commerce as well as public finance, and Robinson had no alternative to propose in this respect. Moreover, Robinson's solution would place an extra financial burden on Upper Canadians as well as Lower Canadians and many members were unwilling to support a measure that was certain to be unpopular with their constituents.

When Robinson's amendment was defeated, Ogle R. Gowan, the Grand Master of the Orange Lodge and editor of the Brockville *Statesman*, tried different tactics. He moved an amendment proposing that a dissolution be requested in order that the question might be taken to the country. Gowan's amendment was supported by most of the Reformers, but the Tories had little faith in the electorate's judgment on important questions and Colonel John Prince was the only one of Gowan's Tory colleagues who favoured an election.[8]

After the amendments had been disposed of, the Assembly proceeded to pass two resolutions to the effect that union, on the terms proposed during the previous session, was "indispensable" and that "further delay must prove ruinous to the best interests of the Canadas."[9] A third resolution authorized the appointment of delegates to represent Upper Canadian interests in England while the Canadian problem was under consideration. Of the thirty-five members who supported the union, twenty-three Tories and seven Reformers were prepared to do so only if it was accompanied by conditions that would ensure both a British majority in the united legislature and a predominant position for Upper Canada. When the Assembly turned to drafting the instructions for the delegates, the particular conditions upon which the "indispensable" union would be acceptable were stated more explicitly and more emphatically than in the previous session.[10] The "decided majority" which Upper Canada would require in the united assembly was now precisely stated as the retention of the existing sixty-two seats while Lower Canadian representation was to be limited to fifty members. After 1845 the franchise was to be restricted to those who held their land in free and common soccage. Other stipulations which had been set forth in 1838 were all reiterated.

An attempt by the Niagara merchant, James Crooks, to secure a similar approval of union in the Legislative Council failed when an amendment declaring that the House adhered to the opinions expressed in the report and address approved in the previous session was carried by two votes. The majority, William Morris reported to Durham on April 8, was, with one exception, composed of residents of Toronto and the immediate vicinity who were motivated, in part, by fear of the removal of the capital.[11] John Henry Dunn and John S. Macaulay, two Toronto members who favoured union, were absent when the vote was taken.

Reporting upon the proceedings in the Legislature, Archdeacon Strachan paid tribute to Moffatt as "an admirable negotiator" who had succeeded in winning over a large majority of the Assembly.[12] "It is true," he continued, "they annex a number of ridiculous conditions to which neither the British Population in Lower Canada nor the Imperial Parliament can ever submit. . . . If the Union is to be entertained it must be on fair and honourable principles, otherwise it would increase the difficulties under which we labour. . . ." He was inclined to think that before the proceedings of the Legislature reached England, the British Government would have decided on the future government of the Canadas. In any case, the Legislative Council had not rejected union outright, but had only refused to put it prominently forward. Under such circumstances, if no decision had been made, the Assembly's proceedings were likely to attract more attention in England and would probably shift the balance in favour of union. If this should happen, Strachan admitted that it would be the duty of all to make the union work as well as possible, but he could not conceal from himself the "anticipation of disastrous consequences." "A general union of all provinces," he concluded, "might . . . be so modified as to regenerate British North America, but a partial union appears to me pregnant with evil." The Archdeacon's opinions were shared by the Lieutenant-Governor who remarked, in forwarding the Assembly's fourteen resolutions on union to Sir John Colborne, that there ought to have been an additional one declaring the independence of Canada—"the obvious consequences of ceding the other 14."[13]

II

Scarcely had the Legislature finished considering the question of union when Lord Durham's Report arrived from England.[14] After reading it, Colborne wrote to Arthur on March 31, "I have no doubt that a Union will be proposed by Ministers, if the measure should be decidedly popular in Upper Canada."[15] He considered the Report to be "full of Hum", but added, "I think, however, it will lead to the adoption of many beneficial measures in both Provinces." Arthur, whose opinion of the Report was much less favourable, replied, "It is much to be regretted that Lord Durham had not tried his hand with a Colonial Legislature— to talk of a strong responsible Government is absurd."[16]

When Arthur received the Report he immediately sent copies to members of his Executive Council for comment. "There should be no factious opposition to the Government, but a calm exposure of Lord Durham's errors," he wrote to John Beverley Robinson. After Durham's frequent denunciations of a Canadian legislative union, Arthur could see only one explanation for the recommendation. "I believe He could work out no other Plan," he declared to Robinson, "and was obliged to have recourse to the Union to save Himself."[17] It appeared probable now that the Imperial Government would make use of the Assembly's declaration that union was "indispensable," but would ignore their annexed conditions. Arthur personally preferred a legislative union of the five provinces, to the plan suggested by Robinson, "but," he added, "to tell you the honest truth, the expectations of a responsible Gvrt. which will be excited by Lord Durham's Report . . . will be too strong to be stem[m]ed[?] by any Measures. . . ."

Although John Beverley Robinson was moved to an immediate counter-attack when he first read the Report in England, it threw many of his fellow Tories into a state of despondency which accentuated the breach in the party. It seemed to ultra Tories that Lord Durham was bent on expelling the elect from paradise, or rather, on creating a new heaven and a new earth in which all true values were inverted. The "true, loyal" element of the population which had sought to maintain the British character given to the province by Lieutenant-Governor Simcoe—those who twice, in their own eyes, had saved Upper Canada for the Empire—now found themselves referred to as the Family Compact—a term of abuse hitherto used by some vociferous Reformers, but not by British statesmen. Lord Durham had even claimed that the "Compact's" efforts to monopolize power and patronage had been a major factor in causing the Upper Canadian rebellion. Durham's attitude was, in Tory eyes, the culmination of a wrong-headed, colonial policy by which the Imperial government had been seeking for a decade to conciliate the disaffected. Sir Allan MacNab picked up the challenge and flung himself vigorously into the fray,[18] but he was the exception—for most High Tories the old ideals had been overturned and there seemed to be no hope for the future. It would be left to the younger, more moderate members of the party to adjust to the new conditions if they could.

Aware that the party faced a crisis, Sir George Arthur sent Christopher Hagerman a copy of Robinson's criticism of the Report in the expectation that it would stimulate him to immediate action, but the Attorney General replied:

For my own part I have slight hopes of benefit to the Country from any measure that may be adopted. The British Ministry are influenced by opinions that must prove fatal to British connection if longer acted upon. They seem to think that it is necessary to render the Colonial Government more *liberal*—that is more *democratic* than it is—and the power of the Crown instead of being strengthened should be relaxed—and that the opinions and wishes of a Provincial House of Assembly is [sic] to guide the administration of public affairs—What chance is there of maintaining that controul, which is essential to the efficient Government of a Colony if this policy is avowed and pursued? the attempt would be utterly hopeless.[19]

He went on to declare that "unless Lord Durham's Report—and the principles and theories it advocates, are openly—plainly—emphatically *denounced*—and declared to be *utterly inadmissible*, these Noble Colonies . . . will cease to be appendages of the British Crown in a *very few years*. . . ." Hagerman's opinions were shared by John Macaulay, a Kingston High Tory, who held the office of Inspector General and sat in the Legislative Council. "The Union seems almost a settled matter—," he wrote disconsolately to his mother, "all our debates & resolutions will go for nothing. The matter will be decided without reference to us."[20]

The Upper Canadian Reformers, on the other hand, found great encouragement for the future in Lord Durham's recommendations. In an instant their respectability had been restored by Durham's endorsement of responsible government. Moderate Reformers, whose loyalty was beyond question and who had either withdrawn from public life or aligned themselves with the Tories as Mackenzie led the extremists down the path to rebellion, now began to play an active role in the party once more. Some divisions and differences of opinion still remained, but a new party spirit was developing. During the late spring and summer of 1839, the Reformers took the offensive, forming Durham clubs throughout the province and holding mass meetings at which resolutions were passed approving Durham's recommendations. Sir George Arthur reported that the Reform revival was attracting even moderate Tories. Among the more prominent converts to responsible government were William Hamilton Merritt, Egerton Ryerson, the editor of the Methodist *Christian Guardian*, and Ogle R. Gowan.[21] Merritt's conversion was due, at least in part, to pressure from his constituents; Ryerson was displeased by the clergy reserves bill passed in the recent session; and Gowan was annoyed by Arthur's attempt to prohibit Orange processions.

In 1836 the Upper Canadian Reformers had been in communication with Papineau and his followers, and before the rebellions occurred there had been the prospect of a working alliance between the two groups. Now, a union of the Canadas had been recommended by Lord Durham, and Francis Hincks, the editor of the reform newspaper, the *Examiner*, saw that such an alliance could produce a solid Reform majority in the united assembly. This spectre had haunted anti-unionists since 1822. With such an alliance as his objective, Hincks wrote the first letter of his celebrated correspondence with Louis H. LaFontaine less than a week after the Report was made public in Toronto. He admitted that union would mean ruin to French Canadians if Lord Durham was correct in his assertion that they were motivated by a desire to remain a separate and distinct nation, but ". . .

If he is wrong," continued Hincks, "& . . . you are really desirous of liberal institutions & economical government, the union would . . . give you all you could desire, as an United Parliament would have an immense Reform Majority."[22] Before the month of April was out, Hincks followed up his initial letter with a second on the same theme. "On the Union question," he wrote, "you should not mind Lord D.['s] motives, but the effect of the scheme. Lord Durham I think wrote more against you than he would have done, in order to carry the British party with him."[23]

When the Upper Canadian Legislature turned officially to the consideration of Lord Durham's Report, there must have been uneasiness in the minds of those members who favoured union only on their own terms. But, despite the apprehension which Durham's proposals aroused, the economic incentives were still sufficiently strong to forestall any tendency to censure the recommendation for union. In both Houses, select committees condemned the inaccuracies of the Report and attacked the recommendation for responsible government, but uttered not a word of criticism against the proposed union.

As spring wore on, Sir George Arthur became increasingly despondent about future prospects. "In place of swamping the French . . ., if all H. M. Subjects cd. be comfortably provided for elsewhere, I doubt whether it were not better to fill the Canadas with French Catholics & allow them to fight it out with Jonathan—," he confessed to Lord Fitzroy Somerset, the Military Secretary at the Horse Guards.[24]

Arthur felt impelled to warn Lord Normanby, who had taken over at the Colonial Office in February, of the Tories' reaction to the Durham Report and to endeavour to explain their position. These were the men who, since the American Revolution, had stood by the imperial connection through thick and thin. In their determination to resist the extension of republican influence and to retain the "Regal Institutions" to which they were devoted, they had steadfastly opposed any extension of popular government despite mounting pressure from the Reformers. In their struggle, the Tories had generally been able to regard the Lieutenant-Governor as an ally, but for a number of years, as public opinion in Great Britain forced a more liberal policy on the Colonial Department, they had felt that the Colonial Secretary was aligning himself with their political opponents. Now, the Durham Report seemed to portend their complete repudiation by the Imperial Government. As a result, Arthur reported, many members of the constitutionalist party "are now anxiously meditating whether a separation from Great Britain would not be most conducive to their peace and future welfare."[25]

If it was imagined that union would produce a better spirit among Lower Canadian members of the Legislature, Arthur continued, he wished to emphasize the counter point that one-third of the population of Upper Canada desired republican institutions. The result of union "must be worse than a mere failure." When first it met, the Assembly had favoured union under certain conditions, he admitted, but after Lord Durham's Report was received "a very different feeling appeared to be entertained." His "humble advice," Arthur concluded, was that Parliament "meddle not at all with the Institutions of Upper Canada. At this time, if it can be had, she needs repose."

The Lieutenant-Governor's opinion that there had been a change of heart regarding the union was probably wishful thinking prompted by his own High

Tory bias. When the Durham Report was under consideration, neither the Assembly nor the Select Committee to which the Report was referred ventured any criticism of the union and no attempt was made to retract the endorsement given to it earlier in the session.

III

In England, the Melbourne Government had awaited Lord Durham's Report with some trepidation. When it was presented, they were undecided concerning the course of action to be adopted. Conscious of their weak position in the House of Commons, they were reluctant to precipitate a debate on the vexed Canadian question. Moreover, there was division within their own ranks. Melbourne and Russell were predisposed to accept Durham's recommendation that French Canada should be assimilated, but there were differences of opinion in the party regarding the means by which this should be accomplished.

While the Whigs pondered their problem, John Beverley Robinson was busy. Robinson had expected to act as the Government's unofficial consultant on the Report. But when he called at the Colonial Office the day after it was presented to Parliament, he was merely handed a copy by James Stephen who commented that the announcement of the "popular policy" recommended by Lord Durham could be regarded as the fulfilment of it.[26] Lord Glenelg had resigned and there was no indication that Robinson's advice, if he saw fit to offer any, would be very seriously considered. Annoyed by Stephen's remarks, Robinson returned home only to have his agitation increased as he read the Report "with mingled feelings of astonishment and regret."[27] "It absolutely made me ill to read it," he declared to Sir George Arthur. "You said rightly to me once, 'Lord Durham is a bad man—'. . . ."[28]

The day after Lord Normanby succeeded Glenelg in office, Robinson waited upon him with a criticism of the Report "almost as long as Coke's upon Littleton."[29] The Chief Justice was critical of Durham's numerous inaccuracies, but at the same time he admitted that the section on Lower Canada contained much sound reasoning, ably expressed. Responsible government he dismissed as an utter impossibility without the counteracting influence of an ancient aristocracy. His criticism of the proposal for union was based upon the objections which he had formulated in 1822 and which had hardened into unalterable convictions during the intervening years. With the existing state of Canadian communications, the united province would present far too vast a territory to be governed satisfactorily by a single executive. Representation based upon population would magnify the problems with which the home government had to contend. The French would combine against the British portion of the legislature and the priests would animate and support them "upon principles and from feelings which could scarcely be subject to reproach."[30] The republican element in a united assembly would be strong enough to constitute a genuine threat to the British connection. To employ the paramount authority of Parliament to make Lower Canada essentially British was one course, asserted the Chief Justice, but it was quite another matter "to leave that to be attained through the agency of a legislature in which French and English, Catholic and Protestant, will be almost equally balanced, and in which, therefore, nothing can be looked forward to but years of bitter, obstinate, dangerous contention, attended with universal jealousy and distrust."[31]

Robinson was encouraged to find that Normanby did not regard the Report as "a document worthy to be implicitly received and acted upon."[32] When he was requested to make suggestions of his own he was well pleased. It was highly desirable, he believed, that an acceptable policy should emanate from the Whig Government and that he should remain obscurely in the background. At the same time, however, he made it quite clear to Normanby that should the Government ignore his advice and decide upon an injudicious policy, he would feel at liberty to lay the case before the British public by publishing his opinions. Under these circumstances he was confident that the dependable Tory party would take up his cause and save Canada for the Empire.

As an alternative to Durham's union, Robinson proposed the old Upper Canadian Tory panacea—the annexation of Montreal Island to Upper Canada. Gaspé, he suggested, should be added to New Brunswick. Government by a governor and council for ten to fifteen years together with provisions to make the English language and civil law prevail was the solution proposed by the Chief Justice for the Lower Canadian problem. Although Lord Normanby was not prepared immediately to adopt his suggestions, Robinson informed Arthur that he found him "reasonable & open to correction in any erroneous opinions he had formed."[33]

During the course of their discussions, Normanby referred to Edward Ellice's plan for a federal union of the Canadas which he had had printed and circulated among his colleagues in the Cabinet.[34] Ellice had proposed that a federal government should be established at Montreal closely resembling that of the United States at Washington. Unlike the model, however, Ellice suggested the Canadian federal government should be made supreme and the provincial governments definitely subordinate. To the federal government he would give jurisdiction over criminal law, general revenue, trade and navigation, the post office, interprovincial communications, banking, currency, and any other objects of general interest. The governor general's office would be the channel of communication between the home government and the lieutenant-governors. Two federal districts would be created consisting of Montreal Island, and the land south of the St. Lawrence River bounded by a line running from St. Regis to Laprairie, and thence following the railroad to Chambly, and up the St. John River to the United States border. The federal districts would be governed by the central government. Perrot Island and the tongue of land between the St. Lawrence and Ottawa Rivers would be given to Upper Canada. Lower Canada could either be divided into Canada North and Canada South or retained for ten years as a single province under a lieutenant-governor and council. The federal legislature would be composed of a congress and a senate. The congress would consist of thirty-two members elected from Upper Canada, twenty-six from Lower Canada, plus two each from Montreal and Quebec, and one from each federal district. Six senators were to be appointed by the Crown, and three each by the Legislature in Upper Canada and the Special Council in Lower Canada. In defining the electoral districts, Ellice suggested, it would be wise to give greater weight to the extent of territory than to the present population, so as to encourage settlement and "above all things to secure a *reasonable* share of the representation in Lower Canada to the British population, and an equal share *at least* in the cities and congressional district." A supreme court with appellate jurisdiction over the provincial courts completed the plan.

Robinson, who was already familiar with Ellice's proposal, remained unimpressed. "It would be complicated, unpalatable from its *republican flavour* & as dangerous as the Union in the other form," he declared to Sir George Arthur. "I am sure it would very soon bring us to a stand still—or rather to a rapid descent."[35] At Normanby's request, Robinson was about to prepare a written criticism of the federal scheme when Ellice solicited an interview to discuss the matter. Robinson agreed and the two men met, but Ellice's renowned persuasive powers were insufficient to convert the Chief Justice.[36]

Robinson was not the only one endeavouring to exert pressure on the indecisive Whigs. During the month of January 1839, British merchants with extensive financial interests in the Canadas continued to press, through their North American Colonial Association, for the solution they desired. Unless a preponderance was given to the opinions of the loyal British population it would be impossible to govern the Canadas, warned Robert Carter, the Association's secretary.[37] In order that Glenelg might see clearly the objectives which the Association had in mind, Carter enclosed a draft bill prepared by Robert Gillespie. By means of franchise qualifications, suspension of writs, redistribution, and the interchange of a number of members from both Houses of the Legislature, the bill attempted to provide an assembly in which the loyal British members would outnumber, by an estimated eighty-seven to thirty-six, the French Canadians and the Upper Canadian Reformers combined. The North American Colonial Association, Carter added, would be pleased to submit observations and suggestions upon any measure which the Government might have under consideration. When the Durham Report was made public, a special meeting of the Association was called to consider its recommendations, and a series of resolutions were passed recognizing Durham's "sincere desire to promote the peace and permanent welfare of the Canadas" and testifying to the accuracy of his account of the French Canadians. The Association warmly endorsed the recommendation that British influence must predominate, but deprecated the basis recommended for representation since it made no distinction between loyal and insurgent inhabitants. A resolution was also passed dissenting from the impression of Upper Canada given by the Report.[38]

Within the Cabinet, Durham's brother-in-law, Lord Howick, was critical of the union recommended in the Report. Early in 1837 Howick had adopted the idea of a federal union for British North America. Undoubtedly he had hoped that Durham would make such a union the basis for his recommendations. To this end, he had endeavoured to insert provisions for a convention of delegates from the North American provinces in both Durham's instructions and the preamble to the bill for the temporary government of Lower Canada. He was pleased with the Report in general, but he was disappointed to find that a legislative, instead of a federal, union had been recommended. Looking ahead to the prospect of British North American union, he foresaw numerous difficulties if there were to be no provincial legislatures. The only subjects in which the provinces had a common interest, Howick suggested, were trade, banking, customs duties, postal services, internal communications, defence, and the creation of an appellate judicature. Under these circumstances, he urged that it would be better to establish a federal legislature with jurisdiction over these matters of common concern and to leave other local matters to the provincial governments. He also objected to the proposal that union should be effected by an act of Parliament, claiming that this would be inconsistent with the recommendation that colonists should be permitted to manage their own internal affairs. As an alternative, he advocated a convention of deputies from Upper and Lower Canada which Parliament could empower to make whatever alterations were necessary in the constitution of 1791.[39]

Both Buller and Wakefield were critical of Howick's suggestions. ". . . The great argument against a federal Union is that it does nothing to attain the main end which we ought to have in view. That end is the keeping Lower Canada quiet now, & making it English as speedily as possible," commented Buller.[40] Wakefield warned that Howick's aim was to substitute a whole scheme of his own, and advised Durham to avoid being drawn into private discussion with him.[41] Howick, nonetheless, clung tenaciously to his federal idea and began to regard Edward Ellice's proposal as a plan more worthy of his support in the Cabinet.

On the evening of March 26, 1839, eight members of the Cabinet met at the home of Lord Lansdowne, President of the Council, in an effort to reach agreement on a Canadian policy. After considerable discussion Howick persuaded them tentatively to set aside the legislative union recommended by Durham in order to give prior consideration to a federal union of the Canadas.[42] The next day Lord Normanby, in "an attempt to reduce into form the results of that meeting," had the heads of a bill drawn up based on Edward Ellice's plan, but with its American terminology deleted.[43] Lord John Russell had been present at the meeting, but he was not in favour of a federal union. When the plan was brought before the Cabinet, on March 28, he attacked it vigorously. By the summer of 1838 Russell and Melbourne had become convinced that French Canada must be assimilated, and Lord Durham's Report had strengthened their conviction. Russell saw that the proposed federation would thwart the objective of assimilation, but he chose to attack it upon other grounds. "Such a mixture in politicks has never yet been. Such a provision for confusion was never yet created," he declared.[44] The division of powers between imperial, federal, and provincial governments would be "most difficult, intricate, & complex." The plan had nothing to support it but "mere theory" for it had neither been sought by the British population of Lower Canada nor recommended by Lord Durham. Russell had a "better and simpler way" of his own. He proposed that the Special Council should be continued for three years with the same powers as the old Council under the Quebec Act. During the interval, commissioners should be appointed by Upper Canada to confer with the Imperial government upon the details of a legislative union which would become effective when sanctioned by Parliament.

Russell's arguments swayed his colleagues to the extent that they agreed to reject the federal plan and have a draft bill, along the lines he suggested, prepared for further consideration.[45] With their approval he proceeded to dictate, to James Stephen, ten principles which were to serve as the basis for the heads of the new bill. That part of the Constitutional Act which separated the two provinces was to be repealed. Each province was to have equal representation in the legislature. The commissioners under the Canada Trade Act, assisted by four or six additional commissioners to be appointed by the provinces, and two to be named by Parliament, were to decide upon the terms of union and the amount of debt to be charged upon the united province. Whatever terms were agreed upon were to be submitted to Parliament for approval. The rights and privileges of the Roman Catholic Church were to be secured. The life of the Special Council in Lower Canada was to be extended until March 1842. Electoral divisions within the two provinces were to be determined by territorial extent as well as population. A civil list was to be established equal to the amount of the Upper Canadian civil list plus a sum for Lower Canada to be determined by the commissioners. Lord Durham's recommendation that the right to originate votes in supply should be controlled by the Executive was to be adopted.⁴⁶

At the Cabinet meeting on March 30, Russell argued for the adoption of his plan and Howick countered with the proposal that a joint committee be established by the legislatures of the two provinces "with a view either to a Legislative Union or a sort of federal Union." After lengthy discussion, the Cabinet found itself deadlocked, seven to seven, on the question of whether the union should be decided upon and the precise terms left till later, or whether the legislatures should be empowered to take measures for a union if they chose to do so. Finally, after Howick had left the meeting, Spring Rice, Chancellor of the Exchequer, came over to Russell's side and his plan was adopted as the Government's policy.⁴⁷ The period of indecision had finally come to an end.

On April 2, Lord Melbourne wrote to Russell commenting upon the decision that had been made: "We feel that we cannot impose this union upon Upper Canada without her consent, and therefore we give her a choice. We give Lower Canada no choice, but we impose it upon her during the suspension of her constitution."⁴⁸ Melbourne and Russell had looked with favour on Durham's recommendation of union and gradual assimilation. To them, it seemed both a feasible and a desirable course. It is doubtful if they ever seriously questioned the validity of the argument presented to support it. The political situation in which they found themselves made it difficult for them to do so. Faced with the task of formulating a Canadian policy which would escape violent criticism from the Radicals on the left and the Tories on the right, they were probably relieved to find that Durham's plan only required the Government to produce a union bill and left the details of assimilation to be worked out and implemented by the Canadian legislature. Melbourne, however, was bothered by Durham's proposal concerning the basis for representation. "If we pass the Union . . . in such a manner which gives the French any power or weight in the representative assembly, we shall not have a man for it in either province," he declared. "We shall not be able to persevere in our measure; and how are we to recede from it." Melbourne was fully aware of the weak position his Government occupied and the last thing he wanted was a storm in the House of Commons over Canadian policy.

Outside the Government, commercial interests on both sides of the Atlantic were endeavouring to press home the advantage gained by Durham's recommendation of union. The Montreal Constitutional Association submitted a draft bill which provided for equal representation in the assembly. Numerous electoral provisions designed to secure a British preponderance were included. English was stipulated as the official language of the legislature, but French was to be permitted in debate.⁴⁹ Robert Gillespie eagerly circulated Moffatt's letters from Toronto describing the enthusiasm for union in the Upper Canadian Assembly.⁵⁰ After reading some of Moffatt's letters which Gillespie had sent to Sir Robert Peel, John Beverley Robinson observed: "The game is begun already for no sooner has

Mr. Moffatt succeeded by his caucusing in obtaining a vote asking for the union upon certain terms which I dare say he did not strenuously object to, than he sets to work (as his letters shew) to counteract in England, any embarrassment that might be thrown in the way by the conditions."[81]

Edward Ellice, remembering the fiasco of 1822, and still favouring his federal plan, feared the Government was rushing precipitately into legislative union. As preparations were being made to introduce the measure in the House of Commons, he wrote to Russell expressing a hope that debate on the bill would be adjourned until the views and sentiments of Upper Canada could be considered. John Beverley Robinson was in England at the moment, Ellice pointed out, and should be consulted.[82]

Robinson was chagrined to find that his relationship with the Government differed completely from that of 1822. To be sure, his advice had been requested and had been freely given, but he had not been taken into the Government's confidence. Weeks after the Cabinet had decided upon a legislative union he left an interview with Normanby under the impression that the decision on Canadian policy was yet to be made.[83] The explanation was quite simple. The Cabinet had decided upon a policy which ran counter to Robinson's advice, and he had already declared what his course would be if this should happen. Simple though the explanation was, it seems never to have occurred to the Chief Justice. He was fully aware of the weak position the Government occupied and became convinced that they would take an early opportunity to resign rather than face the difficult task of formulating a Canadian policy. The numerous rumours circulating among the Tory party were his only source of information. Upon these he reported regularly to Sir George Arthur. He would have to wait for the public announcement of any Whig policy that might be forthcoming, but in the meantime he was freely circulating his criticism of the Durham Report and his counter proposals among the Tory leaders. His objective was to counter the efforts of the merchants by building up anti-unionist sentiment among the opposition in case the Whigs should surprise him by introducing a union bill unexpectedly.

Robinson was wrong in assuming that the Whigs had reached no decision on the Canadian problem, but he had accurately surmised that they would prefer to resign on some less significant issue rather than risk defeat on their Canadian policy. On May 3, the Government announced its intention to bring the Canadian question before Parliament. Two days later, when a bill for the suspension of the Jamaican constitution was carried by a majority of only five, the Whigs seized the opportunity and tendered their resignation. The "bed chamber crisis" ensued when Queen Victoria refused to dismiss the wives and daughters of Whig members who held positions in her household, and Sir Robert Peel, feeling that she would be influenced by them, declined to take office unless she did so. The Melbourne Government found itself back in office, but in an even weaker position than before. The Canadian difficulty would have to be faced, but the Government had no hope of withstanding any sustained opposition in the House of Commons. It was obvious that the Whigs must proceed with their legislative union, but on June 3, the very day appointed for introducing the measure in the House of Commons, Arthur's warning against "meddling" with Upper Canada arrived and provided an opportunity for a respite. After hasty consultation with his colleagues, Russell revised his plans and entered the House of Commons to propose two resolutions. The first

stated that it was "expedient to form a legislative union of the Canadas on principles of free and representative government. . . ." The second resolution proposed
that the Special Council should be continued in Lower Canada until 1842 with
such alteration of powers as was deemed advisable.

Russell outlined the Whigs' Canadian policy and presented their views on
Lord Durham's recommendations. He condemned the division of the old province
of Quebec in 1791 as having served to perpetuate French customs and institutions.
The pre-rebellion situation in Lower Canada he attributed directly to that division.
Parliament was now called upon to provide a solution for a very complex problem.
The restricted form of government in Lower Canada could not be continued indefinitely for it was out of harmony with North American political concepts and
was entirely repugnant to British subjects who had enjoyed representative institutions. He rejected both the oft-suggested annexation of Montreal to Upper Canada,
and the more grandiose scheme for North American union as impracticable. As
far as Russell and the Whigs were concerned there was only one solution—a
legislative union of the Canadas alone.

The Government could not accept Lord Durham's recommendation that representation in the united assembly should be based upon population. Russell recognized that in stating the objective with regard to representation he was, in reality,
stating the basic objective of the union. "I think the true policy of this country . . .,"
he declared, "is to give a British character to the whole province, to allow British
laws and British legislation to have a thorough scope. . . ."[64] This was to be accomplished by combining the two principles of population and territory to "give a
representation which may not be actually suitable to the amount of the population
at present, but which several years hence would more correctly be a representation of the people. . . ." Care must be taken to protect the French population from
oppression and injustice, but he was determined that "their jealousies and their
attachments to their own customs" would not be permitted to impede "that great
progression which . . . Canada is destined to make."

Russell agreed with Durham that a system of elective municipal government
was urgently required and indicated that a provision designed to remedy this defect
would be incorporated in the union bill. Durham's recommendation that a supreme
court should be established with appellate jurisdiction over all the North American
colonies was not unacceptable, but must be reserved for a separate measure. Durham
had recommended that steps should be taken to give the legislative council greater
weight without making it elective. In the absence of any specific suggestions as to
how this was to be accomplished, the Whigs had decided to restrict council appointments to those who had either been members of the assembly or who had held
Crown offices. In accordance with Lord Durham's recommendation, the united
assembly was to be given control over the Crown revenues after provision had
been made for an adequate civil list, but appropriations would be permitted only
for measures which had been recommended by the governor. There was no place
in Whig policy for the concept of responsible government as Durham had outlined
it; the recommendation was rejected as being completely incompatible with colonial
status.

Russell was under the impression that public opinion in Upper Canada was
not opposed to the principle of union, although the Assembly had insisted upon
terms which could not be "reasonably or fairly granted." However, additional in-

formation, which had just been received, indicated that the Upper Canadian Legislature was greatly disturbed that any action should be contemplated before its views had been considered. Under these circumstances, he was prepared only to recommend that Parliament should approve the principle of legislative union. He was ready to introduce a bill, but he did not consider it desirable to proceed with the details before consulting the people of Upper Canada.

Sir Robert Peel voiced the Tory objection that the Government should either introduce legislation for union or propose some alternative plan. He was personally dubious of the wisdom of approving, in principle, a union which was not to become effective until 1842. Beneath the surface of Peel's remarks there was an implicit accusation that the Whigs were endeavouring to shirk their responsibility merely to avoid the risk of defeat in the House.[55]

Charles Buller professed himself a supporter of any bill for union, but regretted that the Government was not prepared to sponsor legislation for British North American union. He was perturbed by the rejection of responsible government, and demanded of Russell whether he advocated that government should be conducted without the support of the majority in the Assembly.[56] The day after the debate he wrote to Durham, "With the exception of an indefinite Union at one time or another all your Report is clear thrown over."[57]

Speaking for a second time in the debate, Russell sought to answer both Peel and Buller. It had been the Government's intention, he asserted, to proceed with legislation upon the assumption that Upper Canada approved the measure and would send delegates to confer upon the details. It now developed that the Government had erred in its assumption, and further discussion would be necessary. It would be of great advantage in that discussion if the Government could assert that Parliament had approved the principle of legislative union. In reply to Buller's question, Russell enunciated a general maxim that was to have a great effect upon the character of the union. He was unwilling to state as a constitutional principle that colonial constitutions should be exact replicas of Great Britain's, but he did believe that "the executive should be carried on in such a way, as that their measures should be acceptable and agreeable to the representatives of the people. . . ."[58]

On June 10, another skirmish occurred in the House of Commons when Stanley gave notice that he intended to call for a vote on the expediency of pledging the House to the abstract principle of union. Realizing the necessity for a change in tactics, Russell declared that if Stanley merely thought that no pledge should be given until the details were revealed, he would withdraw his resolution and ask for leave to bring in the bill. If, however, the Tories were unwilling to accept the principle of union, he was prepared to drop the matter and press only the provision for the government of Lower Canada. When the Tories declined his invitation to reject union completely, Russell brought in the union bill on June 13 together with a bill extending the life of the Special Council in Lower Canada until March 1842.

With the details before them, the Tories were willing to signify their approval of the abstract principle of union by permitting the bill to receive a first reading. Beyond this point, however, Peel had no intention of going. On June 27 he inquired as to the Government's intentions. If the Government planned to limit its action to the Canada bill and insisted on pressing it to a second reading, he declared he would move the previous question.[59]

Despite Russell's previous assertions to the contrary, he was apparently considering a second reading for the union bill. The morning after Peel's announcement in the House of Commons, Charles Poulett Thomson, President of the Board of Trade, wrote a hasty note to Russell. "Surely it would be better *not* to press the Canada Bill to a 2d reading," he urged, "after what was said by Peel last night, and the expression of opinion by some of our friends."[60] Peel had declared himself in favour of the union "in quite as strong terms as we can expect," Thomson pointed out. Russell should now declare his satisfaction with the approval which the House had given, and announce that the recess would be utilized to obtain Canadian concurrence in the details of the plan. If a proper person were sent out to Canada with the bill, he could reconcile the differences of opinion regarding the details and obtain general approval for a measure similar to the one proposed. "But to do that," Thomson warned, "it is far better that he should not be hampered by all sorts of conflicting opinions delivered in Parlt. upon those details. . . ." Acting upon Thomson's advice, Russell announced in the House of Commons that the Government would not push the measure to a second reading. In reply to a further question from Peel, he stated that the bill was to be sent out to Canada with instructions to obtain information and, as far as possible, an approval of the plan. If objections were made to this course, every attention would be paid to the points raised, but, Russell added, much of the difficulty in legislating for Canada was due to factious opposition designed to attain party objectives rather than the good of Canada.

During the debates on union, Russell had outlined the objectives which the Government hoped to attain and had referred in general terms to the provisions by which this was to be accomplished. Some aspects of the bill which he introduced are worthy of closer examination. Although it provided for the repeal of Lord Ripon's Act, the effect was neutralized by a provision which placed all revenue at the disposal of the legislature after prior charges of collection, the civil list, and interest on the provincial debt had been deducted. Gaspé and the Magdalen Islands were to be annexed to New Brunswick. The united province was to be divided into five municipal districts, each of which was to be sub-divided into nine electoral districts. The legislative assembly would consist of ninety-eight members— two from each electoral district plus two each from Quebec, Montreal, Kingston, and Toronto. Tenure of legislative council appointments was set at eight years instead of life, and a president of the council was to be appointed by the governor. Appointments to the council were to be restricted to former judges of the superior court, militia colonels, members of the legislature and the executive council, chairmen of district councils, and mayors of incorporated cities and towns. Municipal government was to be entrusted to district councils which would be empowered to pass ordinances and to raise funds for municipal purposes by local taxation. Each electoral division was to elect three members to the district council. The division of the province into districts and electoral divisions was to be arranged by arbitrators —two to be appointed by the Special Council in Lower Canada and two by the Assembly in Upper Canada. An umpire was to be chosen by the arbitrators to preside over their deliberations, but if they failed to agree on the selection, the appointment would be made by the Crown. In addition, the arbitrators were to determine the amount of the civil list and the portion of the debt of Upper and Lower Canada which would be made a charge on the consolidated revenue of the united province.[61]

IV

Poulett Thomson had persuaded Russell to withdraw the Canada bill, and had proposed that a "proper person" should be sent to Canada to arrange the details and obtain general approval for the measure. Thomson had entered politics in 1826 after spending ten years with his father's Baltic timber company. He had risen rapidly in the Whig party and, although he was not yet forty, he had already held cabinet rank as President of the Board of Trade for five years. Eager for further honours, it is quite possible that he had himself in mind for the Canadian mission when he made the suggestion. Whether such was the case or not, it was to him that Russell first offered the appointment. Thomson was not unwilling to accept, but he demanded a reward in advance. "No one in these days seems disposed to make any sacrifice for the general advantage," Russell complained to Melbourne. "Thomson wants to have a peerage before he consents to go to Canada. This will not do."[62]

The appointment was offered, without success, to Lord Clarendon, the Minister Plenipotentiary to Madrid, and to Lord Dumferline who had only recently been elevated to the peerage upon his retirement from the House of Commons where he had served as Speaker for the past four years. The original negotiations were then renewed and early in August Lord Duncannon informed Edward Ellice that Thomson would probably accept. He had been informed that a peerage was out of the question at the moment, but the successful execution of the mission would almost certainly lead to one.[63] By the end of August it was arranged—Thomson had agreed to accept the appointment. At the same time Russell exchanged offices with Normanby in order to be in direct contact with the Governor General while he was in Canada. Informing Ellice of the arrangement, Russell requested that he give Thomson the benefit of his knowledge of Canadian affairs. The plan was that Thomson should "collect opinions on the way he finds most likely to succeed . . . bending any fancies of . . . [the Government] to meet the general wishes of the provinces."[64] Union was to be the Government's objective, "but not any one kind of Union, should he find another mode of effecting the object more popular."

Ellice agreed to assist Thomson in his preparations, but held out little hope that a legislative union would succeed. "I still maintain my own view of the case—," he informed Russell, "a view which Sir Geo. Grey and Stephen will tell you, was neither adopted hastily, nor to suit the emergency of last session. . . ."[65] He could see nothing but "formidable obstacles" in the way of the Government's plan. "I thought, & still think," he continued, "these were more likely to be overcome— by attempting a federal union to legislate on all objects of general interest—widening the general sphere of legislation as much as possible constantly and gradually— so as at last to absorb almost any local interest, & to make local legislatures more experienced" than in the past.

Simon McGillivray also conferred with Thomson and reported that Thomson had accepted his advice with "laudable docility."[66] McGillivray's opinions ran counter to those of Ellice. For him the only hope of benefit to the Canadas lay in a legislative union of the two provinces. The Family Compact, bent on pre- serving their own local interests and influence at Toronto, would advocate the union of British North America in the hope of defeating all unions, McGillivray warned. There were, however, strong cards which the Governor General could play.

Upper Canada desired union in order to reduce the burden of its debt—the bait for the British party in Lower Canada should be to suppress the French party. If Thomson kept his own counsel and played one party skilfully against the other, he would succeed in obtaining union petitions from both provinces. Lord Durham also co-operated with Thomson, meeting with him on several occasions and giving him the benefit of his advice even to the final hour before he sailed.

To the Cabinet, Thomson had seemed both a logical and a desirable choice for the Canadian appointment, but beyond the narrow Government circle, his selection created a storm of protest. His unpopularity was said to be due to his personal character, "a compound of inordinate vanity, selfishness, and insincerity."[67] Among his most vociferous detractors were the merchants with North American interests, but their objections stemmed from his business connections, especially his interest in Baltic timber, rather than his personal characteristics. The British North American Association of Liverpool passed resolutions recalling his policies in the past and expressing the hope that he would change them. Petitions to the Queen against his appointment were signed by merchants and ship owners in London, Birmingham, and Glasgow. When Russell Ellice, Edward's brother, added his name to the protest, Thomson determined to neutralize the mercantile opposition. In a letter which was published in the *Morning Chronicle* he stated that it was at Edward Ellice's "earnest request" and "acting entirely on his advice" that he accepted the appointment. Thomson greatly exaggerated Ellice's influence, for he had done no more than point out the advantages and disadvantages involved. When Ellice categorically denied Thomson's assertion, a bitterness developed between the two men which lasted almost until Thomson's death.

What were the prospects for Thomson's success in the Canadas? Upon being informed that union was not to be pushed through during the current session, Sir George Arthur had written, "Most heartily do I rejoice that my communication . . . [arrived] in time to lead to the postponemt. of any final measure."[68] The diametrically opposed versions of the rebellion and its causes presented in Lord Durham's Report and Sir Francis Head's *Narrative*, published in 1839, had so inflamed the entire population that "nothing cd. have been done which wd. have satisfied any party." From Lower Canada, however, Sir John Colborne was offering a more objective and a more accurate opinion: the British portion of the population wanted union without delay and the French Canadians were not as strongly opposed to the measure as they had been. In Upper Canada, he was certain that the districts east of the Trent River and the Bay of Quinte strongly favoured the union, as did a majority of the settlers west of the Midland District. There were, however, many in the latter region who were strongly opposed to it.[69]

Commenting on the bill which Russell had introduced, Colborne criticized the innovations which would produce a radical departure from the constitution of 1791. He assumed that these represented an effort to propitiate those "who may not be attached to our Institutions," but recommended that details which would give rise to party conflict in the Canadas should be withdrawn. Instead, the bill should contain only the clauses necessary to allow the union to go safely into operation. Any proposed innovations should be left to the provincial legislature after union had taken place. Rejecting the theory of territorial representation and the new electoral districts involved, he proposed a plan for equal representation which would require but slight modification of the existing electoral divisions. Under this plan, he predicted that one-quarter of the members elected from Lower Canada would be of British origin, and estimating the population at 520,000 French Canadians to 180,000 British, he declared this to be a fair proportion. The vast extent of territory involved would render it almost essential that deputies for the governor, the commissioner of Crown lands, the surveyor general, and the registrar should be appointed to reside at Toronto. Colborne did not favour the expansion of municipal government beyond that which already existed in Upper Canada, but, if it was considered expedient, he felt this could be done by the provincial legislature.

In sending Thomson out on a difficult task the Cabinet had sought to provide him with the means of attaining success. It was recognized that the key to Upper Canadian acquiescence might well be a financial one. The repeated representations of John Beverley Robinson and Receiver General John Henry Dunn during the past year had underscored the financial plight of the province. Thomson was authorized to promise that the Imperial Government would guarantee the interest on a loan of £1,500,000, but such a promise was only to be made in order to obtain approval of a "final and satisfactory settlement." Lord Howick had attempted to make the settlement of the clergy reserves question by the Upper Canadian Legislature a *sine qua non* for the loan, but he was overruled by his colleagues. Commenting on Howick's proposal Thomson wrote, "Of course it might be *tried* and most likely the only important part, namely the utilizing the lands could be obtained, but not the distribution—and to postpone our Union till that question was carried in Upper Canada alone, would be deferring the Union not to 1842, but to the Greek Kalends."[10]

For Thomson's guidance, Russell forwarded Sir John Colborne's comments on the union bill introduced during the last session. In an official despatch Russell outlined the object of the mission and suggested means by which it might be attained. The bill which he had introduced was the product of "deliberate reflection" upon the numerous suggestions made by Lord Durham. Its progress had been delayed as a result of "various circumstances," particularly the representations received from the Legislature of Upper Canada. It would be Thomson's first duty to learn the "deliberate wishes" of the Canadas and "to obtain their co-operation by frank and unreserved personal intercourse." The Government attached minor importance to the subordinate details of the bill that had been introduced, but found "no sufficient reason for distrusting the principles on which it proceeds." Thomson was to endeavour to obtain approval for a legislative union in which the three estates of the provincial legislature would be maintained and a permanent civil list would be provided. A system of freely elected municipal government was also to be considered an essential feature of the union.[11]

Russell suggested that Thomson might commence by appointing representatives from each province to draft articles of union which would be submitted to the Upper Canadian Legislature for approval. Alternatively, he could assemble the Legislature and ask that commissioners be appointed to meet with those to be selected by the Special Council in Lower Canada. If the Assembly proved uncooperative, it could be dissolved and an appeal made directly to the electorate, but in the unsettled state of the province, Russell urged that this course should not be resorted to without the "gravest deliberation." Whatever course was adopted, the Government would expect to receive from Thomson, as soon as possible, a plan of representation based upon competent authority which would enable it to lay the scheme before Parliament "with confidence in the data on which it has been formed and in the justice of the general arrangement."[72] "I will not now argue," Russell continued, "on a further supposition, vizt. that from difficulty of detail, or mutual disinclination, the plan of Union may be found altogether impracticable." If such an impasse was encountered, Thomson was to inform the Government immediately and, at the same time, to outline "the nature of any alternative which may seem . . . more conducive to the general good."

Reports from Upper Canada led Russell to believe that Thomson would be questioned about responsible government. He reiterated his conviction that constitutional principles could not be reduced to positive enactments, but went on to expand upon the admission he had made to Buller in Parliament. The importance of maintaining harmony between the executive and the legislature, he agreed, did not admit of question. Thomson was therefore instructed to call to his councils and employ in the public service individuals "who by their position and character have obtained the general confidence & esteem of the inhabitants of the Province."

On September 13, 1839, his fortieth birthday, Thomson embarked in the frigate *Pique* at Portsmouth. After a final conference with Lord Durham he was off for Canada. As his ship slowly made its way toward the colonies he was to govern, he reflected upon his mission. "I have a better chance of settling things in Canada than any one they could have found to go;" he wrote in his journal, "and if I had not taken it then, as I could not well have got out of the government, I should have shared in the disgrace next session."[73] In mid-ocean, as he planned his course of action, he glanced over his papers and found he was missing a despatch that would quite likely prove useful. While he was preparing for his mission, he had learned that the Colonial Office was in the process of formulating a new policy on the tenure of office.[74] A circular despatch had been drafted stating that colonial offices were not to be considered as life appointments held during good behaviour. Colonial officers could expect, henceforth, to be called upon for their resignations whenever "sufficient motives of public policy may suggest the expediency" of new appointments. The appointment of a new governor was cited as an instance upon which a change of officers might be considered advisable. Thomson had instantly recognized the despatch as a potential weapon to coerce anti-union members of the Family Compact. When he found the despatch was not among his papers, he took the first opportunity to ask that it be sent without delay. ". . . Altho' I shall certainly not hesitate about dismissing any officials who may be opposed to my views," he wrote, "I should liked [sic] to be fortified by that circular."[75]

As the *Pique* approached Quebec, Lord John Russell was writing another despatch devoted entirely to the difficult question of responsible government. Thomson was to refuse any explanation which could be construed "to imply an acquiescence" in the numerous petitions and addresses requesting the concession of a responsible ministry. Russell had long since taken his stand that the governor was responsible to the Imperial government and could not delegate his responsibility to his executive councillors. Nonetheless, he had conceded that it would be a mistake to attempt to govern in opposition to a majority in the assembly. This concession was beginning to assume the proportions of a major concept in his policy. The British government, he informed Thomson, had no desire to thwart the efforts of representative assemblies in North America to institute reform and improvements. Thomson was to maintain harmony between the executive and the legislature and was to oppose the wishes of the assembly only when the "honour of the Crown or the interests of the Empire" were at stake. In terms of action this implied that Thomson was to be his own prime minister. He was free to choose his executive council as he saw fit, but in doing so he must endeavour to ensure that the executive would always have the support of the assembly. This was not responsible government and Russell made no pretence that it was. Nonetheless, it was this new concept which was to change the character of the union.

The union was conceived primarily as the first step in the anglicization of French Canada. Historians have sought to show that this objective was defeated by the attainment of responsible government, but surely this is an erroneous conclusion. When the union was based upon Russell's new "harmony concept" and the principle of equal representation was adopted, anglicization became an unrealistic objective although it was not immediately recognized as such. The French party held the balance of power. In so far as the ultimate character of the union was concerned, the fact that they united with the Upper Canadian Reformers on a responsible government platform is but little more than a coincidence. What is significant is that they were in a position to form a coalition which would thwart assimilation. The terms of union and the constitutional principle upon which it was based contained the seeds of a quasi-federal system within the framework of a legislative union. Nothing short of the creation of a party embracing all members of British origin in the united assembly could have prevented the emergence of that dualism which was a characteristic of the United Province of Canada throughout most of its history.

CHAPTER FOUR

PRELUDE TO UNION

IT WAS NO SIMPLE TASK that Charles Poulett Thomson had been sent to accomplish. Durham's proposal that representation should be based on population had been rejected in favour of giving greater weight to Upper Canada, but with this exception: his plan for a legislative union and gradual assimilation had been adopted. It was Thomson's assignment to gain approval for such a union. Lord John Russell had suggested several modes by which he might proceed, but before the *Pique* reached Canada he had determined upon his course of action. His nature rebelled at the thought of surrendering the initiative by summoning a constitutional convention. No, he would present his own terms for union and seek approval of them. Lower Canada presented no great difficulty, for the Special Council had been appointed by Colborne after the first rebellion and could probably be managed. Upper Canada, however, was quite another matter. Since 1822, Upper Canadian High Tories had shown a deep-rooted antipathy to any suggestion of union, an antipathy based upon religious, political, and social grounds as well as upon those of self-interest. It was true that during the last session of the Legislature the Assembly had approved of union, but only upon terms which were unacceptable if the Durham formula was to be a guide at all. The problem was to obtain Upper Canadian assent for union unencumbered by such conditions. Unknown to Thomson was the fact that Sir George Arthur had increased the difficulty of his task by encouraging the ultra Tories in their opposition. With the aid of Robert Baldwin Sullivan, Christopher Hagerman, and John Macaulay, the Lieutenant-Governor had prepared a detailed criticism of Lord John Russell's union bill.[1] Thomson, nonetheless, proceeded to overcome these difficulties and achieve his objective in a manner which revealed him to be a most competent practitioner of the political arts, if not a statesman. Once he had succeeded in obtaining the desired assent to union, the Whigs no longer encountered any major obstacles in Parliament and easily carried their Canada bill.

I

Thomson landed at Quebec on October 19, 1839, and, after conferring with Sir John Colborne, proceeded to attack the union problem. Before meeting with the Special Council, he had a private interview with at least one of its members. John Neilson, who together with Papineau had waged an anti-union campaign seventeen years before, left no doubt in the Governor's mind that he would never accept the idea of union.

Neilson had come to Canada in 1793 as a boy of seventeen. Through the years he had learned to understand and appreciate his French-Canadian neighbours and they, in turn, had accepted him as virtually one of their own. As the proprietor and editor of the *Quebec Gazette,* which was published in both languages, he exercised considerable influence in Lower Canada, particularly amongst the French-Canadian population. A strict constitutionalist, he had joined the Lower Canadian Reformers in their struggle to gain control of the purse. His firm belief that justice was to be obtained from the British government, if the facts could be made known, exerted a moderating influence on the reform movement in Lower Canada during the 1820's and the early 1830's. When Papineau began to advocate radical solutions for Lower Canadian constitutional problems, Neilson separated from him, in 1834, and retired from politics until he accepted an appointment to the Special Council in 1838. Although he was generally regarded as a Reformer, many of Neilson's opinions were similar to those of the Upper Canadian Tories. He strongly favoured maintaining colonial status for the Canadas and was opposed to responsible government, both because he feared it would lead to independence and because he considered it a constitutional rationalization of the spoils system. Neilson's conservative outlook, his ingrained provincialism, and his sincere appreciation of French-Canadian values predetermined that he would be an implacable foe of the union from the moment it was first suggested.

Despite Neilson's opposition, Thomson easily prevailed upon the Special Council to pass resolutions in favour of the union, a permanent civil list, and the principle that Upper Canada's debt should be charged on the consolidated revenue of the united province. Success had come even more easily than anticipated and Thomson was elated, especially since he had achieved his ends without any alteration in the composition of the Special Council. He was puzzled to find, however, that *Le Canadien* was adopting a resigned attitude: "Si l'Angleterre renonce à la politique de maintenir une nationalité française dans le Bas-Canada, l'Union, malgré tous les sacrifices qu'elle exigera de nous, est ce que tous les Canadiens Français peuvent attendre de mieux pour le présent et pour l'avenir." [2] Was this an accurate presentation of French-Canadian feeling? Lord Durham had predicted that the French Canadians would resign themselves to their fate, but Thomson was dubious that this had happened already. He did not believe the sentiments of the French-Canadian population had changed, but rather that an awareness of both their own weakness and the great power of the Executive restrained them from any acts of insubordination.[3] Actually, he had no wish to concern himself with French-Canadian opinion at the moment. Now that the Special Council had approved of union, the immediate problem lay in Upper Canada and he was anxious to proceed to Toronto as soon as possible.

In preparation for his visit to the upper province, Thomson had summoned Sir George Arthur to confer with him in Montreal while the Special Council was in session. Arthur still considered the union to be an unwise measure, but, as it had been adopted by the Imperial Government, his strong sense of duty demanded that he should render Thomson every assistance. He strongly recommended that the Governor submit his union proposals to the Legislature, rather than dissolve the Assembly and place them directly before the electorate. Thomson would have preferred to sample Upper Canadian opinion by personal residence before making such a decision, but, realizing that time was short, he accepted Arthur's advice. It was agreed that the Legislature should be summoned to meet on December 3.[4]

Upon Arthur's return to Toronto, he had a distinct sense of uneasiness as he contemplated Thomson's approaching visit. While the Governor was in Upper Canada, Arthur's own position would be anomalous, if not superfluous, and he felt this keenly. But more important was his sense of guilt for having previously opposed the union. In letters to both Thomson and Russell, he sought to explain the stand which he had taken. He had only endeavoured to follow his instructions by continuing the policy of Sir Francis Bond Head. Lord Durham had repeatedly condemned a legislative union of the Canadas, and Arthur had endorsed his remarks. Now, he was called upon to reverse his position; he was prepared to do so, but the whole situation was most embarrassing. He had begged Thomson to remain in Lower Canada and permit him to handle the problem of obtaining Upper Canadian assent to union, but the Governor would not consider entrusting the most important aspect of his mission to hands other than his own.[5]

The Upper Canadian Reformers, on the other hand, eagerly awaited Thomson's arrival. An article in the *Colonial Gazette,* which had been copied by Upper Canadian papers, left the impression that the Governor was likely to oppose the High Tories and introduce a new political climate in the province. Seeking to improve upon the occasion, Francis Hincks continued his correspondence with LaFontaine. He was afraid that their "just indignation" over Thomson's failure to release the political prisoners would prevent French Canadians from giving the Governor their support, but he added, "I believe however it will be wise to do so as much as possible. He must displease the Tories and if things are managed right, he may be brought to support liberal measures."[6] When LaFontaine indicated a preference for a federal union, Hincks replied, "As to the federative Union I am entirely of your opinion but I think Lord Durham's idea of District Councils is intended for this end. What would those District Councils be but a Legislature without a Legislative Council & electing their own president?"[7] French-Canadian acceptance of the union was an essential prerequisite of the alliance of Reformers which he was attempting to form and Hincks missed no opportunity to advocate it in his letters. "Be assured the Union is the only chance for us Reformers," he wrote. "I am glad to find that you are cautious in advocating it. I almost fear *Le Canadien* has said too much in its favour. Let the Tories fall into the pit of their own digging."[8]

II

Upon his arrival in Toronto, on November 21, Thomson was coldly received by municipal and provincial officials. The Mayor and Aldermen of the city declared in the address which they presented that any legislative union which was not "predicated upon the ascendency of the loyal portion of the inhabitants" or which gave equal rights to French Canadians would be fatal to the imperial connection. Thomson replied curtly that the Imperial Government had decided upon the policy of union with a "deep conviction that it [would] cement the connexion between the Colonies and the Parent State . . . but to be of permanent advantage, it must be founded upon principles of equal justice to all Her Majesty's Subjects."[9] The warm enthusiasm with which the populace of Toronto had greeted Lord Durham was noticeably absent during Thomson's public appearances. As he went forth to take his oath of office, one observer noted there was "an abortion of a cheer which was worse than silence." [10]

Undeterred by his apparent lack of popularity, the Governor pressed on with his mission. Shortly after his arrival in Toronto he conferred again with Sir George Arthur on the problem that faced them. Arthur foresaw no difficulty in gaining assent for union as an abstract principle, but predicted that opponents of the measure would endeavour to attach conditions which would render it altogether unacceptable. [11] His prejudice against the measure apparently blinded him to the fact that most of those who insisted upon conditions could not be classified accurately as opponents of union. Arthur ignored the fact that his Solicitor General, William Draper, and many other Tories strongly favoured union, but considered it unsafe for Upper Canada unless it was accompanied by adequate safeguards. Attorney General Hagerman, who rejected union in any shape or form, was one of the few real opponents of the measure in the Assembly.

Having experienced considerable embarrassment himself, Arthur could sympathize with Draper and Hagerman in the situation in which they now found themselves. Thomson naturally expected the two principal officers of the Government to introduce and support his union proposals in the Assembly, but both felt they were committed by their course during the previous session. Thomson had little patience with Arthur's explanation that union had not previously been a Government measure. The fact that it was now Government policy was, for him, more than sufficient explanation for any reversals required of the law officers. He would regret having to turn Hagerman out of office for he had some followers in the Assembly, but it might be necessary to do so. He was determined that union should not be regarded as an open question. [12] For the moment he would hold his hand. Perhaps both Draper and Hagerman would be more tractable after he had talked with them and shown them the tenure of office despatch of October 16.

Supremely confident of his own ability to influence men, Thomson proposed that as many members as possible should be interviewed before the session began. This was a task in which Arthur could share; his first-hand knowledge of the individuals concerned would be most useful. As the interviews progressed, Thomson's position was outlined to High Tories, Moderates, and ultra Reformers alike. Re-union was definitely decided upon and must be accepted, but there was at least one important compensating factor. The Upper Canadian debt was to become a charge upon the consolidated revenue of the united province. Each section of the province would have equal representation in the assembly. A permanent civil list was essential. If any stipulations were made regarding the location of the seat of government, Thomson would take "other measures for getting . . . assent to the Union." [13] Assurance was given that the Imperial government would provide assistance for immigration in order that the objective of British predominance might be more speedily attained. Although Thomson made no official pronouncement regarding the guaranteed loan, he must have suggested in his interviews that he had this promise of the Imperial government in his pocket. By the time the Legislature met, it was common knowledge that approval of the union would be rewarded by financial assistance for the public works programme.

Within a few days, Arthur informed Thomson, "Your personal communications are evidently working exactly as you wish." [¹] Henry Sherwood, an eminent High Tory who represented Brockville in the Assembly, was "highly satisfied" with the report he had heard of the Governor's conversation with Hagerman. In his discussions with the Reformers, Thomson avoided the negative aspect of Lord John Russell's views on responsible government and stressed the "harmony concept." It was perhaps more than mere misunderstanding that led the Reformers to conclude that responsible government, as they understood it, was about to be conceded. After his interview Francis Hincks declared, "I am now fully persuaded that the Union will be the only means of securing the liberties of the people." [¹] Hincks suggested that the English Tories might spoil the bill if Upper Canada were to give unconditional assent to union, but Thomson assured him that when the bill was sent home, it would be passed without any major alterations. It was unnecessary to seek out William Hamilton Merritt. Scarcely had Thomson arrived in Upper Canada when Merritt began to bombard him with letters declaring that he had been a constant supporter of union, denying the allegation that Upper Canada's debt could be attributed to an overly ambitious public works programme, and suggesting the means of raising additional loans to complete the waterway to Lake Huron and Lake Michigan. [¹]

Within a few days of his arrival, Thomson recorded his initial impressions for the benefit of Lord John Russell. Upper Canada's need for the union was ten times greater than that of Lower Canada, but, nonetheless, it was not going to be easy to obtain the necessary assent. ". . . Unless there be some great changes, and I know of none that is practicable but the Union, all is up," he warned. [¹] Upper Canadians were so much in the habit of talking about separation that they were beginning to believe it. Despite their professions of loyalty, the High Tories were as bad as the others in this respect. Thomson found public finances to be even more deranged than he had anticipated. In terse, forceful phrases he described Upper Canada's financial predicament: "The deficit of £75,000 a year; more than equal to the income. The Public officers nearly one and all proved to be defaulters by an investigation which is now going on. All Public works suspended & emigration going on fast *from* the Province—Every man's property worth only half what it was. This is a pretty state of things to deal with, and I do not exaggerate it." [¹]

III

When the Legislature met, on December 3, Thomson was still far from satisfied with the attitude of Hagerman and Draper, but he had decided not to ask for their resignations at the moment. His conversations with them led him reluctantly to concede that the situation was an unusual one. In addition, he probably realized that one would neutralize the other in the Assembly. Hagerman would vote in the negative on the abstract question of union and Draper would cancel his vote. Moreover, Thomson required a spokesman to introduce his proposals in the Assembly and Draper appeared to be the only possible choice. His previous support of the union would permit him to act as Government leader up to the moment when resolutions were introduced in favour of the Upper Canadian conditions. Draper felt bound to support such resolutions and thus, at this point, Hagerman would assume the role of Government spokesman and strongly oppose them. It was a situation that Thomson deplored, but he was resolved to try his proposals before the Legislature. If he failed, he could always resort to a dissolution and place the issue directly before the electorate.

Four days after the session opened, the question of union was placed formally before the Legislature in separate messages from the Governor to the Legislative Council and the Assembly. Three specific principles were set forth as the basis upon which the union was to rest: equal representation, a sufficient civil list, and the Upper Canadian debt to be a charge on the consolidated revenue.

In the Legislative Council, which, hitherto, had been considered an impregnable High Tory stronghold, Thomson achieved a major victory, and, in doing so, he drove a wedge between the last-ditch, ultra Tories and the rest of their colleagues. On December 13, just six days after the message had been received, union on the Governor's terms was approved by a vote of fourteen to eight.[19] "They approve the principles on which the union is proposed, assent to the terms on which I offer it . . . and remit the details to the wisdom of the Govt. and Parlt.," Thomson reported to Russell. "I hope you will think this is pretty well managed, considering that last year, they wd. not agree to the union itself even, upon any conditions."[20] Of the eight who recorded their dissent to the measure, six were Toronto men and the other two were under their influence, the Governor explained. "Your confounded Bishop headed the opposition in all things, tho' I taxed him with his promise not to engage in Politics."[21]

Thomson had contributed materially to the success of his measure in the Council. By insisting upon the attendance of the non-Toronto members, he had obtained the "most numerous Council ever assembled" and had, thus, counteracted the perpetual Toronto majority. His interviews and the tenure of office despatch, which he had published two days after the session opened, also had their effect. Robert Baldwin Sullivan, who only a few weeks earlier had condemned the Assembly for "admitting the notice of Union upon any terms," abandoned the ultra Tories on the grounds of personal political expediency, and supported the measure in the Legislative Council with one of the ablest speeches of his career. It was reported that when he was congratulated on the speech Sullivan replied, "Yes it was a good speech, but not half so good as the one I made a year ago from the other point of view."[22] John Macaulay's conversion, paradoxically, was based upon a tenet of High Tory faith. He had voted for union, he explained to his mother, although he entertained "great dread of the consequences," because it had been deliberately adopted by the Cabinet and "I therefore have felt it to be my duty to give up my own opinions & do all in my power to forward the views of the Government whose Servant I am."[23]

Thomson had used every means at his disposal to isolate the ultra Tories. He had aligned moderate members of the party—and those who could be brought to support a moderate position—with erstwhile political opponents who, for personal, geographic, economic, and political reasons, were willing to accept union on his terms. High Toryism had reached its nadir; not only had the Governor denied the ultras the British Government's support, but he had used its full weight against them. He could not have done otherwise. When the Melbourne Government adopted Durham's solution, they were committed both to a union "upon principles of equal justice to all Her Majesty's subjects," and to the proposition that the

English-speaking members of the united assembly would act as a bloc. They had already strayed from Durham's definition of equal justice and would stray further, but they could permit no deviation from the second commitment. If the Tories were allowed to use the power and authority of the Imperial government for their own purposes, as they had done in the past, the continuation of party conflict after the union would be encouraged, and this would lead to the defeat of the assimilation policy. Thomson was dedicated to the eradication of political differences. It would be his objective to create a large Moderate party that would encompass all, save a mere handful of ultra Tories and radical Reformers.

In the Assembly, the proceedings followed the pattern predicted, but Thomson was both surprised and annoyed at the strength of the opposition that his proposals encountered. Draper introduced the Governor's terms for union and gave them his support, but, at the same time, he declared that he could not accept a union arrangement which did not include the conditions approved last session. He was placed at once in an illogical and embarrassing position to the great delight of the Reformers who chided him continually. As Government leader, Draper successfully opposed an attempt by Sherwood and Gowan to have Lord John Russell's union bill presented to the House.[24] Both Draper and Thomson feared that if the Assembly were given the bill, a lengthy and unproductive discussion of its details would ensue. Two days later, however, during Draper's absence from the House, a second request for the bill was passed by a large majority. The Governor's annoyance began to mount. He would have to send the bill, but he would give the Assembly to understand that it was beyond their competence to attempt to arrange the details of union. "If, when they have assented to the terms proposed in my message, they then choose to add any recommendations, they will of course receive the best attention," he informed Sir George Arthur.[25]

Draper pressed on with his unwelcome task despite the embarrassment of his position which he felt had been accentuated by the publication of the despatch of October 16. In moving the adoption of his resolution approving equal representation, he declared that concession on this point would improve the possibility of securing the English language stipulation and the location of the capital in Upper Canada. Henry Sherwood refused to accept this argument and gave notice that he would move in amendment the resolution approved last session. He could not regard equal representation as an application of the principle of equal justice. The representation proposal was clearly designed to produce a British preponderance, Sherwood asserted, and with this he was in complete agreement, but he was determined to ensure that end beyond all doubt.

Throughout most of the debate the Reformers supported Thomson's terms, but, on the question of a permanent civil list, they withheld their support until the grant was restricted to ten years or the life of the Queen.[26] Francis Hincks jubilantly described the result of their firm stand to LaFontaine. "The sol. genl. who is govt. organ asked an adjournment and yesterday stated that tho' *his own opinion remained unchanged* he was instructed by the govt. to propose an amendment to meet the views of the supporters of the measure. You may imagine the . . . Tories and their exasperation."[27]

The real crisis came when John Cartwright, the president of the Commercial Bank of Kingston and a staunch High Tory, attempted to add the Upper Canadian terms to Thomson's three basic principles. Draper supported Cartwright, and

Hagerman momentarily assumed the role of Government leader. In opposing Cartwright, Hagerman declared that if Lord John Russell's bill had been "the Bill" he would have opposed it had he stood alone. But the Governor had made new proposals. "Under all the circumstances of the case," he continued, "I have not the slightest hesitation in saying that the conditions of the [Governor's] Message are just and reasonable in themselves. . . . If a union take place you cannot ask it but upon terms of justice." [28] Lest it be supposed that he was bowing to coercion, Hagerman reiterated his opposition to the whole concept of union. "If the constitution of 1791 cannot be sustained, all that I can say is that I have washed my hands of it, and I shall retire. I was born a British subject and so I will die."

As the debate progressed, Thomson and Arthur were busy behind the scenes soothing the injured pride of Draper and Hagerman, and alternately threatening and reasoning with Sherwood and Cartwright. [29] Repeatedly, Thomson explained that the Assembly would not be permitted to dictate the terms of union. Recommendations, submitted in the proper form, would be quite acceptable, but only after his proposals had been approved. Arthur formed the impression that Sherwood was ready to concede the point, but Cartwright remained obdurate. Finally, on December 19, the vote was taken. After preliminary votes on amendments in which Draper and Hagerman followed their natural inclinations, the principle of union was approved forty-seven to six with Hagerman, Draper, Cartwright, and Sherwood all voting in the affirmative. Equal representation and the amended civil list proposition were passed by large majorities and the debt provision was approved without a division. It was a major triumph for Thomson—the Assembly had accepted union on his terms. The effect of his efforts was plainly visible. An attempt by William Benjamin Robinson to have the union rejected completely was supported by only nine of his fellow Tories, and four of these voted for union once the amendment had been defeated. [30] Cartwright's efforts to incorporate the Upper Canadian terms in the union scheme were opposed by thirty-four members. Of these, sixteen (eleven Tories and five Reformers) had insisted, just nine months before, that without the terms union was totally unacceptable. [31] As a result of Thomson's stand, Tories who had favoured union on their own terms were forced to reconsider their position. Those who remained unwilling to settle for less began to realign themselves with the ultras while the remainder followed Draper's lead to form the nucleus of a Moderate coalition.

The Governor was elated with his success. "I have done my business," he wrote home. "The Union is carried triumphantly through the Legislature of both Provinces. . . . My ministers vote against me. So I govern through the opposition, who are truly 'Her Majesty's'. . . . It is something to have completed my business before I get an answer to my announcement of arrival in the country." [32]

IV

Thomson's success did not cause him to lose sight of the unsatisfactory state of affairs in Upper Canada. Summarizing the situation for Lord John Russell, he reported that the Government had not only "abstained from taking the initiative in measures of Legislation, but it appears to have studiously repudiated those Legitimate means of influence, without which, it could scarcely be carried on." [33] From this source stemmed most of the disorganization, abuses, and dissatisfaction so prevalent in the province. The Assembly was split into half a dozen parties with the Government having *"none* and *no one man* to depend on!"[34]

In essence, Thomson's major criticism was that the Lieutenant-Governor had failed to act as his own prime minister and had shown a tendency to hide behind the Executive Council. As a result, the legitimate power and influence which he should have wielded had passed to the Family Compact on the one hand and the Assembly on the other. Under these circumstances, Thomson was not at all surprised that a demand for responsible government had developed, but he was convinced that in its extreme and inadmissible sense this could be avoided:

By the Union of the Provinces, the important changes which are indispensable will be greatly facilitated. A good departmental organization may be effected,—a more vigorous and efficient system of Government may be established, which, conducted in harmony with the wishes of the People will at the same time be enabled to give a direction to the popular branch of the Legislature, and also to check the encroachments upon the powers and functions of the Executive, which have been carried so far, and have produced so much mischief. . . . The people will be satisfied that whilst there is a steady determination on the part of the Home Government to resist unconstitutional demands, there is no desire, either that the affairs of the Province should be mismanaged for the supposed benefit of the few, or that a minority opposed to them in feeling and principle should govern it, in opposition both to themselves and to the Home Government.[35]

Upon informing Russell of the Assembly's assent to his union proposals, Thomson admitted that the civil list was not to be on as permanent a basis as he had anticipated, but he considered the arrangement to be a fair and reasonable one. Although it was soon to be asserted that the Assembly had merely approved the principle of a civil list and had not abdicated its right to appropriate the fixed amounts, such was not the Governor's opinion at the time. He hoped that the "generous confidence" which had been shown in leaving both the amount and its distribution to the British Government would be appreciated at home and that he would be supported in his endeavours to limit the size of the civil list and to leave as much as possible to the legitimate control of the Assembly.[36]

The Upper Canadian Reformers' hopes for the future were, like the Governor's, based upon the success of the union. They had supported Thomson's project in the Assembly with the firm conviction that by union alone could responsible government and reform be attained. Nonetheless, the Upper Canadian debates were a source of some embarrassment to Hincks in his correspondence with LaFontaine. He agreed that equal representation was unjust to French Canada, but asked, "Can you at present hope for more?"[37] The provision concerning Upper Canada's debt was "downright robbery," he admitted, "but we as Upper Canadians cannot well refuse the measure as a whole on this ground." On the civil list question, everything would depend on the amount. Whatever the arrangement the executive must be financially dependent upon the assembly—this must be regarded as a *"sine qua non."*

LaFontaine was not entirely satisfied with Hincks's explanation of the Reformers' course in the Assembly. In his opinion, it would have been a better policy to have opposed the union and forced a dissolution; an election victory would then have given the Reformers a commanding position. To this Hincks replied that the existing electoral laws and the threat of Tory violence rendered such a victory improbable. Although he had described the debt provision as "downright robbery," he modified his opinion when LaFontaine was critical of the

Reformers for supporting the principle. Most of this money had been spent on extending the St. Lawrence waterway—a project that would benefit both provinces and which would eventually produce a revenue. It was only just that similar improvements in Lower Canada should be given priority, but he could not accept LaFontaine's suggestion that the extinction of seigniorial tenure would make an equitable *quid pro quo*, for such a project would never produce a revenue. Hincks agreed that it was "not improbable" that Thomson had deceived the Reformers as LaFontaine suggested, but he asked him to believe that they had acted "to the best of our Judgement for the good of our common cause." [38] In spite of the French-Canadian leader's criticisms, Hincks remained firm in his oft-repeated conviction. "I am convinced the Union as proposed is the best plan to effect our common object. A representative Govt. & a united Legislature must give us all we want or *Separation*." Some details of the union were admittedly objectionable, but given responsible government, "which we must have," these could be easily altered.

The High Tories saw in union nothing but doom. Not only did it portend the end of British connection, but it also seriously threatened the position of the Church of England in Upper Canada. "The proposition for the Union was carried in the Legislative Council in a manner disgraceful to those who made up the majority," Strachan declared to John Macaulay's brother, the Reverend William Macaulay. "Your Brother does not hesitate to say that since he took place he has no opinion but that of Govt. Accordingly he has given his vote for papal ascendency and may in a few days be called upon to vote away the Clergy Reserves." [39]

V

Strachan might well fear for the safety of his clergy reserves. Lord Durham had reported that the reserves were considered by many to be the primary cause of the rebellion in Upper Canada. Lord John Russell had instructed Thomson to "consult the persons on whose judgment you can most rely" and endeavour to find an acceptable solution for the problem. [40] Thomson required no further urging. He was fully aware that the clergy reserve question was "the root of all the troubles of the Province—the cause of the Rebellion—the never failing watchword at the hustings—the perpetual source of discord, strife and hatred." [41] The problem must be settled before the union took place or it would assuredly imperil its future. During the previous session, Arthur had secured a clergy reserve bill with great difficulty, only to have it disallowed by the home government on a technicality. [42] Could Thomson now hope for success? He was not at all sure for there were "as many minds almost as men" and they were all "dreadfully committed, both in the House and with their constituents, upon this question, for twenty different projects." [43] But, in the flush of his victory on the union question, he resolved to stay on in Toronto and "try my hand at the clergy reserves."

From his discussions with prominent Upper Canadians, it was clear to Thomson that many favored devoting the proceeds of the clergy reserves to education. The Governor would not accept such an objective for his bill because he was convinced it would never escape unchallenged in Parliament. During preliminary discussions, Draper and Hagerman raised objections to Thomson's original proposals and suggested three possibilities of their own. Anxious to secure the unanimous support of his administration, Thomson withdrew his proposition and adopted one of the three plans as the basis for the bill.[44]

It was a compromise measure. The remaining clergy reserves would be sold and the annual proceeds distributed among the various religious denominations of the province. The Church of England and the Church of Scotland were each to have one quarter, and the remaining half was to be available on a semi-voluntary principle to any denomination which might apply. Each denomination would be entitled to apply for an amount equal to that of the offerings contributed by its members.

The bill was introduced in the Assembly by Draper on January 6, 1840. After it was introduced, Hagerman contended that he now discovered an "objectionable principle" in the measure and that he would be forced to oppose it. Thomson was extremely annoyed. He had already written a letter accepting Hagerman's resignation when Arthur proposed a milder, yet more effective, means to silence the recalcitrant Tory. Justice Sherwood was anxious to retire from the bench because of failing eyesight. Could the vacancy not be offered to the Attorney General? Thomson agreed, and Hagerman passed from the scene of active politics.[45] At the same time, Draper was appointed Attorney General and shortly afterwards Robert Baldwin accepted office as Solicitor General.

In the Assembly, Thomson's clergy reserve bill was passed twenty-eight to twenty. The vote marked a further stage in the emergence of a Moderate coalition. The majority that carried the bill was made up of sixteen moderate Tories, seven moderate Reformers, and five of undetermined political affiliation.[46] The opposition consisted of thirteen Tories who declared the bill would both deprive the Church of England of its rightful property and encourage religious competition, and seven Reformers who wished to see the proceeds from the reserves devoted to education or other non-sectarian purposes. The vote was also indicative of the degree of adjustment still going on in the Tory ranks. Six Tories who had steadfastly insisted upon the Upper Canadian terms for union voted for the bill, and two who had been converted from their insistence on these terms now aligned themselves with the ultra opposition. In the Legislative Council, the bill passed thirteen to five with Strachan, DeBlaquière, J. S. Macaulay, Crookshank, and Elmsley recording their dissent.

While the measure was under consideration, a choice was given to the Legislature regarding the division of the second half of the reserves fund. It could be distributed on the semi-voluntary principle proposed in the draft, or it could be divided on a straight per capita basis. The latter alternative was approved by the members.

With characteristic flamboyant enthusiasm Thomson reported his second major success. The bill was "worth ten Unions & was ten times more difficult."[47] Assent could never be looked for again, nor would any future assembly grant such favourable terms for the Church of England or religious instruction. "If the Lords reject the Bill, upon their heads be the consequences. I will not answer for the government of this Province, if the measure should come back," he warned Russell.[48] With a rare flash of humour Sir George Arthur remarked, "It certainly wd. be an Act of kind consideration were the Governor General to send a straight waistcoat [with the bill] for the Bishop of Exeter . . . the bare perusal of it will certainly drive his Lordship mad."[49]

While the clergy reserves bill was still under discussion, Thomson and Chief Justice James Stuart, whom he had summoned to attend him in Toronto, were busy preparing a draft union bill to send home. At the same time, John Cartwright renewed his efforts to gain approval for the Upper Canadian terms by embodying them in an address to the Queen. Although he had previously stated that there would be no objection to recommendations once the union was approved, Thomson was greatly annoyed. After attempting to dissuade Cartwright from his course, Arthur reported that he had consented to many alterations in his proposed address, but he would not give it up.[60] Cartwright's word was "not worth a pinch of snuff," Thomson replied. The only way to treat such a man was to beat him and show him up. At Draper's request, the Governor agreed that members of the Government might support three points: the English language, the seat of government, and life tenure for the Legislative Council. ". . . These are my terms for the Govt. people at least," Thomson declared. "Mr. Cartwright, of course, as leader of the opposition, must take his own course."[61] When the address was finally passed, it went only slightly beyond the three points authorized. Nonetheless, in transmitting it to Russell, Thomson emphasized that these points must be considered only as suggestions; they had been defeated by considerable majorities when presented as conditions. He considered the use of English in the records of the proceedings desirable, but he would not advise going any further than this with language restrictions. He admitted that "circumstances might render it very desirable to remove the meetings of the Legislature from the centre of a French population," but obviously the seat of government ought not to be settled in the bill.[62]

Before the end of January, 1840, Thomson and Stuart had their bill ready to send home. It did not differ in many respects from Lord John Russell's measure, but Thomson believed the differences were extremely significant. The 1839 bill had been drawn up "without a due acquaintance . . . with the Laws of Upper and Lower Canada" and as a result "extreme inconvenience . . . must have resulted."[63] Additional clauses had been inserted in the new draft to avoid the difficulties created by the different judicial systems in the two provinces. Russell's bill had provided that the union should take place on January 1, 1842, but the new draft left this to the Governor's discretion. In view of the desperate state of Upper Canadian finances and the statutory requirement for an election before 1842, Thomson was convinced that the union should be completed as soon as possible. As it was no longer considered desirable to annex Gaspé to New Brunswick, the Governor had deleted this provision.

Several changes relating to the legislature were made in Thomson's bill. The unpopular proposal for an eight-year term of office in the legislative council was abandoned in favour of appointments during good behavior. At the same time, provision was made to permit members to resign if they were unable to attend regularly. The title of president of the legislative council which had appeared in Russell's bill was rejected in the new draft for the more familiar one of speaker.

The most significant alteration was the abandonment of Russell's plan for the creation of five districts in each province to serve as both electoral and municipal divisions. Colborne had been critical of the elaborate means proposed to establish the districts, and Thomson agreed with him completely. In proposing the creation of districts, Russell had been motivated by a desire to provide a statutory rationalization of his equal representation principle. Thomson showed how unrealistic the attempt actually was: "To attempt to measure out representation in proportion to population is impossible. Your very premises forbid it, inasmuch as you set out upon the principle of giving an equal number of Representatives to 650,000 people; and to 400,000. An attempt to adjust the proportions to a mixed calculation of population and area would not be more practicable." [54]

As Colborne had pointed out, the existing electoral divisions, with a few modifications, would serve very nicely. Thomson's bill provided for an assembly of seventy-six members, half to be elected from each province. With some exceptions, each county was to form a riding and elect one member, whereas many had formerly elected two. Among the cities, Toronto, Kingston, Hamilton, Brockville, and London retained their individual representation. In Lower Canada, Montreal and Quebec City had their representation reduced from four to one member each, and Three Rivers was given one member in place of two.

Thomson's bill provided a property qualification of £500 for election to the assembly. He admitted this appeared to be low, but declared that it was sufficient to exert a "wholesome check" in Lower Canada against the introduction of individuals "without property, or any qualification except that of being able to excite the passions or delude the understandings of a very ignorant and inflammable people." [55] The bill contained only a nominal qualification for the franchise, but Thomson urged Russell to consider seriously the advisability of inserting a provision for an educational test to be applied in eight or ten years. Records of the legislature were to be published in English only. Great "inconvenience and embarrassment" had resulted from the necessity of using two languages in the Lower Canadian Legislature, and there could be "no good ground for continuing the practice." The debates could be conducted in either French or English at the speaker's discretion. Chief Justice Stuart had tentatively inserted a clause to extend the English language provision to the proceedings of the courts after a stipulated interval. Thomson endorsed the principle, but doubted that it should be included in a union bill which did not interfere with judicial proceedings in any other respect. Nevertheless, as such a provision had been included in the bill of 1822 and the proposed bill of 1824, he left it for the consideration of the Cabinet.

In Thomson's opinion, Russell's proposed districts would serve no better for municipal purposes than they would for electoral divisions. With such large districts, the assemblies would amount to little parliaments which would soon turn to the discussion of political questions and demand political privileges. Nonetheless, he was firmly convinced of the need for a comprehensive system of municipal government which would make it possible for the cost of local improvements to be defrayed locally. The new provision to restrict the initiation of money bills in the assembly to the government presupposed that such a system would exist. A better solution than Russell's was ready at hand. Upper Canada was already divided into districts for police, judicial, and magisterial purposes; Thomson proposed to utilize these districts and to erect similar divisions in Lower Canada. A lieutenant would be appointed in each district by the governor to preside over council meetings and to act as the representative of the central government. Each district was to have an elected council with powers of taxation for local purposes. A district clerk and treasurer were to be appointed by the governor from a list of three nominees submitted by the council for each office.

The Governor's bill contained no provisions relating to financial arrangements as he felt these clauses could be "more conveniently" framed in England. He did, however, indicate the principles he wished to be incorporated in the bill. The revenue and debt of the two provinces should be combined from a specified date after the union was proclaimed. The original intention had been that only the portion of the Upper Canadian debt due for works which would benefit both provinces was to be charged on the consolidated revenue. Such an arrangement, Thomson now declared to be impossible for no fund would remain to pay other charges.

The principle of a civil list had been approved; permanent provision was to be made for the governor and the judiciary, and annual allotments were to be guaranteed to the other departments during the Queen's lifetime, or for a minimum of ten years. It remained only for Parliament to fix the sum to be allocated under each of these categories. As an aid in making this decision, Thomson submitted figures estimating the revenue of the two provinces (including the proceeds under the Quebec Revenue Act) at £101,799/7/8 and the expenditure at £74,314/18/4. At the same time he warned, "Some considerable margin . . . ought however to be taken for extraordinary Expenses, as I am satisfied that it would not be safe in these colonies to leave the Government dependent on the Assembly altogether for any such charges." [56]

One additional point the Governor made quite clear. He did not wish Parliament to tie his hands by making appropriations for specific offices: ". . . It is clearly understood here that the distribution, except so far as relates to the distinction between what is permanent, and what is temporary shall not be defined at all, and that it will be in the power of the Crown to allot the sums amongst the different offices, or to create new ones, as necessity may arise when the union is completed, and the Government has been remodelled."

The vast extent of the united province—virtually 1,000 miles in length—posed a potential problem which Thomson sought to provide for in his bill. The governor was empowered to appoint one or more deputy governors at distant points to exercise any powers he might delegate to them.

With the union and clergy reserves questions settled and his bill drafted, Thomson's work in Upper Canada was completed for the moment. He prorogued the Legislature and prepared to leave for Lower Canada. Just before his departure, he reported on the prospects for the future: ". . . The Province is in a state of peace and harmony which, three months ago, I thought was utterly hopeless. How long it will last is another matter. But if you will settle the Union Bill as I have sent it home, and the Lords do not reject the Clergy Reserves Bill, I am confident I shall be able to keep the peace, make a strong Government, and get on well." [57]

VII

Thomson returned to Lower Canada to find that an anti-union campaign led by John Neilson was gathering momentum. Even before the Governor's arrival in Canada, Neilson had started to lay the groundwork for opposition to the union. Late in July, the *Quebec Gazette* carried a copy of Lord John Russell's abortive union bill together with Neilson's comments. "A permanent civil list with no power of periodical revision by the legislative body, . . . district councils with the power of local taxation and management do not belong to the constitution of any Government with which we are acquainted." [58]

While Thomson's proposals were before the Upper Canadian Legislature, Neilson increased the tempo of his anti-union crusade. When the Reformers gave their support to the union project in the hope of gaining responsible government, they did not escape his vitriolic pen :

And what do the friends of liberty, the great advocates of a Government conducted in accordance with the *wishes* of the people, "the Responsible Government" men . . . say to this [injustice]? "Oh! it is excellent!" They swallow the bribe and care not a pin for the public liberty, the wishes of the people, the responsibility of the administration to the *majority* of the people. Their professions are all a farce: they expect to get into "the Compact's" places and divide "the spoils" of Lower Canada.[59]

During the debate in the Legislative Council, Robert Baldwin Sullivan had stated bluntly, "The only means of discharging our obligations, of faithfully satisfying our creditors is by uniting Upper Canada and Lower Canada *whose surplus revenue alone can enable us to redeem our obligations."* Neilson eagerly printed Sullivan's pronouncement and added his own editorial comments : "To all this the holders of these obligations or debentures in London, Upper Canada and elsewhere to the amount of a million and a quarter at interest, together with the *expectants* of another million already appropriated or promised, and their respective friends and connexions say *AMEN!"* [60]

Le Canadien. aroused by the opinions expressed in the Upper Canadian Assembly during the debate on Cartwright's resolutions, deserted the union and joined Neilson in opposition. "Il y a quelques mois, l'Union était ce que nos compatriots avaient de moins désavantages à craindre, nous l'acceptâmes alors; aujourd'hui, l'Union ne leur offre que des désavantages sans aucune compensations— nous nous opposons à l'Union." [61]

Thomson would have preferred to ignore the movement entirely, but when anti-union petitions began to circulate he felt obliged to inform the Colonial Secretary of the campaign before it came to the attention of the London newspapers. As he was preparing to leave Toronto, he wrote an official despatch reporting Neilson's activities and, at the same time, expressing the conviction that any petitions which might be sent home would not be "allowed to produce the slightest effect on the deliberations of Parliament." [62] Three weeks after his return to Lower Canada, the Governor found it necessary to go into the question more fully. There were, he explained, two parties who had united against the union—the priests, and the French party who constituted a majority in the last Assembly and who were "more or less implicated in the Rebellion." [63] The priests were animated by a vague fear that union would produce "consequences disastrous to the interests of the Catholic Church," and the intemperate language of the British press in Montreal had increased their fear. He was convinced their real wish was "that the present system of Government should, if possible, be maintained; the powers of the Governor in Council extended, and the Country ruled by a despotism." On the other hand, the French party had supported the union until recently. *Le Canadien* had advocated it warmly, both before he went to Upper Canada and even after the terms were announced in his message to the Upper Canadian Legislature. The changed attitude he attributed to two factors—Neilson's anti-union crusade and the discovery that

Upper Canadian Reformers would not support them in their "ultra designs." Neilson's agitation had led the French party to hope for the restoration of a separate legislature in Lower Canada and a return of French-Canadian ascendancy. Thomson considered that his own efforts in Upper Canada were largely responsible for the French Canadians' realization that "they can look for no assistance in their ulterior views from any party amongst the Upper Canadian People." Using the Durham formula as his guide, he had sought to insure that the English-speaking members of the united assembly would act as a unit. He was unaware of the fact that Hincks was working towards another goal.

It was quite possible that numerous petitions against the union would be presented, Thomson informed Russell, but no great weight should be given to them. Indeed, the agitation and petitions only provided additional arguments for the union. "In the State of ignorance and subserviency . . . in which the French Canadians unfortunately are, it is notorious that any number of signatures might be obtained for any purpose whatever. . . ." The clergy were loyal and desired the preservation of the British connection, but they dreaded the introduction of British feeling and habits among their people. They were deluded by a dream, "for it is worthy of no other name," of retaining the French-Canadian race as a separate people with their primitive and simple habits unsullied by contact with the enterprising British population. Conversely, the aim of the French party, which was imbued with a hatred of everything British, was separation from the mother country. Thus, although both groups had united to demand a restoration of the constitution of 1791, this was not the ultimate objective of either.

Thomson had accepted Durham's assessment of French Canada and, thus, had incorporated Durham's errors into his own reasoning. Like Durham, he saw nothing in French-Canadian culture worthy of preservation and, in any case, he was convinced that it was doomed to be engulfed by the Anglo-American culture which surrounded it. Perhaps with some reservations, he accepted Durham's prediction that a social revolution would take place in French Canada with French-Canadian leaders taking an active and co-operative part in it. Both men failed to see that before this could happen French Canadians would have to reject their own social and cultural values in favour of English values. If French-Canadian leaders changed their values in advance of the people generally, they would cease to be leaders and would become "vendus."

Thomson cared nothing for French Canada's delusive "dreams." His basic premise, and indeed that of the union which he came to implement, was that French Canada had to be assimilated. Upon his return from Upper Canada, in February of 1840, he made a few ineffectual attempts to obtain French-Canadian support, but these were spurned. French-Canadian leaders could not accept the Governor's basic premise which assumed the termination of their culture. When Thomson offered to appoint LaFontaine to office, the latter could only regard it as a hollow attempt to purchase support for a policy which he could not accept.

VIII

Despite the opposition in Lower Canada, Thomson had no real cause to worry for the safety of his union measure in England. The Cabinet stood poised, ready to proceed the moment it received his draft bill. Moreover, a different spirit prevailed in the House of Commons and it was unlikely that the bill would encounter very serious opposition. The Conservatives' bitterness over the bed-chamber episode had had time to abate, but of greater significance was the general conviction that the Canadian problem demanded an immediate solution. Sir Robert Peel and his followers were not certain that union was the perfect answer, but they could suggest no alternative which seemed more likely to succeed. A sense of futility was reflected in Chief Justice Robinson's letters to Arthur and in his diary. He had carried out his threat to publish his "hopes and fears" in a pamphlet[64] and there was nothing more he could do. "I can satisfy myself hereafter with *hoping*," he informed Arthur.[65] He had relied upon strong Conservative opposition to the union and was now forced to admit that such was unlikely to materialize. A few staunch old Tories like the Duke of Wellington, who had promised, "I'll say what I think if the Devil stands in the door," [66] would remain firm, but with the party as a whole it was likely to be an open question. After considering all the factors involved, Peel was unwilling to accept the responsibility for defeating a measure which he approved in principle.

Lord John Russell had long since grown weary of Robinson's presentation of the anti-union case. On one occasion, he had accused the Chief Justice of concerting with Lord Lyndhurst, later Lord Chancellor in the Peel administration, and others to oppose the Government.[67] In the face of Robinson's vigorous objections that he had only given information and stated his opinions, Russell agreed that his position was satisfactory. But he pointed out that, according to the Governor, great inconvenience had resulted in Upper Canada from Robinson's prolonged absence. It would be well if the Chief Justice made plans for his return as soon as possible. There was really no reason why he should remain in England until the union bill came before Parliament. As he prepared to sail aboard the *Quebec*, Robinson recorded in his diary the hope that union "will be somehow defeated" but, he admitted, "appearances are the other way." [68]

When the Cabinet received Thomson's draft bill, only one significant change was made before it was introduced by Russell on March 23, 1840. The series of clauses relating to the establishment of municipal government were deleted to avoid "a great amount of inconvenient detail," and a general enactment, empowering the Governor to create municipal bodies, was substituted. The bill did, however, contain one aspect which Thomson had not anticipated and which annoyed him greatly. He had left it for the Cabinet to frame the financial clauses, but he had expressly asked that only the total amount of the civil list should be stated. Despite Thomson's stipulation, Russell and his colleagues had proceeded to appropriate every penny of the £75,000 civil list to specific offices and purposes. There is no clear indication as to why the Governor's request was ignored, but the Whigs probably were afraid of opposition on the grounds that with £75,000 at his disposal he would be in far too powerful a position. Thomson was furious:

I think your Bill will do, except a few inaccuracies which I have pointed out in a dispatch, and your Civil List clauses & Crown Revenues. But these last are the D---l and all, and *must* be changed. Who on earth framed them? I wish I had sent them myself. The schedule to which you propose to tie me down, as I understand it, would in the first place knock over my Judicature Bill here, the best work ever undertaken in the Province, and next, provide nothing for Upper Canada Justice which of course was included in my estimate. The concession of the Crown revenues *without* any of the charges to which the faith of the Crown is pledged, *without* the expences of carrying the Bill into operation, *without* providing for the necessary retirement of many Public Officers consequent upon the Union would compel me to break faith for the Crown, prevent me from working out the Bill as I ought, and force me to keep the whole of the present vicious system of administration in both Provinces standing, which it is my great object to remodel. . . . Pray have a proviso added to the 53d Clause providing for these charges. . . ."

Russell declined to accede to Thomson's request with the admonition that surely he could do with a £75,000 civil list. "To be sure I could!" retorted the Governor, "But you have placed all sorts of conditions upon the appropriation, and they are what will hamper me and do the mischief. . . . How I am to pay £5,450 pensions to which the faith of the Crown stands pledged when the Bill declares that only £5,000 shall be thus allotted, is more than I can tell! Perhaps you will point out a mode." [70] Despite Thomson's objections, Russell and the Cabinet remained firm. The civil list provisions would stand as introduced and the Governor would have to manage them as best he could.

As the bill progressed through its various stages, minor alterations and additions were made in its provisions. At Thomson's suggestion, a clause was inserted annexing the Magdalen Islands to Prince Edward Island. Robert Gillespie objected that the bill, as introduced, would neither assure a British predominance nor an equitable representation of the mercantile wealth of the province. He suggested that the provisions should be altered to increase the number of representatives from the cities and towns and to ensure that these would be English-speaking members. In the House of Commons, Peel and Ellice advocated greater representation for the commercial element. Although Russell was not prepared to go to the extremes suggested by Gillespie, he did alter the representation scheme to provide an additional member for Montreal and Quebec in Lower Canada. To maintain the balance in Upper Canada, additional members were given to Toronto and Lincoln County. Before the bill was finally passed, the number of representatives was again increased as a result of pressure from Edward Ellice, and Sherbrooke and Bytown were each given a member.

When the bill came up for debate in the House of Commons, it did not encounter serious opposition. Many members had misgivings regarding the general effects of the measure; some questioned the means by which Thomson had gained assent in the Canadas, but most were inclined to agree with Sir Robert Peel that it was essential to take action immediately. The House was called upon to decide between two dangers, Peel declared. For his own part, although he was not free from apprehension, he considered union to be less dangerous than an attempt to preserve the *status quo*. The union might produce religious conflicts in the Canadas, but no measure would be without risk, and he doubted whether he could suggest a better one. Had he heard strong objections from Upper Canadians, he would have deferred to their opinions, but on the contrary, the Special Council in Lower Canada and both Houses of the Legislature in Upper Canada had signified their approval. If Peel had wished, he probably could have defeated the bill, but once he had declared his support, the issue was never in doubt. [71]

Edward Ellice declared that, although he still considered a federal union to be a wiser solution, he was willing to accept the general feeling of the inhabitants. He did object, however, to the provision for district councils as an undesirable innovation which would result in local jobbing. The councils were designed as a means of placing a local tax on wild lands, Ellice asserted. He was not opposed to this in principle, but he felt the provincial legislature was the only body competent to levy such a tax.[12] When Peel and Stanley supported Ellice's opposition to the district councils, Russell acted to preserve the unanimity which had characterized the debate thus far. Parliament, he agreed, should not attempt to do for local legislatures anything which they could do for themselves. If it was the general feeling that neither racial jealousies nor local conditions would prevent the provincial legislature from undertaking the creation of a system of municipal government, then certainly the clauses could be dropped.[13] In thus modifying the bill to meet the wishes of Ellice, Peel, and Stanley, Russell dropped one of the major provisions, but he considered this a reasonable concession in view of the large majority it helped to produce for the bill. He was convinced that Thomson could secure his municipal institutions in the Canadian legislature without difficulty.

In the House of Lords, the bill encountered stronger opposition. The Duke of Wellington and many of the older and more reactionary Tories who sat in the Upper House were convinced that the union could not fail to produce a republican majority in the Canadian assembly. In their eyes, the union could have no other ultimate result than the termination of the British connection. Other Lords were opposed to the anti-French aspects of the bill. Wellington begged that all the circumstances might be carefully reconsidered; if, after doing this, the Government still thought it proper to take the responsibility upon themselves, "in God's name let them do so," but for himself he must say, "not content" to this bill.[14] Speaking from his personal experience as Governor of Lower Canada in the two years preceding the rebellion, Lord Gosford declared that the great body of French Canadians were loyal, and he condemned the measure as "arbitrary and unfair."[15] Lord Ellenborough attempted to have the equal representation provision removed, asserting that at the moment it amounted to disenfranchisement of the French Canadians and that it would eventually react to the disadvantage of Upper Canada. The bill, he declared, was "pregnant with injustice to Lower Canada" and would never attain any of its objectives.[16] The opinion of Lord Seaton (formerly Sir John Colborne) carried considerable weight for he had only recently returned from Canada and was regarded as the best-informed member of the House. It was true, he stated, that the bill had been decided upon and introduced before Durham, Arthur, or he had been consulted. He felt great apprehension and alarm concerning the possible results of union, but, under the present circumstances, he believed that it would be more injurious both to the provinces and to England not to proceed with the measure. The present suspension of the constitution in Lower Canada could not be continued, nor could the constitution of 1791 be restored. Union was the only alternative.[17]

On the eve of the crucial vote in the House of Lords, a large number of peers assembled at the Duke of Wellington's home. Wellington declared that he would oppose the bill to the end, but implored his friends not to be influenced by his vote. It was a question which each man must decide for himself. Many who were not prepared to support the union and yet were unwilling to accept the responsibility for killing it determined to be absent when the vote was taken and thus to leave the Government in a majority.[18] The bill passed easily with Wellington and Ellenborough officially recording their dissent upon the journals. On July 23, it received the royal assent and only a proclamation by the Governor was required to make union a constitutional reality.

In a sense the policy of union was carried by default. There was a large body of potential opposition in England, but, when no acceptable alternative was brought forward, few public men were willing to take a strong stand against the union. When John Beverley Robinson's departure became imminent, Sir Francis Bond Head tried to rally anti-union sentiment, but both the Archbishop of Canterbury and Sir Robert Peel denied him their support.[19] Many had doubts regarding the ultimate results of union—even Lord Melbourne had admitted some misgivings during the debates—but almost everyone agreed that the *status quo* could not be maintained.

In the light of subsequent events, it is obvious that a federal, rather than a legislative, union would have been a wiser policy. However, a federal union would have been possible only if it were generally recognized that French Canada did not constitute a threat to the imperial connection, and even then it would have been most difficult to persuade the English minority in Lower Canada to accept a federal solution. In 1840, there were very few members who did not see French Canada as a political menace. Political considerations, both in the Canadas and in England, militated against the adoption of coercive measures by Parliament, but it was generally agreed that a basis for assimilation must be established. Yet, ironically, the union that Parliament had just approved was to provide the basis upon which an embryo federalism would soon develop.

CHAPTER FIVE

FINAL PREPARATION

THOMSON HAD SUCCESSFULLY completed his difficult assignment of obtaining unencumbered Canadian assent for union, and Parliament had duly passed the necessary Act in July 1840.[1] According to the Durham formula, the next step was to establish an effective union which would reveal to French Canada the utter futility of resisting the process of assimilation. This was actually an impossible task, for French Canadians would never accept assimilation and the means of resisting it were ready at hand. In his more reflective moments Thomson seemed to sense this, and as a result he was inclined to apply more pressure and to proceed at a more rapid pace than Durham had recommended. He realized that the Special Council could be used as an instrument to undermine French-Canadian culture—in the name of progress—before the union was carried into effect. His main attention, however, was directed at the establishment of a functioning union which he regarded as his primary task. With a display of administrative efficiency that reflected his early business training, he quickly produced a union in accordance with the terms of the Act. But, in reality, his union was only a gleaming veneer applied over elements which would soon cause it to crack and peel until it became clear that a federal arrangement was the only satisfactory solution. Thomson realized that the first test of any union he might achieve would occur when the Legislature met. For almost a year after the Act was passed, he devoted most of his attention and energy to preparing for that test.

I

When the Governor first received a copy of the Act of Union, he was completely disgusted. He had reluctantly accepted the civil list restrictions and the alterations to his representation scheme, but the abandonment of the municipal government provisions could only be condemned as sheer folly. ". . . I defy you to govern these Provinces without such a system, & you have by the abandonment of its enactment by Parliament thrown away . . . the opportunity of securing good Government in the Canadas," he informed Russell.[2] His first impulse was to throw up his appointment and return home, but upon further consideration he changed his mind. He had taken a great personal interest in the problem of producing a Canadian union and he was reluctant to leave the task uncompleted. Moreover, if he did so, he was unlikely to receive the peerage which he so greatly desired. It was characteristic of Thomson that, even after he had made his decision to remain, he was at pains to impress upon Russell that, because of the Government's blunder, the difficulties with which he was confronted had increased enormously. In the absence of any explanation from Russell, Thomson had read and re-read the debates, but found only "a representation against the proposed scheme" by Edward Ellice whose notorious "ignorance of all that concerns Canadian affairs" and avowed opposition both to the union and to the Governor ought "to have deprived his authority of any weight."[3]

By the time that Russell's explanation of the Government's action arrived, Thomson had learned of his elevation to the peerage as Baron Sydenham and his annoyance had abated considerably. He would need to adjust himself to the new aspects of his problem and amend his plan of action, but as long as he was not to be denied municipal government the situation was not impossible. Although the Clergy Reserves Act had been thrown out on a technicality, Russell had obtained the passage of a new Act which the Governor admitted was an improvement upon his own. The only new problem was that of creating a system of municipal government. Russell suggested that this should be accomplished through the provincial legislature after union, but Sydenham considered the Special Council to be a much more reliable instrument for the purpose.

He had already discovered that the Council provided an excellent means of making preliminary preparations for union. During the spring and early summer of 1840, while he waited for Parliament to produce the Act of Union, Thomson had been busy with his own local legislation. Ordinances were passed establishing district courts, reforming the judicature, providing for a more efficient and economical police force, incorporating the cities of Montreal and Quebec, and providing for public works projects in Lower Canada. The French-Canadian newspapers and Neilson's *Quebec Gazette* had been critical both of the enactments and the means by which they had been obtained, but the Governor was well pleased with his reforms. In his opinion, they were all part of the necessary preparation for union in order "to admit of its being brought into operation with safety,"[4] but to French Canadians they were steps in the direction of assimilation, taken without consulting them and without their approval. Whether he realized it or not, Thomson was departing from the Durham formula and, perhaps, beginning to question Durham's basic assumption that French Canada could be controlled by an English-speaking bloc in the legislature until it was ready to accept assimilation.

When Thomson prorogued the Special Council, at the end of June, his legislative programme had not been completed and he planned to call the Council back for a fall session. Before the union took place he wished to obtain legislation establishing registry offices, and possibly an educational system. As a result of Parliament's failure to provide for municipal government, this subject would have to be added to the Special Council's agenda.

Thomson had already decided that Kingston should be the capital of the united province. Quebec, Montreal, Toronto, and Bytown were all considered briefly and rejected for various political and geographical reasons. Kingston was ideally located and although there was some doubt that accommodation could be prepared in time for the first session, Thomson considered it to be undoubtedly the best location for the permanent seat of government. By bringing French-Canadian members into an English-speaking community, he would "instil English Ideas into their minds" and "destroy the immediate influence upon their actions of the host of little Lawyers, notaries & Doctors."[5] Moreover, the selection of Kingston as the capital would symbolize the break with the old High Tory tradition and the intention to forge a new moderate policy.

In addition to his formal preparations for the union, Thomson started to ease the restrictions that had been imposed in Lower Canada. In May, old Denis Benjamin Viger, who had remained in prison since the second outbreak of the rebellion rather than post the security demanded of him, was released unconditionally. A month later, when the ordinance for the suspension of *habeas corpus* expired, the Governor decided there was no necessity to renew it.

Upon proroguing the Special Council at the end of June, Thomson prepared for a hasty trip to Halifax. In Nova Scotia, Lieutenant-Governor Sir Colin Campbell had clashed with his Assembly on the question of responsible government and Russell had asked Thomson to endeavour to secure a reconciliation. He begrudged the time required to visit Nova Scotia for he wished to make an extended tour of Upper Canada. "It will be sharp work to get it into the summer," he wrote to Russell, "but I must try, as the Elections all depend on my going up." [6] After a successful month in Nova Scotia, Thomson returned to Montreal, pausing to visit the Eastern Townships on his way. On August 19, he set out from Montreal for Upper Canada. In just over a month he was back at Government House, having visited all the settled areas in the upper province "from the province line to Amherstburg and Sandwich, from Lake Erie to Penetanguishine." [7] As he descended the Ottawa River on his way back to Montreal, he learned of his elevation to the peerage and must have considered it a fitting climax to a most successful tour.

As preparation for union, his visit to Upper Canada was all Lord Sydenham could have wished. While he was in Nova Scotia, Sir George Arthur had informed him that Robert Baldwin had united the full responsible government men with the more moderate Reformers and would very likely cause further trouble. He would advance towards the goal of responsible government, step by step, as he felt his strength. The tour convinced Lord Sydenham that Arthur had been unduly alarmed. ". . . I have everywhere found a determination to forget past differences and to unite in an endeavour to obtain, under the Act of Union, those practical Measures for the improvement of the country which have been too long neglected in the struggle for party and personal objects," he reported to Russell. [8] The prospects for a Moderate coalition party appeared to be very good indeed. Even in Toronto he had received a cordial reception and had an opportunity to soften the "asperities" which existed. From Toronto he wrote, "I . . . have satisfied myself that I can beat both the Ultra Tories and the extreme Radicals at the Elections in Upper Canada." [9] In the fifty or sixty addresses presented to him, the same spirit prevailed: "confidence in my Govt. and a determination to support me." His original analysis of the Upper Canadian problem was, he considered, fully upheld by the evidence of his tour. The people wanted only "the vigorous interference of a well-intentioned Government, strong enough to control both the extreme parties, and to proclaim wholesome truths, and act for the benefit of the country at large, in defiance of ultras on either side." [10]

Upon his return, Lord Sydenham was pleased to discover that the spirit of co-operation which had prevailed in Upper Canada also extended to the mercantile interests of Montreal: "They are slow to learn, but they have yielded to the practical conviction of better roads, better streets, Quays building—Police cheaper and yet more efficient—Justice well administered by a Police magistrate instead of a set of ignorant Unpaid—A Corporation to manage their own matters—and the public servants made to work—besides the general measures, which I have given them in common with the Province and which they are now beginning to understand.'"

For all his enthusiasm, Lord Sydenham could not delude himself that a majority of the French Canadians would welcome the union. Nothing but time would do anything with them, he declared. "They hate British rule—British connexion—improvement of all kinds whether in their Laws or their roads. So they sulk, and will try, that is, their Leaders, to do all the mischief they can.'" He expected no serious trouble, however, for the habitants had suffered to such an extent in the rebellions that they would support no further violence. Before proclaiming the union, Sydenham intended to complete the work of reforming the system of law and government, and, in time, he trusted this would produce "a more improved state of things as well as of feelings."

The Governor plunged immediately into the task of preparing for a final session with his Special Council. "There will be a vast deal to do," he wrote to Russell, ". . . before the Union, or at least before the Parlt. can meet, in the entire reconstruction of offices as well as in carrying into effect the different things required by the Act to be done before that can be summoned—Limits of Towns, etc., etc. So you must not be impatient.'"

By the end of November, he was well advanced with his programme of legislation. He informed Russell that he had before the Council a good measure for municipal government which was popular with Canadians except for the extreme Tories and the "Agitators amongst the French party who see that it will deprive them of power.'" A Registry Bill, "a much greater work even," had already been passed. This Act, which had been the "Pons Asinorum" of Lower Canadian legislation for years, was so interwoven with old French law and custom that he could not pretend to understand its details. However, it had been prepared by Chief Justice James Stuart, "the most competent person perhaps in the world from his thorough knowledge of both French and English Law," and when circulated for criticism and comment it had received almost universal approbation. When the Special Council was finally dissolved, Sydenham had secured a total of thirty-two ordinances relating to highways, harbours and navigation, railways, alien regulations, the erection of jails, and the administration of justice, in addition to those concerned with municipal government and the establishment of registry offices.'" The session had taken longer than he had anticipated, but now Lord Sydenham could feel that every possible legislative preparation had been made for the union.

The new judicial system, established under the ordinance passed in June, was originally intended to become effective in December. It had to be delayed, however, until the provincial legislature revised the judges' salaries as established by the Act of Union. Aware of the importance of education to the process of assimilation, Sydenham would have liked to include provision for a school system in his pre-union legislation, but he complained that lack of funds and the Roman Catholic clergy's failure to agree on any feasible scheme prevented him from doing so. "They pretend to be in favour of something," he wrote, "but are in reality opposed to teaching the people at all, being weak enough to think that so long as they are ignorant they are under their control.'"

It was generally agreed that a large influx of English-speaking immigrants would materially increase the union's chances of success, but there was little that

Sydenham could do to attain this end. Dr. Thomas Rolph had acted as an unofficial emigration agent while visiting Great Britain in 1839; Sydenham planned to
give him an official appointment and send him back again. But he considered it
impossible to "frame any great plan such as people seem to look for, and which
has been hinted at but never *explained* in Lord Durham's report."[17] Wakefield's
theory of financing emigration from the proceeds of land sales was not, in Sydenham's opinion, applicable to Canada because the revenue from this source amounted
to less than £20,000 per year. The only sound policy was to encourage voluntary
emigration by providing transportation to Upper Canada upon arrival. The practice
of throwing "starving and diseased paupers under the rock at Quebec ought to be
punishable as *murder.*" He wanted "good stout English peasants who know what
work is," or some yeomen with a few hundred pounds each.[18] Emigration, he informed Russell, was "no lottery with a few exorbitant prizes, and a large majority
of blanks—but a secure and certain investment in which a prudent and reasonable
man may safely embark."[19] With the assistance of Sir George Arthur, R. B. Sullivan, and S. B. Harrison, Sydenham prepared a plan for free land grants of fifty
acres along the Garafraxa Road, from Garafraxa Township to Owen Sound, as an
additional means of encouraging immigration.

Sir George Arthur had suggested the establishment of a newspaper to present
the Government's point of view in Upper Canada, only to be discouraged by Lord
Normanby, but Sydenham soon discovered merit in the proposal. A government
organ would serve to present the Governor and his union to the public in the
proper light and would also prove useful during the election campaign after the
union was proclaimed. With Sydenham's active encouragement, Robert Baldwin
Sullivan embarked upon the publication of the *Monthly Review.* "I am glad to hear
that you have taken up the Periodical again," the Governor wrote to Sullivan,
"as I am satisfied that it will be most useful. . . ."[20] Although Egerton Ryerson
had declined the offer to edit the review, Sydenham was quite certain that he would
be unable "to keep his fingers off Politics" and would probably be useful in the
periodical's management. Sydenham promised to see to it that Christopher Dunkin,
the former editor of the Montreal *Morning Courier,* contributed an article on
Lower Canadian politics when Sullivan was ready. In what was obviously a suggestion regarding editorial policy, the Governor expressed the hope that with "good
management" such political extremists as High Tories George Boulton and Sir
Allan MacNab and ultra Reformers Francis Hincks, Henry Boulton, and James
Durand would be defeated.

II

Lord Sydenham had been far from satisfied with the Act of Union in its final
form, but many Canadians were positively shocked when they read the details for
the first time in their local newspapers. The Governor had sent his draft bill home
without showing it to anyone in Canada and had given no indication of its provisions. It was the middle of May before the bill that Lord John Russell had
introduced was published in Canadian papers.

In French Canada the publication of the bill banished any faint hopes that
might have been nourished. "La mesure de l'iniquité est comblée dans ce Bill,"
declared *Le Canadien,* but after all perhaps this was for the best: "Si le plan

d'Union eût été supportable on aurait eu moins de chance et de facilité à s'en débarraser, par la suite. Tel qu'il est, on est certain qu'il ne pourra opérer, et que la première session de la législature unie laissera les affaires dans un état plus embarrassant, plus embrouillé, plus critique que jamais." [21] John Neilson's *Quebec Gazette* continued its uncompromising opposition to the union and threatened that 150,000 voters would be heard at the next election. Monarchy was preferable to republicanism, Neilson asserted, but inadequate representation, the great distance from any capital, and the dissimilarity of the laws and usages could not be ignored.

In Upper Canada the bill naturally created less excitement, but Bishop Strachan wrote that the measure gave "offence to all parties" and was opposed by nine out of twelve. He declared that he would not be surprised to see an address for repeal carried on the first or second day after the united Legislature met.[22] Sir George Arthur, on the other hand, admitted there were "various objections," but saw no reason to think they would prevent the union being "fully and fairly carried into operation."[23]

The Upper Canadian Reformers had been under the impression that they had gained a victory on the civil list question; a brief perusal of the bill soon disillusioned them. The Legislature was denied the right of establishing the amount of the civil list, and thus, effective control of the purse was in jeopardy. The bill was "abominable," Hincks wrote to LaFontaine: "I should be very glad indeed that the Union bill was thrown over this session if it is as I understand it. My impressions however is [*sic*] that it will pass and thus we must work it if we can, and afterwards improve it. *What else can we do?*"[24]

In truth, the only alternative was to campaign for repeal and this was a course to which Hincks was decidedly opposed. The Reformers of Upper Canada, he promised, would assist French Canada in its efforts to have the language restriction and other objectionable features modified. The Reformers in both provinces needed each other's support and only by means of the union could they join forces. "After what has taken place your countrymen would never obtain their rights in a Lower Canadian Legislature," he wrote. "You want our help as much as we do yours."[25]

Hincks's arguments gradually overcame LaFontaine's initial preference for repeal. In retrospect the French leader recalled: "After having carefully examined the rod by which it was intended to destroy my countrymen, I beseeched some of the most influential of them to permit me to use it to save those whom it was unjustly designed to punish."[26] The changing attitude of LaFontaine and his followers was reflected in *Le Canadien* which commented: "Ainsi nos enragés d'Unionaires qui avaient rêvé la dégradation, l'ilotisme du peuple Canadien, n'auront fait que donner à ce peuple de nouveau protecteurs, un appui des plus puissants dans le parti réformiste du Haut-Canada; c'est le sort que méritent tous les projets conçus dans l'iniquité." [27]

Throughout the second half of 1840, Francis Hincks laboured industriously to expand his entente with LaFontaine into a solid working alliance with a concrete policy. He sought to interpret the policy of the Upper Canadian Reformers for LaFontaine's benefit and endeavoured to keep him informed on political developments. When Baldwin accepted the appointment as Solicitor General early in the year, Hincks had hastened to assure his French-Canadian friend that no principle had been sacrificed. Hincks was not aware of it, but there had been a mutual misunderstanding in connection with Baldwin's appointment. Sydenham believed that

Baldwin was prepared to accept Russell's "harmony concept" instead of demanding full responsible government and that he could, therefore, be considered a moderate Reformer. Baldwin's understanding, on the other hand, was that he intended only to give the Governor a fair chance and not to force him into the hands of the Tories. "We shall be able to use the Govr. Genl's name on *our side* at the next election to promote the return of *good men and true*," Hincks informed LaFontaine, "and if His Excellency should prove a deceiver, on his own head be the consequence."[28] When word reached Toronto that the Act of Union had been passed, Hincks wrote, "Now for the elections & the death strugle [sic] of Toryisme [sic]."[29]

During the summer and autumn of 1840, Hincks's letters were primarily concerned with election strategy. Bidwell and others at a distance seemed to think the Reformers should unite with the party disposed to act with the Governor General, he informed LaFontaine, but, he added, "a more mistaken idea cannot exist." No Reform county would return a doubtful man. "If there is any shampooing in the business it is we that are *'using'* the *Moderate* party as they call themselves." There were, of course, certain Tory constituencies where there was no hope of electing a Reformer, and in such instances the moderate candidate would be given Reform support in an effort to turn out leading Tories such as Sherwood, MacNab, and Draper. Toronto was likely to be a difficult constituency for the Reformers. In order to secure Baldwin's election, Hincks thought it would be necessary "to take some Half Tory, I may almost say full Tory"[30] as his running mate. Such a contingency did not materialize, for, when the Tory candidate triumphed over the Reformer in the municipal election, Baldwin considered it an ominous portent and decided not to seek election in Toronto.

Although Hincks had suggested that it would be best to leave plans for the strategy to be employed during the first session until after the elections were over and the character of the House was known, he occasionally turned to this subject in his letters. "Not only will it be necessary to protest against the Union bill," he asserted, "but also the Clergy Reserves Bill, a most *unconstitutional* measure."[31] When Neilson implied, in the *Quebec Gazette*, that LaFontaine was returning to the ranks of the anti-unionists, Hincks turned again to the civil list question:

Would you object to a permanent civil list for the Judges & Governor alone & his *private* secretary – putting all the rest in an *annual* supply bill, *all* to be voted by the Prov. Parliament – your judges to be *independant* [sic] – the civil list clause in the Imperial statute to be repealed. – I think myself it is unconstitutional & cannot be acted on.[32]

Towards the end of the year, Hincks began to look beyond the elections and consider the composition of an executive council which would be acceptable to the Reformers in both provinces. As a basis for discussion, he suggested a list of possible candidates to LaFontaine.[33] The French-Canadian leader curtly replied that he would not join any cabinet containing the Lower Canadians listed. "I quite concur in your views as to not Joining a cabinet with the men described," Hincks answered, but some compromise might be necessary. "Suppose Stewart & Ogden got rid of and that Day should join the Reform party in sincerity would it not be well to take him."[34] Such a case was only hypothetical for Day might well commit himself so that no liberal man could act with him, but it seemed to Hincks that the Reformers might very possibly make use of such men as Harrison, Sullivan, and perhaps Day.

LaFontaine replied that, although he would not join such an administration, he would not offer it factious opposition. Upon receiving this letter, Hincks must have heaved a sigh and decided that it was time for another lecture on the refinements of responsible government:

I really can hardly answer your letter on the subject of the provincial cabinet. . . . Now I think that we as a party should be prepared to crush any administration in which we have no confidence & as a necessary consequence to be prepared to take the government into our own hands if strong enough. . . . I should like to know from you whether you would consent *to any compromise,* that is would you act with any of our old enemies provided they agree *to carry out our policy.*[35]

Hincks urged LaFontaine and his followers to emulate the Upper Canadian Reformers in planning for the elections and to avoid alienating Lord Sydenham. He agreed that LaFontaine should offer unflinching opposition to the Governor's bad measures, but implored him to avoid any personal clashes. "This will only add to our difficulties."[36]

LaFontaine could not follow Hincks's advice unreservedly, for he had problems of his own in Lower Canada and had to speak out against those aspects of the union which implied assimilation to his compatriots. Hincks had virtually convinced him that rigid opposition to the union would be futile, and that its character could be altered with the support of Upper Canadian Reformers and the attainment of responsible government. But prominent French-Canadian leaders in Quebec did not share this opinion, and there was a danger that French-Canadian representation in the united Assembly would be divided.[37] John Neilson had been urging that French-Canadian members stand firm and demand repeal of the union when the Legislature met. After A. N. Morin conferred with him on LaFontaine's behalf, Neilson agreed that the position regarding the union might be left an open question, but he remained uneasy about the prospect of co-operation with the Upper Canadian Reformers and continued to consider responsible government an undesirable objective. Napoléon Aubin, the editor of *Le Fantasque*, fully appreciated the strength of French Canada's position and advised against any commitment to the Upper Canadian Reformers: "Ces réformistes s'occupent beaucoup plus de vous faire payer leurs dettes qu'ils s'occupent de vous, de vos malheurs et du moyen de vous retirer d'où l'on vous a plongés. . . . Ce que je voudrais que vous fissiez, il n'est pas difficile à vous le dire: vous placer là au milieu des partis et n'aider qu'à celui qui voudra vous aider."[38] Aubin's opinion was shared by Denis Benjamin Viger, whose extended stay in prison had enhanced his reputation, and *L'Aurore*, which he controlled, was strongly opposed to union. Many French Canadians preferred ". . . the O'Connell-tail-system, to unite with one party or the other as momentary alliance or expediency may suggest."[39]

With LaFontaine's approval, Etienne Parent argued, in *Le Canadien*, against both agitating for repeal of the union and maintaining an independent position in the Legislature. At the same time, however, he warned that French Canadians would have no alternative but to agitate for repeal if they were not supported by the Upper Canadian Reformers in an attempt to remedy the objectionable terms of union.[40] Ultimately, French Canada would follow LaFontaine's lead, but, in the autumn of 1840, he found it necessary to pick his steps very carefully.

As Sydenham continued to make extensive use of the Special Council in preparation for the union, LaFontaine's criticism of the Upper Canadian Reformers' trust in the Governor began to have its effect on Hincks. The *Examiner's* editorials became increasingly critical of Sydenham's policy and finally condemned it as tyrannical and deliberately anti-French. John Neilson's *Quebec Gazette* and the French-Canadian press had already protested vigorously against the use of an admittedly temporary legislative body to pass permanent legislation. Hincks agreed with them and warned that, if the Governor was dedicated to an anti-French policy, the Reformers from both provinces would unite in the first session to para- lyse the Government by stopping supplies. Baldwin soon felt obliged to caution Hincks that the Upper Canadian Reformers did not intend to unite with French- Canadian members for the purpose of following "a course of proceeding leading necessarily to collision and tending to stop inevitably the whole machinery of the Constitution."⁴¹ On the contrary, the "just and necessary object" of restoring French Canadians to the same footing as their fellow subjects was to be attained by means of the application of the principle of responsible government to the practical workings of the constitution. In reply Hincks declared that, to a great degree, he had lost confidence in Lord Sydenham; he believed the Governor had decided not only upon an anti-French policy, but also upon the subversion of the Reformers in the upper province unless he could corrupt or deceive them. He did not wish to create a collision with Sydenham, but he felt that French Canadians would have just grounds for complaint if no protest were made against the Gover- nor's *"monstrously oppressive and unjust"* measures.⁴²

III

On February 10, 1841, the union took place. It was, as Lord Sydenham re- marked to Arthur, a day with many charms for the "lovers of coincidences"—the anniversary date of the Queen's marriage, of the last prorogation of the Upper Canadian Legislature, and of the introduction of resolutions for the suspension of the constitution in Lower Canada—the day of the royal christening—exactly six months after the Act of Union became law—"in short quite a constellation of events."⁴³ Napoléon Aubin, with a different perspective, commented: "Le jour choisi pour nous installer dans l'Union est un mercredi. Les érudits vous diront que ce mot signifie *jour de mercure:* or Mercure est le dieu des marchands et des voleurs. Singulière coincidence. . . ."⁴⁴

In Montreal, the ceremonies commenced with a twenty-one gun salute fired at noon from the Champ de Mars. At one o'clock, military and civil dignitaries assembled at Government House while the Governor's new commission was read and the oaths of office were administered. Lord Sydenham read a proclamation urging French Canadians not to be misled by efforts which had been sedulously made to convince them that the union would be injurious and that its provisions were susceptible of change. Such attempts could only prove as mischievous as they must be useless. He appealed to the inhabitants of Lower Canada to use the power now restored to their hands in a manner which would justify their Sovereign's trust in them. He predicted advantages for Upper Canada from the union which could be attained by no other means. "In your hands now rests your own fate; and by the use which you will make of the opportunity must it be decided," he concluded.⁴⁵ After the formal ceremonies were completed, a levee was held at Government House with a guard of honour and a band in attendance.⁴⁶

Toronto had just learned that Kingston was to be the new capital and the despondent population was in no mood for joyous celebrations. But Sir George Arthur, with his strong sense of duty, felt that some display was required and ordered a royal salute to be fired in honour of the occasion. The only alternative, he told Lord Sydenham, would have been to fall in with the prevailing melancholy and fire minute guns." It is doubtful if many Torontonians noted the difference in the artillery performance. "The guns have just done firing—it is the day of the dinner to Sir George, the people are in low spirits," Helen Macaulay observed." That evening, at the banquet given in his honour, Sir George Arthur continued his valiant efforts to preserve appearances. Despite a splitting headache, he forced himself to drink thirteen bumper toasts with the customary enthusiasm as the band blared forth its accompaniment." The banquet was an ordeal. It had been planned to honour Sir George Arthur, but everyone present clearly recognized that, whatever its significance in this respect, it symbolized the end of an era in Upper Canada.

IV

Once the union had been proclaimed, Sydenham gave orders for the election writs to be issued and turned to the first stages of a political and administrative reorganization which he had been contemplating for more than a year. He prepared a list of thirty-three possible candidates for appointment to the Legislative Council and asked Russell to send him separate instruments under the royal sign manual for each. He explained that he planned to restrict the appointments to twenty-four or five, but, as it was impossible to know in advance that all would accept and agree to attend regularly, he had allowed himself a margin. Those named in the list were the most "distinguished and respected in the Province for their character—their position—and their independent circumstances—of Loyalty to their Sovereign [and] of . . . attachment to British Connexion."" The extremists from both parties were not excluded from the list, but a preference had been given to moderate men intent on improving the country. Because of the stigma which had been attached to the Legislative Council, Lord Sydenham had listed scarcely any holding office under the Crown. With the exception of Vice-Chancellor Robert S. Jameson, both the judiciary and the clergy had been excluded. An effort had been made to name men from different parts of the province in order to provide representation for local interests. In Upper Canada this was accomplished easily enough, but the difficulty in finding French Canadians "whose Loyalty is undoubted and who possess the qualifications of Fortune and Education" had resulted in a larger number of names from Montreal and Quebec than he would have preferred. He hoped that "some time hence, as opportunities offer—of which I shall readily avail myself," he would be able to submit the names of additional French Canadians.

Both Russell and Sydenham thoroughly endorsed Durham's comments on the need for administrative reform in Canada, and, immediately after the union had taken place, the Governor turned his attention to this problem. In order that routine business might not be delayed, he appointed John Henry Dunn receiver general, and Samuel Bealey Harrison and Dominick Daly joint provincial secretaries. At the same time, he nominated Draper, Baldwin, Ogden, and Day, the former law officers, as members of the new Executive Council. These initial appointments—

two provincial secretaries, and two sets of law officers—may have amounted to a subconscious recognition that the union was unlikely ever to become an absolute reality. They were the outward and visible signs of that dualism which, as J. E. Hodgetts has pointed out,[51] was soon to become an important characteristic of the union. In his efforts to provide sectional representation in the Legislative Council, and by his recognition of the need for dual offices, Sydenham unconsciously supported the claim of Ellice and Howick that the Canadian situation demanded a federal, rather than a legislative union. Lord Sydenham undoubtedly would have explained the creation of dual offices in terms of the vast extent of the territory involved, as he had done when stating the need for deputy governors. He had no thought of providing a ministerial framework which would lend itself to the protection of French Canada's separate and distinct interests. Nonetheless, it must be remembered that extent of territory was one of the secondary elements which created the need for a federal solution, and in taking it into consideration, he provided the means of expression for the more positive aspects of federalism.

Sydenham's reconstruction involved a change of status and function for many public offices which still retained their pre-union titles. In Lower Canada the attorney general had previously received a small annual salary that was greatly augmented by fees for each individual service rendered. His average annual income up to 1839 was £3,256. The solicitor general also had a small annual salary, but, unlike the attorney general, he had few duties to perform and his emoluments were insufficient. In his reorganization, Lord Sydenham followed the practice which had been adopted in Upper Canada several years before and abolished the fee system. The duties of the solicitor general were increased and the presence of one law officer from each section of the province was required at the seat of government at all times. The attorney general from Upper Canada was given a salary of £1,080 while the solicitor general was to receive £540. Their counterparts from Lower Canada were paid at the higher rate of £1,500 and £1,000 because, not being members of the Upper Canadian bar, they would be unable to supplement their incomes by taking private cases while they were in Kingston. For some time, the law officers had been members of the Executive Council and in addition to their legal duties they had advised the Governor upon the conduct of general business. Upon making his first appointments after the union, Sydenham asserted that such was now to be considered the rule rather than the custom.

The reorganization of the Provincial Secretary's Office was considered by Lord Sydenham to be one of his major administrative reforms. A Provincial Secretary's Office had existed from the establishment of civil government after the conquest, but it had never been very significant. The tendency to correspond directly with the head of government on even the most trivial matters had resulted in the governor's civil secretary becoming the principal channel of communication. The provincial secretary, who was also registrar, found his duties almost entirely restricted to the registration of land grants and other formal documents. After the union, Sydenham determined to make the office the primary channel of internal communication. Under his reorganization, the civil secretary was to become the governor's private secretary, "the Confidential Servant of the Governor . . . whose tenure of Office should therefore terminate with the Governor's."[52] He would assist the governor in the conduct of correspondence with the colonial secretary, the lieutenant-governors, the minister at Washington, and all foreign authorities and individuals.

Virtually every major public office was touched in some degree by Sydenham's administrative reforms, but little that he instituted was entirely new. Observing that much of the Executive Council's time was consumed in considering land petitions and scrutinizing public accounts, he established subcommittees to perform these functions and to make recommendations to Council. Such committees had existed in the past, but the significant factor was the appointment of Robert Baldwin Sullivan to preside over their meetings. Sullivan had previously held the office of commissioner of Crown lands in Upper Canada and was thoroughly familiar with much of the work.

The status of the inspector general of public accounts was to be increased to make him the senior financial officer in the province—a fore-runner of the minister of finance. For this appointment, Sydenham wanted a man who was well acquainted with accounts and competent to superintend the routine business of his office, and who was also capable of proposing, explaining, and vindicating financial arrangements in the Assembly. John Macaulay would have been the Governor's choice had he not refused to seek election on the grounds that he had no ability as a public speaker. Macaulay's political philosophy represented one strain of Toryism. Subscribing fully to the concept of government by an élite, Macaulay saw himself as a servant of the Crown, not of the people. To him, the idea that an official should seek popular election was extremely repugnant, and probably seemed to be almost a perversion of the constitution.

The first session was almost over before Sydenham came to the conclusion that Francis Hincks was the best man available for the office of inspector general of public accounts. When the Governor's sudden death intervened, it was left to Sir Charles Bagot to make the appointment.

In the spring of 1840, Lord Sydenham had established a Board of Works for the better supervision of all public works in Lower Canada. After the union, H. H. Killaly, who had just completed a survey of public works for Sydenham, was appointed president of the Board in preparation for the extension of its authority to both sections of the province. Before the union, Upper Canada had had one commissioner of Crown lands and Lower Canada two. Sydenham decided that in this instance there was no necessity for dual offices and established a single department for the whole province. John Davidson was appointed commissioner of Crown lands, having held the same office in Lower Canada since 1837, and Thomas Parke, an Upper Canadian Reformer, was made surveyor general, but neither was given a seat in the Executive Council.

In the middle of July 1841, with the first session of the Legislature well advanced, Lord Sydenham reported on his reorganization. He was satisfied that the business of the province would now be performed efficiently and economically. The responsibility which he had previously declared to be lacking was now established in the various departments. By insisting that the heads of departments should be members either of the Assembly or the Legislative Council, he had provided the public with "a wholesome control over their acts, and a security . . . for the general administration of Affairs being in accordance with the wishes of the Legislature."[ss] At the time, all the heads of departments were members of the Assembly with the single exception of Sullivan who was in the Legislative Council. Sydenham did not consider it necessary that such should be rigidly insisted upon in the future, but it was desirable that a reasonable number of the principal public officers should be members of the Legislature. If they were unable to obtain seats they should be required to make way for those who could. Lord Sydenham had thus given a practical application to Lord John Russell's "harmony concept." In doing so, he had taken a long step on the road to responsible government, as numerous constitutional monographs have pointed out. But it was also a step which would lend itself to the further development of federal characteristics within the framework of the legislative union.

Occasionally, Lord Sydenham would extend his thoughts on reform, reorganization, and assimilation beyond political and administrative considerations to contemplate the position of the Roman Catholic Church in Canada. From the moment of his arrival, he had recognized that the Church was a very powerful influence in the country. Care should be taken that this influence was aligned in support of the interests of Great Britain. Writing to Russell, late in May 1841, he reported, "In this Country, more perhaps than in any other, the direction which the opinions and feelings of the People may take depends on the Catholic Clergy, and therefore, upon the Heads of that Church."[44] The British government could not exercise any direct authority over the choice of Roman Catholic bishops, but it could, and should, do so indirectly. The practice had developed for each bishop to have a coadjutor who succeeded him automatically. Thus, approval of the coadjutor amounted to approval of the next bishop. Sydenham greatly lamented the succession of Bishops Bourget in Montreal and Gaulin, as Bishop Regiopolis, in Upper Canada. He regarded both men as Lower Canadian priests of "little ability, imbued with all the little Provincial feelings and prejudices of their Countrymen." He realized it was considered only just that Lower Canadian bishops should be of French-Canadian extraction. If men like Bishop Plessis were readily available, he would have no objections to the principle, but actually few French-Canadian priests combining ability and attachment to the British connection could be found. Under these circumstances, he suggested that the British government should endeavour to have appointments made from the Sulpician Order, which enjoyed a high reputation in the province. If this were done, Lower Canada would be given bishops with "large and extended views in place of little petty provincial feelings— a reasoned and, therefore, a steady attachment to British connexion and British rule, and a thorough contempt for those miserable antipathies of race which so universally prevail among the native Canadians. . . ." Sydenham was also concerned with the manner in which the influence of the Lower Canadian clergy was extending into Upper Canada. He favoured the recognition of a separate See in Upper Canada, not only because it would restrict this influence, but also because it would result in the appointment of Michael Power, the parish priest in Laprairie and a man whom he held in great esteem.

As he prepared for the union in administrative, economic, and cultural terms, Lord Sydenham was also making purely political preparations which will be considered in the next chapter. Whatever criticism may be made of his administration, his endeavours cannot be condemned as incomplete or inefficient. Had there been any real possibility of a complete union and the assimilation it was designed to promote, Sydenham almost certainly would have accomplished it. Everything that could be done immediately was done, and, where he found himself unable to act, he made recommendations and suggestions for the future. He may have doubted that the Durham formula could achieve its objective, but he had gone beyond Durham's recommendations. Because he never doubted for a moment that assimilation was possible, he could honestly believe that he was about to complete his mission by providing a framework in which the process of anglicization could operate with little or no impediment.

CHAPTER SIX

A THIN VEIL OF SUCCESS

WHILE MAKING HIS FINAL preparations for the union, Lord Sydenham never lost sight of the fact that an unco-operative Assembly, during the first session of the Legislature, could deny him that full measure of success which appeared to be within his grasp. From mid-summer 1840 the predominant thought in his mind, and in the minds of all Canadian politicians, was the election that would follow the proclamation of union. The Governor regarded the election as a preview of the session. His union could come under attack from three possible sources. The ultra Tories of Upper Canada would quite likely continue the obstructionist tactics displayed during the last session of the Legislature. The ultra Reformers, who were not satisfied with the "harmony concept" and insisted upon the full measure of responsible government, might endeavour to force through unacceptable constitutional innovations, or they might unite with the French party to pervert the character and purpose of the union. The third threat to the union was French Canada, but Sydenham felt that there would be no real danger from this quarter provided his Moderate party was able to defeat the ultra Reformers and the High Tories in Upper Canada. With the enthusiasm and vigour which characterized all of his endeavours, Lord Sydenham took up the anticipated challenge. In both the election and the first session, he achieved what at first sight appeared to be a complete success, but closer examination and subsequent events would reveal that this was more apparent than real.

I

Shortly after the Act of Union was passed, the Lower Canadian forces began to organize. Early in September 1840, R. Adamson, one of LaFontaine's supporters in New Glasgow, wrote declaring that the sole object of the Act was "to secure if possible a British Tory House." It was not too soon to get "some influential and competent person" to start speaking outside the parish churches each Sunday. Every means, "Clergy and all" would be used in an attempt to prevent LaFontaine's election, Adamson warned.[1]

During the autumn, a committee of electors was formed at Quebec, under Neilson's leadership, for the avowed purpose of securing the election of members opposed to the union. In a circular, addressed to the electors of Quebec, the committee declared :

The Election of Representatives . . . enables us to express in an unquestionable shape, our reprobation of the injustice which is done to this Province. Acts of violence can serve the ends of the authors of this injustice, and prove fatal to the welfare of the country and of all classes of its inhabitants. The law and the precepts of morality which we are convinced are yet powerful with the majority of the Electors permit of only lawful means for lawful ends.[2]

The electorate was urged to see that "perfect tranquillity" prevailed during the elections. The use of intoxicating liquors should be banished from the campaigns. "Every Elector must proceed to the place of Elections with the same zeal as he performs a religious duty or an act of charity for, under the present circumstances, our duty to the country is equally obligatory."

The emphasis on candidates who were opposed to the union would naturally lead to the conclusion that Neilson and the committee stood for repeal. Undoubtedly, Neilson and many of his followers would have favoured such a result, but he, at least, recognized that it would be virtually impossible to obtain. His immediate objective was to secure a strong condemnation of what he considered to be injustices perpetrated upon Lower Canada by the union arrangements and by Sydenham's ordinances.[3] His position did not differ materially from that of LaFontaine for both men considered that the union could only be rendered acceptable by great changes— changes which would alter its character profoundly. The difference which separated them was their attitude to responsible government. LaFontaine's understanding of responsible government was imperfect, and his faith in it as a means of remedying the unacceptable features of the union was inclined to waver. Nonetheless, he was resolved to give the gospel of Francis Hincks a trial. Neilson, on the other hand, had absolutely no faith in such a remedy. He believed that Sydenham was attempting to humbug the people with responsible government and a supposed liberality.[4] But even if such were not the case, the attainment of responsible government would mean the introduction of all the evils of rampant democracy and the spoils system. The only true happiness for Canada lay in a full observance of colonial status. To Neilson, the imperial connection was the best guarantee of individual rights and he wanted nothing to do with any movement in the direction of national autonomy. Perhaps with a memory of his success in the 1820's, Neilson wished to present the British government with an accurate account of Lower Canadian opinion and leave the rest to it.

Five days after he had proclaimed the union, Lord Sydenham ordered the election writs to be issued, returnable April 8. With the election definitely announced, the tempo of campaigning accelerated on all sides. A meeting was held in the Albion Hotel at Quebec to form a committee for the purpose of counter-acting Neilson's efforts by enlisting support for candidates pledged to give the union a fair trial.

II

While the Act of Union was before Parliament, the original representation plan had been altered to give the urban commercial element greater weight. Montreal and Quebec were each given two members instead of one, and Three Rivers and Sherbrooke were set apart from their counties as separate constituencies with one member each. Early in March, Sydenham issued a proclamation defining the limits of these urban constituencies in a manner designed to attain the objective behind the alterations. The suburbs of Quebec and Montreal were cut off from the cities, and "pretty extensive limits" were assigned to Sherbrooke in order to include the village of Lennoxville three miles away.[5] Although Russell declared that Sydenham had done "what was intended by the Union Act," to Neilson and LaFontaine the

Governor's action was another glaring example of the injustice embodied in the policy of the union.

Lord Sydenham did not deceive himself concerning election prospects in Lower Canada. ". . . Except in the Townships and perhaps one or two counties where the English prevail," he wrote to Russell, "we shall not have a man returned who does not hate British connexion, British rule, British improvements, and everything which has a taint of British feeling. . . ." It was upon Upper Canada that he was relying for a majority which would enable him to work the union successfully. To this end he sought to combine moderate men from the Tories and the Reformers into what was virtually a party of his own. In a very real sense, the tour of Upper Canada the previous summer had been his pre-election campaign as leader of that party.

After obtaining Reform support for his union proposals in the Upper Canadian Assembly, Sydenham decided that, if Baldwin would drop his insistence on full responsible government and accept the "harmony concept" instead, he would be a useful member of the Moderate party. Not only would he make a good solicitor general, but more important, he could probably carry Toronto, the ultra Tory stronghold, in the elections. After an interview at which Baldwin and the Governor apparently misunderstood each other, the appointment was made. By the spring of 1841, however, Sydenham was beginning to have second thoughts about his solicitor general. Baldwin's decision not to stand as a candidate for Toronto after the Tories carried the municipal election was most annoying—"an act of great folly." "Why he has given his opponents ten times as great a triumph as he would have done by going to the Poll!" Sydenham declared to S. B. Harrison.

Even more disturbing was the thought of the extent to which the Reform leader might try to carry his theory of responsible government if he were elected. Although Baldwin had accepted Russell's despatches on the subject, Arthur continued to warn that he was really an ultra Reformer and would soon be demanding the full degree of responsibility recommended by Durham. At first, Sydenham had been inclined to discount Arthur's warnings, but, when Baldwin declared his lack of confidence in his fellow councillors shortly after the union was proclaimed, the Governor began to change his mind. "Was there ever such an ass!" he exclaimed. In criticizing Baldwin's action, Sydenham asserted that there would be time enough for the declaration of opinions if the Council should be unable to agree upon the advice to be offered to the Governor. Baldwin replied that his action, if accepted in the proper sense, would only serve to clarify the relationship of the members of Council to each other. He felt certain that the opinions of Lord John Russell and the Governor on constitutional principles were in complete accord with his own. In effect, Baldwin's letter denied the existence of any party cohesion or loyalty among the members of the Executive Council, but Sydenham failed to observe this. "I am very glad you think I nailed Baldwin in the correspondence," he informed Arthur. "I really believe that when away from that mischievous old ass, his Father, good may be made of him. However, if I cannot, I shall make no bones of ejecting him."

Actually, both men were working at cross purposes and neither really understood the other. The objective of Baldwin and the ultra Reformers in the election was a victory for responsible government. Baldwin hoped that this was also Sydenham's objective and he wished to support him until it was clearly revealed that such was not the case. Hincks, however, could supply a more practical reason for Baldwin remaining in office with men like Draper, Day, and Ogden. He pointed out to LaFontaine that Baldwin's resignation at the moment would not only be injurious to the Reformers' election prospects, but would also separate him from such potential allies as Harrison, Dunn, and Daly. "On the whole looking on the appointments as merely temporary I have myself advised the delay of the split which I foresee," he wrote.[12]

In so far as the election was concerned, Lord Sydenham had both general and specific objectives. He was most anxious to secure the return of moderate men who would concentrate on public improvements and not indulge in racial quarrels or flights of constitutional theory. The defeat of the ultra Tories and the extreme Reformers would be a victory for the union and its basic objective. In many constituencies, the Governor had selected a favoured candidate. He had also insisted that the members of his Executive Council, with the exception of Robert Baldwin Sullivan, should find seats in the Assembly. By the time the elections were held, Robert Baldwin's election was no longer considered vital, but the other members of Council headed the list of favoured candidates. Sydenham was particularly interested in the election of Samuel Bealey Harrison who was running against Sir Allan MacNab in Hamilton. Harrison had attracted Sydenham's favourable attention while serving as Sir George Arthur's secretary, and the Governor now had an important role for him to fill. Somewhat less than satisfied with Draper's performance as Government leader in the Assembly, Sydenham planned to replace him in this capacity with Harrison. In addition, MacNab was a prominent ultra Tory and was to be numbered among the enemy.

Lord Sydenham was prepared to use as much influence as was necessary to secure his objectives in the election, but unlike Sir Francis Bond Head, he preferred to operate behind the scenes. In Upper Canada, much of the election management was delegated to Sir George Arthur; Major Campbell, the Governor's Military Secretary, acted as his campaign manager in Montreal. Just as the election campaign was about to get under way in earnest, orders were received for Campbell to rejoin his regiment. ". . . At this juncture his loss would be most disastrous to me," Sydenham protested, "as he manages the *Members* for me, both as to their Elections and their votes, and is the sole reliance I have."[13] To Arthur, Sydenham wrote, "Many thanks for your Electioneering news. *Your* letters are the only accounts I get worth anything, and yet the cry is that I meddle in the Elections. I wish I could do so more effectually!"[14] Two days later, perhaps in an attempt to meddle "more effectually," he suggested the exchange of militia regiments stationed at Cornwall and Hamilton, commenting, "It is certainly a point to get rid of Sir Allan's Tory Militia supporters if possible."[15]

When it began to appear that MacNab was a formidable opponent for Harrison, Sydenham decided that he should be removed, "if he can be conciliated, (Anglicé bought) upon decent terms."[16] It was rumoured that MacNab's price for withdrawing from the election would be the speakership of the Legislative Council. To this, Sydenham objected that he was neither "Lawyer enough" nor sufficiently familiar with the French language. Draper suggested an appointment such as surveyor of forests, but Sydenham preferred to offer the Tory knight a seat in the Legislative Council and the restoration of his militia regiment. After considering the proposition briefly, MacNab rejected it and continued to stand as Harrison's opponent. In Sydenham's mind, Harrison's election was far more important than MacNab's defeat. He had sought to couple the two objectives, but now he began to fear that, if a miscalculation had been made regarding Hamilton, Harrison could be sure of no other constituency. His uncertainty made him increasingly sensitive to any opposition to his favourite. When the Clerk of the Peace of the Gore District publicly announced that the former Civil Secretary was too much under the Governor's influence and thus was not a fit representative of the people, Sydenham ordered his immediate dismissal.

The influence exerted on behalf of Harrison was the exception rather than the general rule. For the most part, Sydenham's methods were more subtle. His favoured candidates were made known by indirect means at the local level. One letter from Chatham inquiring which was the approved candidate bears the endorsement in Sydenham's hand, "Private, Thanks—Say that Mr. Foster knows my views of the election." [17] It should not be imagined, however, that the Governor's influence and organization extended into every constituency. When both candidates had declared their intention of supporting his administration and neither was associated with the extreme parties, he preferred to leave the decision to the electorate.[18] In most instances the Governor's candidates were supported by the newspapers that enjoyed Government patronage. Efforts were made to convince the electorate that local public works were contingent upon the success of the approved candidate. Polling stations were located and returning officers appointed upon the advice of the candidates endorsed by the Governor. In Lower Canada, polling stations were strategically located to give the maximum advantage to the English-speaking minority. The elections were held over a period of several days and an effort was made to arrange them in a sequence that would create the appearance of a trend in favour of the Governor's Moderates. Within this pattern, the approved candidates were permitted to select the dates for their own elections.

Lord Sydenham's election strategy was even more successful than he had expected. The absence of well-defined party lines makes an exact summary of the results impossible, but Civil Secretary T. W. C. Murdoch's analysis is sufficiently accurate for general purposes: Government members, 24; French members, 20; moderate Reformers, 20; ultra Reformers, 5; Compact party, 7; doubtful, 6.[19] Lord Sydenham's prediction that the ultra Reformers and High Tories would be defeated in Upper Canada had been fulfilled. With the support of the moderate Reformers, which he was certain he could obtain, the Government would be in a safe position during the first session. The results contained one major disappointment : Harrison was defeated in Hamilton and had failed in a second hasty attempt in Kent. Sydenham was still resolved, however, that Harrison should be his spokesman in the Assembly. The Kingston seat was reopened by the appointment of the successful candidate, Manahan, as an inspector of customs, and this time the direct use of the Governor's influence secured Harrison's return by acclamation.

Although both Sydenham and Arthur reported to the contrary, the elections were marred by frequent displays of violence. Orange mobs sought to intimidate voters in several Upper Canadian constituencies. Deaths occurred in Toronto, Hamilton, and Durham County as the result of election violence. In Lower Canada, violence was restricted for the most part to the District of Montreal where Irish canal labourers and French Canadians vied for control of the polls. The threat of violence coupled with the remoteness of the polling stations resulted in the return of pro-union candidates for the French counties of Montreal, Rouville, Terrebonne, Vaudreuil, and Chambly. In Terrebonne, LaFontaine's supporters arrived at New Glasgow prepared to defend themselves, but their leader forfeited the election rather than engage in a pitched battle with his opponent's men who had taken possession of high ground guarding the approach to the polling station. Upon returning home, LaFontaine issued an address to his constituents criticizing the iniquities of the union in general and the role played by the Governor in the elections in particular. New Glasgow, "dans les bois, à l'extremité des limites de ce comté," had been selected as the location of the poll purely for the purpose of perverting the election. The French-Canadian leader described his interview with the Governor, early in 1840, when he had been offered and had rejected the office of solicitor general. His real opponent in the Terrebonne election had not been Dr. McCulloch: "Un fait a constater c'est que là lui, Lord Sydenham, est descendu dans l'arene pour combattre corps à corps avec un simple individu. C'est lui qui engageait la lutte avec moi; le Dr. McCulloch n'étant qu'un prête-nom." [20]

LaFontaine's opinion was naturally biased, but even Samuel Gerrard, who reported that LaFontaine "cut a sorry figure," wrote, "I do not say that any undue influence has been used by the Executive, but if His Excellency had been supine, the results would have been less flattering." [21]

III

Having attained his election victory, Lord Sydenham was able to concentrate upon the approaching session. He fully realized that one of the immediate problems to be faced was the financial plight of the country and he hoped to be able to make some definite pronouncement concerning the guaranteed loan in his speech from the throne. Shortly after the union was proclaimed, he had submitted a plan for the Cabinet's consideration. He proposed that a loan of £1,500,000 should be raised by the Treasury on the security of Canada's consolidated revenue and with the interest guaranteed by the Imperial Government. The holders of Canadian securities should be compelled to redeem them at par or accept new stock at a corresponding price. He estimated that by this transaction the cost of servicing the debt would be reduced from 5¾ per cent to 3¾ per cent because of the British guarantee behind the new loan. After the debt had been refinanced in this manner, a sum of more than £200,000 would remain to be applied to public works projects.

Lord Sydenham admitted that the enforced redemption of securities before their maturity date might be considered a breach of contract, but it was his opinion that if the creditors of Canada were offered such a proposition "not one of them would reject" it. [22] "How would a traveller reject such an offer from a highwayman," commented Lord John Russell. The Government was ready to give any assistance "not inconsistent with good faith," Sydenham was informed. His other recommendations would be accepted, but there was no support in the Cabinet for compulsory redemption. The Canadian Legislature should pass an act providing for repayment of the debt on terms sufficiently attractive to induce creditors to accept. Upon learning that creditors were ready to redeem their securities, the British Government would proceed to raise the necessary funds. [23] With characteristic annoyance, Sydenham complained to Russell, "Your squeamishness about the repayment of the Canada Bond holders greatly increases my difficulty. . . . With a vote of the

House of Commons I could have opened brilliantly; now, I shall have nothing but promises to give them. . . ." [24] He agreed, however, that he would endeavour to prepare a measure and send it home.

In addition to the question of the loan, Russell's despatch also referred to the British Government's views on defence and emigration. A sum of £100,000 was allocated annually for defence. If this money was administered with greater economy and efficiency, a considerable surplus might be left to be utilized for military communications. Russell tacitly recognized a degree of responsibility for the support of emigrants from Great Britain. If the province were to revive the emigrant tax, consideration would be given to encouraging emigration by paying the tax imposed on British immigrants.

Lord Sydenham planned to give the three topics—finance, defence, and emigration—a prominent place in his speech from the throne. With the opening of the session three weeks away, he anticipated that the first month would "probably be a little stormy." The Upper Canadian ultra Reformers would likely join the French "in opposition to the Civil List and some other crotchets," but the prospect did not worry him for he had "great hopes of keeping things right with the Members" by means of his personal influence with the Upper Canadians. [25]

IV

While the Governor was considering policy and a legislative programme for the session, the Reformers were discussing tactics. Writing to LaFontaine after his unhappy experience in the Terrebonne election, Hincks urged the French-Canadian Reformers to adopt a more realistic approach to the coming session. The question of a nominee for speaker was a case in point. LaFontaine's preference for A. N. Morin, his lieutenant in Quebec City, over Augustin Cuvillier was understandable; Cuvillier was somewhat suspect because of his Montreal business and banking interests. But, Hincks reminded LaFontaine, there was no chance of Morin being elected, and Cuvillier was *"just of your own mind* regarding the Bill, opposed to the civil list, representation, debt, proscription of language." [26] If he were nominated by the French-Canadian Reformers, his election would be a blow against the existing terms of union. A more realistic view should also be taken regarding the question of representation. Parliament would never alter the basis of representation to give French Canadians the majority they ought to have "on strict principles of justice." Separation from the Empire was the only means of attaining such an end and even then it would be doubtful. "But," Hincks added, "you would gain the same object by joining us to increase *our county representation* along with yours & thus increase the power of the people." If such a coalition was to become effective, however, LaFontaine would have to overcome his prejudice against men like Dunn and Harrison, both of whom were friendly to French Canada. He would also have to make a greater effort to appreciate the difficult position of the Upper Canadian Reformers who were divided among themselves and faced with strong opposition.

As LaFontaine would not have a seat in the Assembly when the session opened, Hincks began writing also to A. N. Morin concerning tactics. ". . . I am against the Union and against the main features, as I think every honest Lower Canadian should be," Morin replied. [27] Union had been widely advocated as the "surest means of destroying the political rights and social institutions of half a million people. No other principle but that can be squeezed out of it." He was not for violence or haste, however, and did not expect direct repeal immediately. Rather, he hoped that men of good will acting together could render the union acceptable to French Canada. *L'Aurore* had proposed that French-speaking members should refrain from taking their seats in the Assembly until repeal was recognized as a *"sine qua non* question," but *Le Canadien* had attacked this negative policy. Morin was certain that "not two, or perhaps not one" of the Quebec members would support such a stand, and he believed the Montreal members were of a similar mind. Although he had at one time thought that Neilson planned to try to break the union, Morin was now convinced of his "pacific dispositions."

Looking towards the session, Morin saw a union of the Reformers as the most natural of several possible alignments. In Lower Canada it was thought that the right wing of the Tory party led by MacNab and Cartwright might join such an alliance and Morin inquired if this were really a possibility. It had also been rumoured that MacNab and Cartwright might join with the French Canadians "to upset the Union at once, and be at warfare until an absolute repeal comes," but he rejected the idea as both unlikely and undesirable. Such an alignment would take place only if Upper Canadian Reformers deserted their French-Canadian friends. "Should we, in the beginning, in claiming our rights as Canadians and as British subjects, be abandoned by you and helped by the Conservatives, that circumstance would be more painful to me than I could express," he informed Hincks. The speakership should not be made a political question. As far as French Canada was concerned Viger, Cuvillier, Quesnel, Neilson, MacNab or Merritt would be acceptable. He agreed with Hincks's views on responsible government, but appeared to be afraid that many moderate Reformers would be satisfied with something quite different. "Mind that there be no misunderstanding in terms when speaking of responsible government," he warned. A reformation of the Executive Council was an obvious necessity and Morin promised his support for any effort to replace Ogden, Day, Draper, and Sullivan by "more able, more disinterested, more honest, and more popular men, alike ready to respect all and do justice to all."

During the last week of May, the Upper Canadian Reformers were faced with a dilemma. There was general agreement that Ogden, Day, Draper, and Sullivan must resign from the Executive Council and that some of the vacancies thus created should be filled by French Canadians, but there was no unanimity as to how such a reorganization of the Government was to be obtained. The Reformers could, of course, threaten to submit their own resignations unless the Tory members of Council were dismissed, but Baldwin, Price, and Hincks were the only ones who favoured such an extreme course. Parke proposed that an attempt should be made, first, to obtain good measures from the present men. Both Dunn and Small felt that the country would reject the Reformers if they resorted to extreme measures. Upon informing LaFontaine of the different opinions among Upper Canadian Reformers, Hincks predicted that Baldwin would resign before the session began unless the Council was remodelled to include some French Canadians and to exclude the objectionable Tories. Although they all agreed that justice must be obtained for Lower Canada, Hincks very much doubted that Dunn, Daly, Harrison, or Killaly would resign with Baldwin.[28]

As Hincks had anticipated, Baldwin resigned alone on the day the session opened. In Sydenham's eyes Baldwin's action was a double attack; by demanding full responsible government, he had revealed that he was an ultra Reformer who would not accept the Governor's concept of a Moderate party, and by insisting upon the appointment of French-Canadian Reformers to the Executive Council, he was virtually demanding the renunciation of assimilation as the union's primary objective. If French-Canadian leaders could have been found who would accept the union without altering the provisions designed to promote assimilation, Sydenham would have been pleased to appoint them, but, under the circumstances, he was bound to resist Baldwin's demands. On the other hand, if Baldwin had not resigned, it is entirely likely the alliance that Hincks had been endeavouring to forge would have disintegrated completely. As Morin had clearly indicated in his letter to Hincks, the Upper Canadian Reformers had no hope of obtaining responsible government without the assistance of the French-Canadian members, but there was more than one means by which *la survivance* could be assured.

Edward Gibbon Wakefield, who had recently arrived in Canada to promote a land and emigration scheme, was in despair at the news of Baldwin's resignation, but Sydenham was not greatly concerned. "I feel confident that I can lick this Ultra-party completely," he informed Russell.[28] Nonetheless, he regretted that the impression of agitation would likely weaken Canadian credit in England. He expected to have "motions on responsible Govt., want of confidence, the details of the Union, and everything that is most mischievous." He was certain, however, that Baldwin could command the support of no more than six members from Upper Canada who, with the French Canadians, would constitute a maximum opposition of thirty. Before the session was two weeks old, Sydenham reported a complete victory. "I have got rid of Baldwin and finished him as a public man for ever."[29] Only two Upper Canadian members were voting with him, and the Governor boasted that he could prevent the return of both "to-morrow if they went to their constituents." He frankly admitted that he felt obliged to act as *"Leader"* because none of the members of his Executive Council had the "slightest notion of carrying on a Govt. in the House." Much of his time was spent "lecturing Members every morning & schooling my Cabinet every day."

v

Regarding the first session of the Legislature as "the touchstone"[31] of his union, Lord Sydenham approached it with two predominant objectives in mind. Any attempt to render the union ineffective as an instrument of assimilation must be rigidly opposed, and, secondly, no extension of the "harmony concept" into a full theory of responsible government could be permitted. The threat to union from French Canada had been reduced by the fact that the number of French Canadians returned was considerably fewer than had been expected. In Lower Canada it was alleged that this was the result of the disfranchisement of French-speaking electors in Montreal and Quebec, the inconvenient location of polling stations, and violence at the polls. There would be election petitions to be considered later on this score; for the moment, the French Canadians could do no harm unless they were supported by the Upper Canadian Reformers. Baldwin might remain firm in his determination to obtain justice for French Canada, but the majority of his followers could be transformed into Government supporters by a programme of practical measures. If this happened, the danger of an attempt to indulge in constitutional theorizing would be greatly diminished.

The month of June was the testing period. Hincks's attempt to have Cuvillier's election as speaker recognized as a declaration against the terms of union fell rather flat when the Government members also supported Cuvillier. The speech from the throne gave a preview of Sydenham's practical measures : the development of natural resources by an extensive public works programme backed by the guaranteed loan, assistance for immigration, reduction in postal rates and improved postal facilities, a system of municipal government for Upper Canada, and provision for education. The throne speech permitted Sydenham to present his programme, but it also provided the opposition with an opportunity to introduce the threats to union which he feared. During the debate on the speech, Draper endeavoured to avoid any concrete admissions concerning responsible government, but finally, in reply to a direct question, he was forced to concede that if the Government was unable to retain the support of the Assembly, either a dissolution would result or some members of the Executive Council would be replaced. Neilson introduced the other threat to the union when he proposed an amendment to the effect that the Act of Union contained features which were "inconsistent with justice, and the common rights of British subjects." [32] Speaking in support of Neilson's amendment, Hincks bitterly attacked the civil list provisions and the basis for representation. When the vote was taken, however, only four Upper Canadian Reformers joined with Baldwin and Hincks in support of the French-Canadian point of view.

When Neilson's amendment was defeated fifty to twenty-five, Sydenham felt certain the crisis had passed. Some "rather ambiguous words about the Union" had been adopted in committee, "in spite of my Cabinet," he reported, but, "I sent for the Members who I knew had voted only from ignorance, not intention, and away they went directly and voted the words out again upon the report, by a very large majority!" At the end of June, he informed Lord John Russell, "Whoever follows me may now, with management, keep everything quiet and rule with comfort." [33] All the contentious issues had been raised and "the agitators have entirely and signally failed. . . . Thus we shall go quietly to work at the measures of improvement which I have prepared, and we are sure of a peaceable and useful session." His successor, he declared, should be a man with parliamentary experience—"a person who will not shrink from work, and who will govern, as I do, *himself.*" Such a man would find everything "in grooves running of itself, and only requiring general direction." [34]

July and August were devoted to Lord Sydenham's programme of practical measures and he was delighted with the results. On July 27, he wrote to Russell that even Wakefield, "a grumbler by trade" was convinced that "the Union is firmly and irrevocably established." [35] A month later, as the session was drawing to its close, he described the success of his legislative programme to his brother : "The five great works I aimed at have been got through—the establishment of a board of works with ample powers; the admission of aliens; a new system of county courts; the regulation of the public lands ceded by the Crown under the Union Act; and lastly, this District Council Bill." [36]

In addition to his "five great works," a School Act, legislation to increase the customs revenue, and several minor measures were passed. Sydenham had also hoped to obtain a Currency Act establishing a government bank of issue. He calculated that merely by giving the state a monopoly on the issuance of paper currency, a sum of at least £750,000 would be made immediately available for public works without the necessity or expense of going into the money market to borrow it.[37] The scheme was strongly opposed, however, by mercantile interests in Montreal and Toronto and the Governor was not prepared to force it through the Legislature.

The Currency Bill was defeated by a combination of French Canadians, High Tories, ultra Reformers, and the moderate Reformers who had been supporting the Government throughout the session. Some members were inclined to regard the bill's defeat as a great triumph. "We are now in our glory," wrote John Johnston, "we beat the ministry 41-29." Referring either to the reduced preference on Canadian timber or to local improvements, he continued, "No Rag manufactory to be established for this session. They look small. I will learn them to be more just in distributing there [sic] mercy towards the Ottawa, I hit them hard blows." [38]

A similar combination of forces earlier in the session administered the only other rebuff that Sydenham received. When it became evident that a technicality would prevent the reception of Lower Canadian contested election petitions, Sir Allan MacNab introduced a bill to provide for the trial of these elections. As leader of the High Tories, MacNab had been endeavouring throughout the session to obstruct most of the Government's measures designed to facilitate the functioning of the union. In this instance, his motives were threefold : he had a genuine concern for the privileges and integrity of the Assembly and felt that it should not be denied the opportunity to determine whether its members had been properly elected; in addition, he had both personal and party reasons for desiring to embarrass Sydenham; and finally, he was alive to the possibility of an alliance between Tories and French Canadians for the purpose of overturning the union.[39] In spite of Sydenham's opposition, MacNab's bill was passed thirty-two to twenty-two in the Assembly, but it was thrown out by the Legislative Council. MacNab, however, refused to let the matter drop and secured a committee on privilege, with himself as chairman, to investigate the Council's action. After receiving the committee's report, the Assembly decided, without division, that a public enquiry should examine the petitioners' complaints at the beginning of the next session.

Lord Sydenham had good reason to consider the session a victory for his union and the policy of assimilation. The French-Canadian members had been unable to effect any alteration in the terms of union, and the moderate Reformers had been enticed away from Baldwin. A split had even developed between Baldwin and Hincks, and the latter had voted with the Government on the Currency Bill. There were, however, some slight indications that the Governor had been premature in declaring the union to be "irrevocably established," at least in the sense in which it was originally intended. Early in September, Baldwin proposed a series of resolutions on responsible government. Sydenham counteracted the Reform leader's action by authorizing Harrison to propose, in amendment, resolutions that were very similar. Baldwin was caught on the horns of a dilemma. By voting with the Tories he could defeat Harrison's amendment, but the Tories would then combine with the Government to defeat his resolutions. He had no choice but to vote for the amendment which was easily carried. On the surface, it appeared to be another victory for the Governor, but, in reality, it amounted to a concession which he had not intended to make. It is true that, by a strict interpretation, the Harrison resoluions conceded no more than Russell's "harmony concept," but they were also capable of a more fluid interpretation and could be used to justify virtually all that Baldwin demanded.

Still later in the session, when many of the members had returned home, an address was carried requesting the Queen to locate the seat of government alternately at Quebec and Toronto. Although it was not to be taken seriously this time, here was the emergence of that dualism which was to defeat the primary purpose of the union.

By the time the address was passed, Lord Sydenham was too ill to transmit it to the Colonial Secretary. He had suffered what was at first thought to be a minor injury when he fell from his horse on September 4. But his condition grew steadily worse and he died on September 19, exactly one month less than two years from the date of his arrival in Canada. Lord Sydenham died firmly convinced that his mission was a complete success and that the Province of Canada, which was already a constitutional and geographical unit, would ultimately become a political and social one as well. Had he been able to transmit the address, he probably would have discounted it as entirely unrepresentative of Canadian opinion. The future was to reveal how wrong he would have been.

What estimate can be made of Lord Sydenham's achievements in Canada? The very least that can be said is that in the administrative and financial spheres he brought order out of chaos. His realignment of the functions to be performed by the civil and provincial secretaries, and the creation of a Board of Works were major administrative achievements. Through Lord Sydenham's efforts, plans were made for the development of Canada's resources on a sound financial basis. In the realm of politics he had prevented, by various devices, any strong assertion of the dualism which was inherent in the situation facing him upon his arrival in Canada.

He had certainly created the appearance of success, but even before his death some men were questioning the depth to which that success penetrated. Upon reaching England, Sir George Arthur informed Russell that one session of the Legislature would prove nothing. Rather, considering Lord Sydenham's powers, any failure would be a surprise. The real test of union and Lord Sydenham's measures would only come after two general elections had taken place.[40] To Sydenham, Arthur made the prediction that "the Machine will soon be out of its Grooves" and that future governors would have a difficult task.[41] After taking over the office of prime minister, Sir Robert Peel commented, "I am afraid Lord Sydenham has acted on the principle of purchasing present acquiescence and support by large promises which he foresaw others would have to fulfil."[42] From their Tory bias both Arthur and Peel were thinking in terms of the threat of responsible government to the British connection, but the same judgments could have been pronounced with regard to the policy of assimilation.

In so far as assimilation was concerned, Sydenham had certainly satisfied the conditions set forth in the Durham formula and had even gone somewhat beyond. He had carried the union and, by political manipulation and an expansive public works programme, he had left the French-Canadian members isolated in the Assembly except for the ineffectual support of a mere handful of ultra Reformers from Upper Canada. The Durham formula required that this situation be maintained until French Canadians recognized the futility of resisting the assimilation process. In reality, this was an impossibility, but Sydenham would not have admitted such was the case. He did not realize that there were limits to what a policy of "management" could accomplish. Durham had stated that he would be surprised "if the more reflecting part of the French Canadians entertained, at present, any hope of continuing to preserve their nationality." Sydenham had searched for French-Canadian leaders with such views to assist, as Durham had predicted they would, in preparing the way for assimilation, and he had failed to find any. Neither LaFontaine nor any other French-Canadian leader could agree to participate in an attempt to exterminate French-Canadian culture. Sydenham's failure, in this respect, may have caused him to doubt the accuracy of Durham's prediction, but it did not lead him to recognize that assimilation was an unrealistic objective. After his vctories in the first session, he would have maintained that, with proper management, the Assembly could now be used to implement a policy of assimilation with, or without, the assistance of the French-Canadian members.

By manipulation the French-Canadian members had been deprived of any political significance during the first session, but within a few days of Sydenham's death, LaFontaine was elected for the fourth riding of York in Upper Canada. His election could be regarded as a portent of the re-emergence of French Canada as a political factor, but it was more than that; it symbolized the personal bond that had been established between Baldwin and LaFontaine. Baldwin's resignation, his steadfast support of the French-Canadian members during the session, and his efforts to have LaFontaine elected for an Upper Canadian constituency had made a lasting impression on the French-Canadian leader. As the moderate Reformers had been seduced away from Baldwin's leadership, it would be inaccurate to claim that an alliance between the Upper Canadian Reformers and the French party had been formed, but the basis for such an alliance had been established. It was not the only course open to the French party, but for LaFontaine it had always seemed the most natural one and henceforth it would be the only one he would consider.

CHAPTER SEVEN

TRANSFORMATION

IN THE LATE . SUMMER of 1841, the long expected defeat of the Melbourne Government occurred and the Conservatives took office under Sir Robert Peel. Neither Peel nor his Colonial Secretary, Lord Stanley, contemplated any major change in Canadian policy; both men had endorsed Durham's recommendations in favour of union and gradual assimilation. The first session of the Canadian Legislature seemed to them to indicate that French Canada had accepted the union or, at least, was incapable of effectual opposition to it. It had been necessary to force the union on French Canada, but, now that it was a *fait accompli*, surely French-Canadian leaders would realize that there was no alternative but to accept it and all its implications. If this were true, justice demanded that French Canada should be represented in the Government and, moreover, such a policy would be in accordance with the Durham formula.

Initially, the decision to appoint French-Canadian executive councillors had been taken on the basis of a preconceived policy, but the question was soon reduced to the level of political expediency when Sir Charles Bagot, who had succeeded Sydenham, reported that without French-Canadian support his Government would likely be defeated in the Assembly. With Sydenham's guiding hand removed and no further developmental projects in the offing, Draper's Moderate coalition was beginning to break up. There was a basic difference between the two components of the coalition—the moderate Tories were opposed to the concept of responsible government, and the moderate Reformers were not. The latter had not been prepared to stand with Baldwin in giving responsible government top priority, but now that the anticipated benefits of the union were assured they were ready to support his efforts to obtain the constitutional objective he had constantly advocated, and one by one they were returning to his leadership. As this realignment progressed it became increasingly clear that the French party would hold the balance of power and that their support would be vital to any government. Bagot's despatch introduced a new perspective that continued to haunt Peel and Stanley as long as they remained in office. Repeatedly, they were confronted with requests from Bagot and his successor, Sir Charles Metcalfe, for authority to make concessions magnanimously before the French Canadians used their power in the Assembly to extort them. But Stanley and his colleagues clearly recognized that concessions would amount to a retreat from the union settlement and the policy of assimilation. Repeatedly, they renounced all thought of magnanimity and urged the Governor to stand firm. Nonetheless, in each instance, they subsequently found themselves obliged to accept the advice they had previously rejected. The reluctant retreat continued until, by the end of Metcalfe's administration, the objective of assimilation was abandoned and the way was open for all the elements of sectionalism and bi-culturalism to express themselves politically and administratively.

I

Sir Charles Bagot sailed for Canada on October 20, 1841, but was driven back to port by contrary winds, and it was January 10, 1842, before he finally reached Kingston. He had originally intended to meet the Legislature as soon as possible after his arrival, but, after consultation with Daly and Harrison, he decided this would not be the wisest course. No great local inconvenience would occur if the Legislature did not meet immediately and there were several excellent reasons for postponing the session. He had not yet heard from Stanley regarding the important legislation that had been reserved during the previous session. Until this information was received, the programme for the coming session could not be fully prepared. Bagot wished to increase the membership of the Legislative Council and this would occasion a delay while his nominations were sent home and the necessary instruments were returned. It would also be desirable to fill the vacant offices of solicitor general for Canada West and inspector general before summoning the Legislature. Moreover, if the session were delayed, the Governor could utilize the interval to become better acquainted with the people and to put his policy before them in replies to their addresses. There were some indications that the French Canadians were awaiting an opportunity of returning to "better allegiance than God knows they have been lately in the practise [sic] of bearing."[1] This tendency should be permitted time to develop.

Bagot was conscious that any political success he might attain would have to rest on the fulfilment of Sydenham's promised public works programme. Less than a month after he took office he advertised the contracts for the Welland Canal and improvements on the St. Lawrence River. At the same time, to emphasize his impartiality, he made arrangements for equivalent works in Lower Canada. "I shall therefore be much disappointed," he declared to Lord Stanley, "if the mere shewing that I am actively and earnestly engaged in advancing them [public works], does not produce immediately, and very generally throughout the Colony, a good effect as regards the Government."[2]

The question of the guaranteed loan was a necessary feature of any consideration of the projected public works programme, and Bagot lost no time in placing it before Lord Stanley. He assumed that the Government would honour the Whigs' pledge, for any decision to the contrary would be fatal to the hope of governing Canada successfully. On the other hand, fulfilment of the pledge would be regarded by the people of Canada as "an earnest of future consideration and protection, and a proof that among the larger questions which engage the attention of the Imperial Government, their interests are not overlooked."[3]

After some procrastination, Stanley agreed that the pledge should be honoured, but he proposed a major alteration in Sydenham's plan. The proceeds of the guaranteed loan would be used to finance public works of general importance rather than to pay off the existing debt. Bagot admitted that Stanley's proposal was, in some respects, more advantageous to the province, but voiced strenuous objections to it on two grounds. He would have to suspend the public works which were about to proceed until new legislation could be passed and funds provided.

Such a suspension was certain to react to the detriment of the Government. Moreover, Sydenham had piloted a public works bill through the Legislature and Bagot was extremely reluctant to throw the whole question open for debate again. In the face of Bagot's objections, Stanley relented to the extent of agreeing that the Legislature should be permitted to choose between the two plans, and in addition he promised Bagot that he would not have to halt the works for lack of funds.[4]

Sectionalist elements, concealed beneath the surface of the Canadian union, soon began to present Bagot with another problem. Less than three weeks after his arrival, he reported to Stanley that he was in the "greatest perplexity" about the office of superintendent of education. The School Act, passed during the previous session, should be implemented immediately. But how was it possible to appoint a superintendent of education "without exciting . . . the apprehensions of every sect and denomination in the Country except that to which the person appointed may belong. . . ." [5] Bagot felt this difficulty should have been foreseen, and, if the office was considered "indispensably necessary," provision should have been made for two superintendents of education. The only solution, now, appeared to be to make a member of the Executive Council the nominal superintendent, and to appoint a Roman Catholic deputy superintendent in Lower Canada and a Protestant in Upper Canada, but he was uncertain of the legality of such a course. Four months later, Bagot reported that he had adopted this solution because he could see no alternative. The selection of a single person for a province "composed of so heterogeneous a population, was surrounded by difficulties of the gravest nature." R. S. Jameson, Vice-Chancellor of Upper Canada and Speaker of the Legislative Council, was appointed Superintendent of Education without salary. Jean Baptiste Meilleur, the founder of L'Assomption Collège in Lower Canada, was made Deputy Superintendent for Canada East, and Robert Murray, "a Member of the Scotch Church—and originally intended for the Clergy—but who has no cure of souls," was given a similar appointment for Canada West.[6]

Towards the end of the first session of the Legislature, the Assembly had passed an address requesting that the seat of government should alternate between Quebec and Toronto. Although it was premature, the address was nothing less than an expression of the dualistic tendencies implicit in the Canadian situation. When the question was referred to Bagot, however, the impracticability of the request prevented him from recognizing its full significance. He agreed that it had been wise to bring the French-Canadian members into Upper Canada for the first session, but he was not satisfied that the capital must necessarily remain at Kingston forever. The Governor declared that he would quietly endeavour to learn the wishes of the majority during the coming session. At the moment, he could only remind Stanley that it was essential the Government should not commit itself to a location which would be opposed by a majority of the members because, ultimately, the necessary funds for permanent buildings would have to be voted by the Legislature.

At the root of almost every aspect of dualism lay the question of French Canada's survival as a separate entity. Sir Charles Bagot was slow to realize this fact for, like Lord Stanley, he assumed that French Canadians had no alternative but to accept the assimilation implicit in the union. Some months after his arrival in Canada, he related to Lord Stanley his sentiments upon accepting the appointment: "I felt that, in fact, I was the first Governor who was called upon to put practically into operation, and endeavour to give effect, to the great measure of the Union, and to work out the experiment of fusing and identifying, so far as it might be possible, the very discordant elements to be reconciled by that irrevocable and unalterable Act—." [1]

During his first months in the province, Bagot had little personal contact with French Canada, but the reports that he received gave him some grounds for optimism. Quebec City's address of welcome represented almost the first occasion since the rebellion when the French and English populations had acted together. Bagot suggested to Stanley that this might be "a first step towards an obliteration of the barrier which has so long divided the English and French races." [8] Since Lord Sydenham's death, Morin, H. S. Huot, and C. J. E. Mondelet had accepted judgeships and C. S. Cherrier and Duncan Fisher had been made Queen's Counsel. The altered tone of *Le Canadien* appeared to offer additional evidence that French Canada was not prepared "to persist in an uncompromising and unreasoning resistance." In his initial enthusiasm over the prospect of a successful attempt to conciliate French Canada, Bagot considered appointing D. B. Viger and John Neilson to the Legislative Council. He was even encouraged to hope that the "unnatural" alliance between the French party and Baldwin's radicals might be broken up before the next session.

The prompt and vigorous efforts of the Montreal Police Magistrate to suppress *La Rebelle Histoire canadienne* annoyed the Governor for he feared the incident would impair relations with French Canada. Bagot admitted to Stanley that the booklet was intended to extol the insurgents and disparage the British government, but added that it was of "so contemptible [a] character that if left to itself it would scarcely have attracted any public notice." [9]

As he became more familiar with French Canada, Bagot began to realize that his original assessment of the situation had been "too sanguine." At the end of March, he reported to Stanley that there were indications that "we have only scotched the snake." [10] French Canada was adopting a "sulky course" with regard to the district councils and local taxation that "sufficiently shows in itself the stubborn ill humour, and provoking stupidity which still prevail there." Moreover, John Neilson, whom he had recently considered for appointment to the Legislative Council, had refused to accept the union as a *fait accompli* and was revealing himself to be a "lover of all mischief for its own sake." In the columns of the *Quebec Gazette* "all the old agitation and inflammatory topics" were being suggested as "proper munitions de guerre for all future sessions of the Legislature."

Among the subjects featured by Neilson was one which had equal appeal to both French- and English-speaking Canadians—the civil list question. [11] Upon leaving England, Bagot had assumed that this problem was settled, but he now realized that he had been completely misinformed. The Imperial Government's action in making a civil list of £75,000 an integral part of the Act of Union was generally resented throughout the province, he reported, and it was likely to come under attack during the forthcoming session. He urged that if an address were presented for the repeal of the relevant clauses in the Act of Union, it should be acceded to on condition that the Legislature provide an acceptable civil list.

Bagot's optimism regarding French Canada soon returned. He paid a visit to Montreal in May and was pleased to find that he was well received even by "the Frondeurs, and the turbulent of the Province." [12] At the same time, he began to contemplate a "stroke" which would assist in "keeping up the present good humour and propitiating the French in these parts." Sydenham's Judicature Ordinance, which was intended to introduce a court of common pleas and numerous other aspects of British civil law, had remained inoperative for want of the necessary proclamation. Bagot proposed to let the Ordinance die simply by neglecting to issue the proclamation until the time limit had expired, and declared that this would be "one of the most popular negative Acts which the Government could adopt." As an indication that the judicature was not to be remodelled, he would offer the appointment of chief justice of the Montreal District to Joseph Rémi Vallière de Saint-Réal. He also planned to promote C. D. Day to the bench and to offer the solicitor generalship to a French Canadian.

Lord Stanley had instructed Bagot to pursue a policy of conciliation towards French Canada, but the Colonial Secretary became alarmed when he thought he detected signs of outright concessions. He wished to see French Canada represented in the Government, but he abhorred the thought of appointing anyone who had been suspect during the rebellion. When Bagot suggested Viger as a possible member of the Legislative Council, Stanley reminded him that the only passport to favour was to be loyalty to the Crown and attachment to the British connection. "How can you then place in the Legislative Council, as one of your first acts, a man who notoriously fails in both these particulars?" he objected.[13] He might also have added that Vallière de Saint-Réal had been suspended, for a time, for issuing a writ of *habeas corpus* to prisoners arrested during the rebellion. Commenting upon Bagot's intention to let the Judicature Ordinance die, Stanley remarked that the "assimilation of the French to the English practice, though certainly not to be forced without due deliberation is an object to be kept in view. . . ."[14] Moreover, he refused to authorize any concession regarding the civil list or any other aspect of the Act of Union. Assimilation would not be forced, at least not without "due deliberation," but it would remain the ultimate objective.

In his anxiety to govern with complete impartiality towards French and English, Sir Charles Bagot tended to lose sight of assimilation as the objective, and to concentrate on concessions that he considered reasonable, but when he was brought up short by Lord Stanley, he denied that such was the case. He accepted Stanley's objections to Viger as "conclusive" and assured him that, although he still intended to let the Judicature Ordinance expire unproclaimed because it was both faulty and unpopular, he had "by no means lost sight of the expediency of assimilating hereafter, and whenever the fit time should arrive, the French to the English judicial practise [sic]."[15]

II

From the purely political point of view, French Canada was but one aspect of a complex problem. Bagot soon came to the conclusion that Sydenham's apparent success during the first session could be attributed to the promised loan plus "unscrupulous personal interference," and measures "which I would not use, and Your Lordship would not recommend."[16] He agreed with his Executive Council that the Government must be strengthened if it was to endure another session. The opposition was made up of three distinct groups—the old Family Compact, Robert Baldwin and his small following of ultra Reformers from Upper Canada who were being constantly reinforced by the return of moderate Reformers to their original allegiance, and the French party—all of which, with the exception of the moderate Reformers, had been shunned by Sydenham in his efforts to construct a moderate party. Bagot was convinced that Sydenham's reliance on moderate men had created a Government with too narrow a base. He believed that the Government would be strengthened materially if he were able to persuade representatives from each of the opposition groups to accept appointments to the Executive Council.

Shortly after his arrival in Canada, the Governor perceived an opportunity to initiate this new policy. He learned that, a week before his death, Lord Sydenham had been about to appoint Francis Hincks as inspector general, but had held his hand when Attorney General Draper threatened to resign if the appointment were made. Now, however, in recognition of the need to strengthen the Government, Draper was ready to accept Hincks's appointment provided it was counterbalanced by the appointment of a prominent High Tory, such as John S. Cartwright.

Bagot welcomed the opportunity to align the High Tories in support of the Government. He believed that experience must now have taught them to "mitigate those exclusive views which formerly entailed upon them the dislike and distrust of the Country. . . ." [17] Moreover, some members of his Government feared that Sir Allan MacNab's sponsoring of the Lower Canada election bill [18] might be the prelude of an anti-union alliance between the High Tories and the French party. Bagot was inclined to discount this threat for he expected to be able to obtain the support of the French party also. But he took the precaution of requesting Lord Stanley to use his influence with MacNab who was on a visit to England. Bagot planned to remove MacNab as a threat by appointing him adjutant general of militia. When Stanley informed MacNab of Bagot's offer, he accepted the office immediately, but declared that he still entertained hopes of a baronetcy in recognition of his services to the Empire. Unfortunately, the office of adjutant general of militia did not become vacant as Bagot had anticipated, and when MacNab returned home, with neither the baronetcy nor the promised appointment, he was in no mood for co-operation.

The attempt to form a coalition government was almost a complete failure. To Bagot's annoyance, Cartwright not only rejected the offer to join the Government, but based his rejection upon self-righteous moral and spiritual grounds. In what might be considered a typical example of High Toryism's swan-song, Cartwright explained, on May 16, that the Conservatives (the use of the new term rather than Tories or Constitutionalists was significant) felt they had been deserted, if not betrayed, by their former friends, and that they would regard his taking office with Hincks as a further betrayal. Three weeks later he amplified the explanation of his refusal to associate himself with Hincks, declaring that, because he regarded "political influence as a talent entrusted to us by the Almighty and for which we are accountable," he felt it to be his duty "to take every honourable method to retain it and leave the result in the hands of that Being who orders everything for the best." [19] After prolonged negotiations, Henry Sherwood agreed to accept the office of solicitor general for Upper Canada, but, as Harrison was soon to point out, this did little or nothing to strengthen the Government.

Of much greater significance was the failure to obtain the support of the French party. Cherrier had declined the solicitor generalship of Lower Canada, and Bagot now began to realize that even if he had accepted, he would not have carried the French-Canadian people with him. The Governor recognized that it was a matter of "just complaint" that French Canada was not represented in the Government.

"But how," he asked Lord Stanley, "is this to be rectified in a manner that would satisfy them?" [20] If he were to approach the French Canadians as a race, through their most influential leaders, and ask what it was they really wanted, he would likely be met by demands for the repeal of the union, the abolition of taxes imposed under ordinances of the Special Council, an alteration of the system of representation, "or some proposal of the kind which must immediately put an end to all further discussion upon the subject." On the other hand, if he were to ignore the French Canadians and wait for English-speaking immigrants to overwhelm them, he would probably lose his small majority in the Assembly and a fresh start would have to be made. "In short it is perplexing—infinitely perplexing," Bagot declared.

Provincial Secretary Harrison appreciated the Governor's perplexity, but he felt that the situation would permit no further delay. In a letter dated July 11, 1842, he placed the problem before Sir Charles Bagot with unmistakable clarity. The attempt to construct a ministry of all talents had been a failure. The key to the entire situation was the French Canadians, and their support must be obtained or the Government was virtually certain to be defeated in the Assembly. Harrison warned that if this happened most of the Executive Council would feel obliged to resign, and Bagot would then be in desperate straits. There was no alternative; a leader of the French party would have to be taken into the Government, and if the appointment of Robert Baldwin was demanded as the price of French-Canadian support, it would have to be accepted. Harrison realized that an attempt to work with the French party could be dangerous, but it was a risk which was inherent in the union and one which must be met and overcome. In any case, it was likely to prove far less dangerous than a Tory-French alliance which would be controlled by the latter because of their greater strength in the Assembly. [21]

Less than a week later, Bagot received similar advice from Attorney General Draper. It was possible that Baldwin would agree to the French Canadians taking office without him, and, in this event, Draper would be pleased to remain in the Government. If it was necessary, however, to appoint Baldwin in order to obtain French-Canadian support, the Attorney General was ready to resign at any time. [22]

III

Bagot pondered the advice of Harrison and Draper for almost two weeks before he passed it on to Lord Stanley as his own opinion. [23] To accept such advice required a radical change in perspective—one which was difficult for Bagot and almost impossible for Stanley. For the first time since the union was contemplated, the Governor and the Colonial Secretary were struck with the full significance of equal representation and the "harmony concept." It was no longer possible to contemplate the appointment of an occasional French Canadian as a benevolent gesture.

Lord Stanley was totally unprepared for the proposal which Bagot submitted to him. He had been convinced that the Government, with assistance from the Conservatives, could produce a majority capable of withstanding any combination of Reformers and French Canadians. If such was not the case, he could only regard the union as a failure: "The main Argument for the Union was the hope of converting the British minority in the Lower Province into a Majority by the infusion of the British Majority of the Upper Province; & the experiment will have woefully failed if the result be to throw British interests into a minority in the United Legis-lature." ²⁴ Stanley's views were shared by Peel and the other members of the Cabinet; Bagot was instructed to stand firm, and not to admit Baldwin or the French-Canadian leaders to his Government until it was clearly demonstrated, by a succession of defeats in the Assembly, that he had no alternative.

It is well known that Bagot felt obliged to act before he received these instruc-tions. By the time Stanley's despatch arrived, the Governor had embarked upon his "great measure," and Baldwin and LaFontaine were members of the Government. The details of Bagot's negotiations with LaFontaine have been related in numerous constitutional studies, and there is no necessity to repeat them here. It will be useful, however, to re-examine the significance of the "great measure." The entry of Baldwin and LaFontaine into the Government is generally presented as a victory for responsible government, and there can be no doubt that indirectly it was. But constitutional historians, in their anxiety to pursue their main theme, have paid scant attention to the fact that Bagot's action marked the beginning of a re-definition of the union's primary purpose. An admission that it was impossible to govern the province without French-Canadian support was tantamount to a renunciation of assimilation. It was a recognition of this fact that caused Lord Stanley to declare, ". . . I own I fear the Union is a failure, & the Canadas are gone." ²⁵

Bagot never considered that he had surrendered to the responsible government movement. Within the limitations set by equal representation and the "harmony concept," he had succeeded in obtaining French-Canadian support by what he regarded as a minimum of concession. He would have preferred not to have appointed Robert Baldwin, but the appointment had been made because the French party had demanded it and not because of the strength of the responsible government movement in Upper Canada. The appointment of LaFontaine and Morin because they were French Canadians was, of course, a political manifestation of the dual character of the Province of Canada, but the "great measure" went beyond this. The appointment of Etienne Parent, the former editor of Le Canadien, as clerk of the Executive Council for the same reason was an indication that dualism would express itself administratively as well as politically.

Although Bagot realized that the course which he had taken implied an abandonment of assimilation, he did not share Lord Stanley's forebodings about the result. He believed that once the French Canadians were given the share in the government to which they were "theoretically at least, justly entitled," they would be reasonable about such questions as the union, the special ordinances, and repre-sentation. He did not expect them to abandon their abstract notions on these points, but he felt they would "consider them as now definitely fixed, and no longer subjects of discussion as first principles." ²⁶ He made no attempt, however, to conceal the fact that they would probably regard some features of the union arrangement as "still susceptible of occasional, and perhaps in some respects, necessary modifica-tions hereafter." Bagot believed that, if the policy of assimilation were abandoned, French Canadians would accept the union, and that it could then provide the means of governing the Canadas successfully.

IV

The Legislature was only in session from September 8 to October 12 in 1842, but it produced ample evidence of the trend away from assimilation. When John

Neilson raised the question of an amnesty for those implicated in the late rebellion, Bagot discovered, to his consternation, that an address which had been passed on the subject during the last session had never been transmitted to England. The Governor recommended the idea of an amnesty to Lord Stanley's consideration: "The good and settled state of the public temper here, and many other considerations combine, in my opinion, strongly to recommend a general act of perfect oblivion . . . so far as regards all persons against whom no legal proceedings . . . have been taken." [27] Stanley replied that, while his natural inclination was to grant as large a degree of clemency as possible, the public should not be encouraged to look lightly upon treasonable offences. He declined to approve a general amnesty and reserved his decision on Bagot's request for discretionary powers until he was given more specific information on the individuals concerned. [28]

Debate in the Assembly on the location of the seat of government produced two resolutions: one recognizing the Queen's undoubted prerogative to determine the location, and a second condemning Kingston in general and the present accommodation in particular as "insufficient and incommodious." [29] After attempts to secure amendments in favour of Toronto, Bytown, Quebec, and Montreal had failed, the second resolution was carried on a sectional vote with twenty Upper Canadians in opposition. For his own part, Bagot preferred Montreal as the ultimate capital, but he wished to delay a decision on the question until his "great measure" had been given time to allay the suspicions and hostility of French Canada. "If the Union be not a mockery," he wrote to Lord Stanley, "the fact of that City being just beyond the limit of the Upper Province cannot, or ought not to be allowed to outweigh the advantages which it offers as the Capital of the United Province." [30]

The question of the contested elections in Lower Canada had been shelved during the first session, but it was revived by Baldwin and Neilson. A select committee was appointed to inquire into election irregularities in the Districts of Montreal, Vaudreuil, Terrebonne, Beauharnois, Chambly, and Rouville. Although the short duration of the session prevented the committee from hearing witnesses, it submitted a report recommending that the investigation should be continued during the next session. In addition, a new Election Act was passed for the purpose of preventing any further manipulation of polling stations and election dates after the fashion of Lord Sydenham. The old municipal boundaries of Montreal and Quebec were restored for electoral purposes by another statute. Several of the ordinances of the Special Council which had created much annoyance and inconvenience among French Canadians were amended, partially suspended, or repealed outright.

Bagot had intended to meet the Legislature again as soon as possible after the new members of his Government had returned from seeking re-election, but shortly after the session terminated he was seized with an illness which was to prove fatal, and it soon became apparent that he would have to be relieved of his duties. From his death-bed he wrote to Lord Stanley, "I leave this world, not satisfied that my measures will be successful, but that I had no choice in regard to them if the Union was to be maintained." [31] In spite of his expressed doubts, Bagot had come to believe that the assimilation of French Canada was not essential to the maintenance of British connection. Stanley and his colleagues in the Conservative Government did not share Bagot's optimism and consequently they prepared to fight a rear-guard action in their retreat from the original objective of the union.

V

Sir Charles Metcalfe arrived in Kingston at the end of March 1843, to take over the administration from Sir Charles Bagot. During his first week in Canada, three contentious items of unfinished business—the seat of government, the amnesty, and the civil list—were brought before him in the Executive Council. In reporting upon these subjects, Metcalfe revealed a spirit of conciliation and a realistic understanding of French Canada for which he has never been given credit.

While admitting that there might be some regrettable circumstances connected with Bagot's "great measure," Metcalfe found that it appeared to have produced "many beneficial effects." The exclusion of the French-Canadian population from office was an "injustice and would have been a perpetual cause of disaffection," Metcalfe declared to Stanley.[32]

When his Council recommended Montreal as the permanent seat of government, Metcalfe forwarded the recommendation with the observation that it was "decidedly the fittest place." He was aware that one of the reasons for the selection of Kingston had been the belief that the process of anglicization could be accelerated by locating the capital in Upper Canada, but he denounced the entire policy of enforced assimilation:

If the French Canadians are to be ruled to their satisfaction, and who could desire to rule them otherwise? every attempt to metamorphose them systematically into English must be abandoned, and the attainment of that object, whether to be accomplished or not, must be left to time and the natural effect of the expected increase and predominance . . . of the English over the French Population. The desired result cannot be produced by measures which rouse an indignant spirit against it.[33]

Metcalfe admitted that the selection of Montreal as the capital would not be popular in Upper Canada; Harrison had already made a vigorous presentation of the Upper Canadian point of view in the Executive Council and had refused to concur with his colleagues in their recommendation. But the Governor considered it obvious that no location could be selected which would meet with general approval in both sections of the province.

Metcalfe took up the amnesty question where it had been left by Bagot. He forwarded all the information available on the individuals concerned and urged that past troubles and dissentions should be buried under a general amnesty, excepting only those who were guilty of cold-blooded murder.[34] Before the Legislature met, the Governor provided additional evidence of his desire to effect a complete reconciliation with French Canada. The language clause of the Act of Union, he informed Lord Stanley, was resented by French Canadians "as one of the supposed attempts to destroy their nationality and anglify them by Force." [35] The repeal of this offensive symbol of assimilation would produce a good effect and, at the same time, remove a cause of discontent "which as long as it exists will excite bad feeling and be made use of by designing Men for that purpose." If the concession were not made, Metcalfe declared that there was little doubt the language question would be agitated in the approaching session.

Sir Charles Metcalfe's recommendation that the policy of enforced assimilation should be abandoned was dictated in part by a sympathetic appreciation of the French-Canadian view, but he had other, and perhaps stronger, motives. Although his first confidential despatch reveals that he came to Canada prepared to accept the degree of responsible government which had been attained under Bagot,[36] both he and Lord Stanley were determined that no further concessions would be made. Shortly after his arrival he began to realize that when the Legislature met, his Government would probably resign and force a test of the responsible government principle on one of four issues: control of patronage, location of the seat of government, the amnesty question, or the civil list. In this situation, it would be surprising indeed if the Governor did not perceive that concession upon two of these points might provide a basis for an alliance with French Canada designed to resist any further extension of responsible government. He recognized that although the French Canadians and the Upper Canadian Reformers were acting together, their alliance was based upon the personal friendship of Baldwin and LaFontaine and not upon common objectives: "They [the French party] may act with other parties on the principle of reciprocity, support for support, but their own views are purely French Canadian, including in their objects the preservation of their own Laws and Language—They strongly resent every attempt that has been made to anglify them." [37]

Metcalfe did not fear the challenge that he foresaw, but he hoped to avoid it if possible, and, if it were inevitable, he would meet it upon grounds of his own choosing. After carefully reviewing the situation, he advised Stanley against permitting the civil list to be the point of issue in any responsible government test.[38] He requested authority to announce to the Legislature that, if an adequate civil list were provided under a provincial act, steps would be taken to repeal the relevant clauses in the Act of Union. By a process of elimination, Metcalfe had decided that, of the probable issues, patronage presented the only favourable grounds for a contest.

Although he entertained some hope of being able to win over the French party, Metcalfe had no illusions about LaFontaine whom he reported had been "inoculated with . . . [responsible government] and has taken it in its utmost violence." [39] "I wish to do justice in every respect to the French-Canadian People, and to consult their feelings as much as possible. But I have no expectation that I shall thereby conciliate their Leader," he informed Stanley.[40] If LaFontaine could not be won, he would have to be replaced as the leader of French Canada, and Metcalfe soon began to see D. B. Viger in this role. Despite Stanley's vigorous denunciation of Viger when Bagot had suggested his appointment to the Legislative Council, Metcalfe renewed the nomination with the observation that his exclusion was "a sore which rankles in the Hearts of the French Canadians, and I trust that Your Lordship will permit me to heal it." [41]

VI

In England, Stanley and his colleagues appreciated the difficulty of Metcalfe's position, but they urged him to stand firm and "play the game, which we recommended to Sir Charles Bagot." [42] They were afraid they could detect in Metcalfe the same readiness to recommend concessions that they had criticized in his predecessor. The Governor was authorized to make many of the concessions which he had recommended, but the authorization was granted so reluctantly that he hesitated to make use of it.

Stanley informed Metcalfe that, while the Cabinet had no serious objections to an amnesty from a purely Canadian point of view, the prevalence of minor disturbances in the United Kingdom made it necessary to avoid creating the impression that treason would be treated lightly. If Metcalfe felt, however, that a general amnesty was essential to the peace of Canada; if a unanimous demand for it developed; if the resignation of his Council on this point would render it impossible to carry on the government; if nothing less would satisfy public opinion; and, above all, if he found it impossible to delay taking the step at once, the Cabinet would support him in proclaiming a general amnesty for all except those guilty of murder and arson." Upon receiving Lord Stanley's despatch, Metcalfe remarked that the authorization was so hedged around with conditions that he felt obliged to resist a general amnesty as long as possible. He had hoped to be able to proclaim it as a magnanimous gesture on the part of the Crown, but now he could do nothing more than consider each application as it was submitted and grant pardons in worthy cases that fell within his jurisdiction.

Metcalfe was also denied authority to make the spontaneous concession he had recommended regarding the civil list. The Legislature was at liberty to address Parliament on the subject if it wished to do so, but the Governor was not to give the project an appearance of royal approval by introducing it in a message to the Assembly.

Stanley was not opposed to the proposal that Montreal should become the provincial capital, but he refused to accept Metcalfe's recommendation that its selection should be announced immediately as a decision taken by the Crown. He noted Metcalfe's observation that the removal of the seat of government would likely produce an outcry in Upper Canada and refused to permit the Executive Council to avoid it by hiding behind the Crown." In reply, Metcalfe stressed the danger of repeal agitation in Upper Canada: "The only hope left for the British Party in Upper Canada is in a dissolution of the Union; and this conviction aided by exasperation if the Seat of Government should be placed in Lower Canada, will produce a strong desire for that remedy." [45]

For a brief moment Metcalfe considered placing the question before the province in a general election. He suggested to Stanley that, by this means, the French party might be placed in a minority in the Assembly "which could only happen at present on a question in which Upper Canada would be all united." [46] Stanley advised against a dissolution and remained firm in his original decision. If the Executive Council wished the capital to be moved to Montreal, an address to that effect would have to be carried in the Legislature." [47]

In recognition of the difficulties which Metcalfe faced, Stanley withdrew his objections to the appointment of Viger as a member of the Legislative Council, but his rejection of Metcalfe's recommendation for the repeal of the restrictions on the use of the French language revealed the British Government's great reluctance to admit that assimilation was not a realistic objective: "The avowed purpose of the Enactment was to promote the amalgamation of the French & English races. Its repeal therefore would I think be viewed in no other light than as an abandonment of that purpose, & would I apprehend be so considered by the British Population." [48] Stanley declared that the British Government was "unfeignedly anxious" to preserve to the French population all their rights and privileges and to avoid any measure that would "violate their feelings of nationality or shock their prejudices." Nonetheless, it was of great importance that Canada should gradually become a British province, and the Cabinet was "unwilling to take a course which would be understood as affirming an opinion on their part that such an amalgamation could not be hoped for." [49]

With the limitations placed upon Metcalfe's proposed concessions, it is somewhat surprising that he was not forced to face a test of the responsible government theory on some more contentious issue than the control of patronage. At least once before the Legislature met, he was threatened with the resignation of LaFontaine and his colleagues. When pardons were granted to Upper Canadian rebels John Rolph, Charles Duncombe, and John Montgomery, LaFontaine demanded that a writ of *nolle prosequi* be entered on behalf of Papineau and two other French Canadians. Metcalfe resisted, but, after four interviews with LaFontaine, he yielded rather than face the consequences of a resignation on this question.[50] By way of explanation, Metcalfe informed Lord Stanley that he had considered pardoning the three prominent Upper Canadian rebels "a wise and unobjectionable act on the part of Her Majesty's Government, calculated to produce beneficial effects in the Province by tending to bury past troubles and dissentions in oblivion." [51] He admitted, however, that he had "lost sight of due caution" and had not taken into consideration the jealousy of the races. Stanley was critical of the Governor's lack of foresight: "You must excuse me for expressing my regret that before selecting for pardon three of the most notorious offenders, the natural and inevitable results were not more deliberately weighed than they appear to have been." [52]

Despite his efforts to avoid a collision, Metcalfe's relations with the members of his Executive Council had never been cordial. He realized that the "harmony concept" demanded that he should do his best to work with them, but all his natural sympathy lay with the staunch Tories whose loyalty had never been in doubt. From the opening of the session of the Legislature at the end of September 1843, the gap between the Governor and his Council widened with increasing rapidity, until the celebrated resignation occurred two months later.

Before their resignation took place, Baldwin and LaFontaine introduced and carried a motion for an address requesting that the capital should be transferred to Montreal. Although the question failed to produce the repeal agitation that Metcalfe had anticipated, it clearly revealed the clash of sectional interests inherent in the union. Just before the session began, Harrison resigned when his colleagues refused to permit the location of the capital to be an open question. The resolutions introduced by Baldwin and seconded by LaFontaine passed by large majorities, but not before attempts were made to retain the capital in Upper Canada, to hold a referendum, and to refer the question back to the British Government for decision.

Early in the session, before many Lower Canadian members had arrived, the Legislative Council had passed an address requesting that the seat of government should be permanently located in Upper Canada. When the Council was invited to concur in the Assembly's address later in the session, several members protested that it was contrary to parliamentary procedure to consider a question twice in one session. When they were voted down, fourteen Upper Canadians, including the Speaker, R. S. Jameson, walked out of the Council Chamber in protest. At the same time, Jameson resigned as Speaker, but, four days later, Metcalfe replaced him with R. E. Caron, and, with the protesting members still absent, the Council voted unanimously to concur in the Assembly's address.

Because of the pardons which he had granted, Metcalfe got through the session of 1843 without an address in favour of a general amnesty, but he could not avoid one on the civil list question. Early in December, resolutions were adopted in favour of an address expressing the Assembly's willingness to provide a civil list if the relevant clauses of the Act of Union were repealed. Metcalfe forwarded the address to Stanley with the recommendation that the offer should be accepted.

VIII

When the long-anticipated test of responsible government came, Metcalfe turned to D. B. Viger. It was the Governor's hope that the high regard in which Viger was held by his compatriots would enable him to supplant LaFontaine as leader, or at least to split the solid French party. Although Viger earnestly endeavoured to accomplish this task from December 1843 until August of the following year, he met with almost no success. From the beginning Metcalfe had feared that such would be the case, and yet he was at a loss to provide himself with a satisfactory explanation of Viger's failure:

The pardons of their Countrymen convicted of Treason which have taken place, as well as the whole conduct of the Government towards them during my administration, ought to have given me some influence among them, as Her Majesty's representative, but I see no symptoms of any such effect. There seems to be a perverse readiness to oppose the British Government which requires only the opportunity to display itself. It may proceed from the habitual distrust which is said to form part of their character. It will eventually be seen whether this will be counteracted by the personal influence of Mr. Viger.[53]

Metcalfe was sincere in his endeavours to abandon the policy of assimilation; he felt that he had given ample evidence of his good intentions, and he could not understand why French Canada should doubt his sincerity. With a sense of injury, he informed Stanley that the French Canadians only had doubts regarding Viger— they were quite certain the Governor was opposed to their interests. He began to suspect that the French party was determined to dominate Lower Canada completely, with no consideration being given to the English-speaking minority. If this were their objective, he would resist it to the end.

The Governor failed to realize that, when his quarrel with the former members of his Council degenerated to the level of personalities, many French Canadians became convinced that *la survivance* was dependent upon responsible government as personified by Baldwin and LaFontaine. Coupled with this, the reluctance of influential French Canadians to take the risk of being labelled a *"vendu"* was sufficient to defeat Viger's efforts.

By the end of July 1844, it was obvious that Viger's success would be limited to the acquisition of D. B. Papineau, a brother of the rebel leader and a close relation of his own. Metcalfe had no hope of forming a government which would be sustained in the Assembly, and there was no course open to him but an appeal to the province in a general election. The loyalty theme, which had been introduced by Metcalfe in his replies to addresses and which had been stressed by pamphleteers supporting his stand, had its effect in Upper Canada. Baldwin was elected for the fourth riding of York, but the ranks of his supporters were seriously depleted. As a result, the Government was able to command a small majority in the new Assembly.

Reporting the election results to Stanley, Metcalfe declared they revealed that British feeling and loyalty prevailed in Upper Canada and the Eastern Townships, but "disaffection" was widespread in the French-Canadian constituencies. He explained that by disaffection he meant the "anti-British feeling, by whatever name it ought to be called, or whatever be its foundation, which induces habitually a readiness to oppose Her Majesty's Government."⁵⁴ He assured Stanley, however, that the French party did not aim at immediate separation from the Empire, union with the United States, or the formation of an independent republic. "If it has any definite object, it is the ascendancy of the French-Canadian Nationality," he added.

Metcalfe was naturally disappointed that the measures which had been adopted during his administration had failed to reduce the anti-British sentiments of French Canada, but he saw quite clearly that the answer was neither exclusion from office nor a return to assimilation:

It is my belief that by a consistent conduct steadily pursued for a series of years, this hostile phalanx might be successfully combated [sic] and dispersed. The course which I would recommend would be to leave the French Race no pretext for complaint, to treat all as if they were well affected; to give office, emolument and privileges equally to the French or British Race; equal fitness being presumed, and to avoid any exclusion, even of those ranged in opposition, whenever the occasion might justify a selection from among them, but to be careful to distinguish and reward those of the French Race who shew a loyal disposition and a desire to support Her Majesty's Government. I entertain a strong conviction that this course would in a short time lead the French-Canadian politicians to perceive that a pertinacious opposition to Her Majesty's Government would not tend to promote their own interests.⁵⁵

During the session of 1844-45, Metcalfe felt obliged to sanction an assault upon the restrictions on the use of the French language despite his instructions to the contrary. With the Governor's approval, D. B. Papineau introduced an address, requesting repeal of the restrictions, which was carried unanimously in both Houses. Metcalfe frankly admitted to Stanley that he had disregarded his instructions, but claimed that there were extenuating circumstances. From the opening of the session, it was obvious that LaFontaine and his followers intended to make the restrictions on the French language "a claptrap for popularity." If they had been left to introduce the address, and if Metcalfe had ordered the members of his Government to oppose it, LaFontaine would have succeeded in the "double game of producing a feeling of hatred against the Government, and of ruining in the estimation of their Countrymen the French-Canadian Members of the Executive Council."⁵⁶ D. B. Papineau was well aware of the trap which LaFontaine was preparing for him as the only French-Canadian member of the Government sitting in the Assembly. He had already been placed in the embarrassing position of being required to vote for MacNab as speaker instead of his countryman, Morin. He urged Metcalfe to permit him to steal a march on the opposition by initiating the movement for the repeal of the language restrictions. The Governor agreed because he was unwilling to force Papineau into an untenable position. In justifying his action to Stanley, Metcalfe argued that English predominated in the province and would continue to do so to a gradually increasing degree as British immigration flowed in. But the use of English was retarded rather than promoted by the existing restrictions on French. They were seized upon "in order to incense the minds of the People, and rouse a spirit of counteraction calculated to diminish the use of the English Language."[37] Metcalfe was not prepared to predict that the concession he recommended would remove the "malignity of the misleaders" of French Canada, but he asserted "it would at least deprive them of what is apparently the only remaining plea on which they can ground their excitement of general discontent."

In England, G. W. Hope, Stanley's Under Secretary, approved Metcalfe's views, but they found no favour with Sir Robert Peel. In a memorandum prepared for the Cabinet, Peel asserted that an application to Parliament on the subject would be "ill timed." He considered Metcalfe to have acted imprudently in permitting the application to be made with the Government's sanction. "The reason he alleges for doing so—will justify the *anticipation* in the same way—of still more objectionable proposals by his opponents," Peel declared.[58] The Prime Minister realized that it would be difficult now to negative the request, but he hoped that the application to Parliament for an amendment of the Act of Union could be postponed at least. Peel's opinion prevailed. Almost a year passed before a despatch[59] was written authorizing Cathcart, Metcalfe's successor, to inform the Legislature that the language restrictions would be repealed, and it was two years more before the amendment to the Act of Union was actually passed.[60] The real significance, however, lay not in the delay involved, but in the fact that by the time Sir Charles Metcalfe left Canada the policy of deliberate assimilation had been completely, albeit reluctantly, abandoned.

IX

Because he was not wedded to the policy of assimilation, Metcalfe soon became aware of the basic weaknesses of the union. When he had been in the province just three months, he wrote to Lord Stanley: "I wish that I could anticipate the day when all would be reconciled, and United Canada [would] be really united in Internal Harmony and Attachment to the British Crown. Such a consummation is I fear remote and uncertain. . . ."[61] He realized that assimilation was neither possible nor essential, and he sensed that without it there was no justification for the union. To John Beverley Robinson he confided: "My own opinion of the Union, formed since I came to Canada, is that it was an unwise measure, fraught with much mischief, that has naturally resulted from it. . . . My present duty is to work the Union as well as I can, and not to find fault with it [but] my best endeavours to do that, or to administer the Government of this Province with any good effect, are I fear likely to end in complete failure."[62]

When Metcalfe looked to the future, he saw the break-up of the union. He apparently never realized that he had cleared the way for the operation of a quasi-federalism which would permit the union to continue for another twenty years. LaFontaine, however, was acutely aware of the dualistic elements implicit in the Canadian situation from the beginning. Early in his correspondence with Hincks, he had suggested that a federal union would more adequately answer Canadian requirements than a legislative one. While admitting the validity of LaFontaine's claim, Hincks had brushed it aside with the assertion that the contemplated municipal councils would provide the federal system which he sought. The close affinity that developed between Baldwin and LaFontaine caused the French-Canadian leader temporarily to lose sight of the federal solution, but the situation created by the election of 1844 brought it to the fore again. The French-Canadian members continued to hold a large majority of the Lower Canadian seats in the Assembly, but among the Upper Canadian members Baldwin's supporters were in a decided minority. From 1845 to 1847, in a sporadic correspondence with Caron, Draper continued Metcalfe's efforts to align the French party in support of the Government. Upon being asked for his advice, LaFontaine suggested that the French party should insist that the Government be constructed upon a double majority basis. In other words, he advocated the creation of a quasi-federal system within the framework of the legislative union. Caron's reply to Draper was based entirely upon the advice which LaFontaine had given: "It has been assumed as a principle that the direction of affairs should be in the hands of the two prevailing parties in each section of the Province, that the administration ought no more to govern Lower Canada by means of a majority obtained in Upper Canada, than it ought to govern the majority of Upper Canada by means of the aid that Lower Canada should give to it."[43] The Upper Canadian members of the Executive Council were supported by a majority from their section of the province, but just the opposite was true of the Lower Canadian representatives in the Council. As a *sine qua non*, Caron demanded the Lower Canadian seats in the Council should be placed at the disposal of the French party.

Although Draper and his colleagues were prepared to go a long way to meet Caron's demands, they were reluctant to accept a full scale reorganization of the Lower Canadian section of the Government, and as a result the alliance was not achieved. Even if Draper had accepted Caron's terms, the evidence of the 1860's would suggest that the double majority principle could not have operated satisfactorily in the Assembly. The prominence of the principle in the Draper–Caron negotiations, however, is indicative of the strength of the federal concept in the United Province of Canada. The legislative form of the union prevented a full assertion of the federalist tendencies as envisaged by the double majority concept, but it still left room for the development of a modified federal system which expressed itself in political and administrative dualism.

An objective evaluation of Sir Charles Metcalfe's administration remains to be written. His biographer sought to create the image of a strong man standing resolutely against the attempts of ultra democratic politicians to encroach upon the royal prerogative.[44] There is much truth in the picture which Kaye has given, but it is incomplete. He failed to show that Metcalfe, even more than Bagot, realized that assimilation was an unrealistic objective and dragged a reluctant, piecemeal admission of the fact from the British Government. By the end of his administration, there remained no justification for preferring a legislative over a federal union, and the natural federalistic character of the Canadian union soon began to emerge without encountering opposition from the Imperial Government or the Governor.

The failure of Metcalfe and Draper to effect an alliance with the French party has induced Canadian historians to accept Kaye's lead and perpetuate the myth that Metcalfe, as an opponent of Baldwin and LaFontaine, was *ipso facto* an opponent of *la survivance*. From such a thesis it follows naturally that the survival of French Canada was obtained through the achievement of responsible government and that the two themes are virtually inseparable. A review of the evidence suggests a new perspective. Assimilation was abandoned before responsible government was conceded. Indeed, it might be asserted that, by depriving the union of its original purpose, Metcalfe had unwittingly made it easier for the British Government to concede the full degree of responsibility claimed by Baldwin. In any event, it is quite clear that there was no essential association of the two themes—responsible government and *la survivance*. Admittedly, the question of responsible government was a major factor in the realignment of the moderate Reformers with Baldwin's ultras after the death of Sydenham, but once that realignment had taken place, the French party held the balance of power and thus was in a position to assure the survival of French-Canadian culture whether responsible government was attained or not.

Responsible government has been given the greater predominance in Canadian historiography, but the emergence of the federal concept, which was primarily the result of the survival of French Canada, merits much more attention than it has received. It was the pressure of sectional and bi-cultural forces and the extent of the territory involved which shaped the ultimate character of the union, and it was the same forces which determined the character of the national union in 1867.

EPILOGUE

THE ADVENT OF THE United Empire Loyalists created the elements of a bi-cultural problem in the old province of Quebec, but it was almost seventy years before the full significance of this fact began to be recognized. In 1791, the division of the province was an attempt to find a solution for the problem of two distinct cultures endeavouring to exist within a single geographic unit. But it was a solution which side-stepped the basic question of whether French Canada was to be assimilated, or the two cultures were to continue to exist side by side. During the debate on the Constitutional Act, Charles James Fox called for measures which would "form the two descriptions of people into one body, and endeavour to annihilate all national distinctions," but William Pitt replied that any attempt to implement such a policy would produce "a perpetual scene of factious altercation." [1] Nonetheless, Pitt sanguinely predicted that assimilation would take place indirectly through Lower Canada's emulation of Upper Canada.

Although the ensuing years revealed the fallacy of Pitt's prediction, they failed to produce any positive indication of the British Government's ultimate objective. Had the attempted union of 1822 been carried through, it would have amounted to a decision in favour of assimilation, but the rapidity with which it was dropped when opposition developed was indicative both of the Government's reluctance to bring thorny colonial problems before Parliament and of the force of ethnological and social opposition to the union. The French Revolution and the Napoleonic Wars, together with the growing reform movement in Great Britain, left British statesmen with little leisure to contemplate Canadian problems. Those who did concern themselves with Canada were inclined to view the clash between the Executive and the Assembly in Lower Canada as a constitutional question rather than as the struggle of French Canada to survive as a separate entity. Consequently, little thought was given to whether assimilation was possible, or to the implications of the survival of two cultures in Canada if it were not. Before the rebellions occurred, only Roebuck and Glenelg seem to have sensed the potentialities of a federal solution.

The rebellions focused attention on the Canadian problem and, at the same time, fostered the conviction that the assimilation of French Canada was essential to the maintenance of the British connection. Against such a background, it is not surprising that few men caught a glimpse of the federal concept. One of the few was Edward Ellice, who had learned a great deal from the unsuccessful attempt at union in 1822. In 1860, as dualism asserted itself ever more strongly in Canada, Ellice reminded LaFontaine of his foresight: "All that has since occurred in Canada, confirms the advice, I gave in vain to the Govt. at the time of the Union Bill. . . . I saw the difficulty that would sooner or later, arise, from the dissimilarity in habits & institutions, of the two Provinces, after the feelings that had been called into action, at the crisis. . . ."[2]

Although Lord Howick and James Stephen shared Ellice's preference for a federal union, they were unable to exert any significant influence on the Government. Lord Durham saw the national possibilities in a federal union of British North America, but when this proved to be beyond his grasp, he could not bring himself to recommend a federal union of the Canadas alone. He believed that responsible government was the only solution for Canadian problems, but that it could not be safely conceded, nor could it function properly, unless French Canada was assimilated in a complete legislative union with Upper Canada. Of Durham's several recommendations, it is probable that the idea of assimilation was most in accord with the views of Melbourne and Russell. Some members of Parliament may have doubted that assimilation could be achieved by means of the Durham formula, but most admitted that, given the influence of the United States in North America and the state of public opinion in England, they could not suggest a better means.

The assimilation of French Canada would have been difficult, if not impossible, in 1791—fifty years later it was an entirely unrealistic objective. Lord Sydenham was able to convey the impression that the union had been successfully inaugurated and that French Canada had no alternative but to submit to anglicization. Under Bagot and Metcalfe, however, it became clear that Canada was likely to remain a bi-cultural province, and the Imperial Government was forced, reluctantly, to abandon the union's primary objective.

Paradoxically, the union, which had been designed for precisely the opposite purpose, left considerable room for the development of federal characteristics. Once assimilation was rejected, equal representation assumed the guise of a political guarantee for the continued existence of two distinct cultures. It was soon discovered that the "harmony concept" could be subdivided to produce the fascinating, though impractical, theory of double harmony or double majority. The existence of duplicate law offices paved the way for the creation of hyphenated ministries which symbolized the dual character of the Canadian population. With the appointment of French Canadians to the Executive Council during Bagot's administration, the federal concept began to emerge and, within a few years, it gained wide recognition. The concept did not, however, become the all pervading force within the union; there were some aspects of politics and many areas of administration which remained unaffected by the principle of dualism. Even Baldwin and LaFontaine, who were deeply committed to the principle, exerted pressure to replace the two separate provincial secretaries with a single one in the interest of economy. Nonetheless, there is ample evidence to support the claim that dualism did become a significant characteristic of the union.

When Lord Sydenham was making the administrative arrangements for the union, he was necessarily thinking in terms of a province in which cultural differences would eventually disappear. Consequently the continuation of separate administrative establishments in each section of the province for some departments was dictated primarily by the vast extent of territory involved. Assimilation was only prospective, however, and he could not entirely ignore the fact that, initially at least, each section would differ from the other in language, religion, civil code, judicial system, and the form of land tenure. These factors must have had some influence on Sydenham's decision that dual administrative establishments should be maintained by the law officers, the provincial secretaries, and the commissioner of Crown lands. In 1842, Bagot's decision to appoint two deputy superintendents of education was based entirely on the religious differences between the two sections of the province. As the federal concept developed, this administrative framework permitted the manifestation of dualism in the public service. Other departments maintained a single establishment, but, as J. E. Hodgetts has noted, some of these were "split right down the middle, starting at the top with the political head and going down to the subdivisions of the various branches." [3] One of the most striking applications of the principle of dualism was the rotation of the capital between Toronto and Quebec in the years after 1849.

If the Durham formula had functioned as its originator had anticipated, French Canadians would have joined the Government not to protect the particular interests of their compatriots, but rather to assist in the process of assimilation. When the continued existence of French Canada as a separate cultural entity was accepted as a recognized fact, however, French-Canadian politicians and public servants became the representatives of a separate unit of the population with its own rights and interests. It was in this context that dualism became a significant characteristic of the United Province of Canada.

Within the political arena, the union functioned well only when its federal aspects were dominant. This fact was recognized by John A. Macdonald during the Confederation debates:

We, in Canada, already know something of the advantages and disadvantages of a Federal Union. Although we have nominally a Legislative Union in Canada—although we sit in one Parliament, supposed constitutionally to represent the people without regard to sections or localities, yet we know, as a matter of fact, that since the union in 1841, we have had a Federal Union; that in matters affecting Upper Canada solely, members from that section claimed and generally exercised the right of exclusive legislation, while members from Lower Canada legislated in matters affecting only their own section. We have had a Federal Union in fact, though a Legislative Union in name. [4]

Despite Macdonald's testimony, there were occasions when measures affecting only one half of the province were passed or rejected by a minority from that section with the aid of a majority from the other section. Equal representation proved to be an insufficient guarantee for the protection of sectional interests, and it was this fact which ultimately doomed the union. For more than a quarter of a century the union managed to function as a quasi-federal system, but eventually the forces of dualism came into direct conflict with the unitary character of the constitution. During the early years of the union, it was Lower Canada that complained of interference; the LaFontaine Papers contain a list of seventeen votes taken during the years 1844 to 1846 in which Lower Canadian matters were decided by a majority from the upper province. Among the subjects listed are damages caused by the construction of the Beauharnois Canal, the Montreal election of 1844, the Lower Canada Election Bill, Lower Canadian rebellion losses, amendments to the Winter Roads Bill, land titles of naturalized persons, claims of the Chambly Canal contractors, the Lower Canada School Bill, and the Jesuits' estates. [5] The shoe began to pinch on the other foot in the 1850's and the charge was made that Upper Canada was suffering from French-Canadian domination. The suspicion grew that the secularization of the clergy reserves was being retarded by the influence of French-Canadian members of the Government. More positive evidence was presented when

Upper Canadian school legislation was amended, by a Lower Canadian majority, to extend the provision for separate schools.

This situation, coupled with the fact that Upper Canada now had the larger population, produced the Clear Grit demand for representation by population which rapidly gained in popularity. G. F. G. Stanley has quite correctly observed that representation by population implied "the collapse of the federal concept." * However, it should be recognized that from another point of view, "Rep. by Pop." was a protest against the fact that the union could still assume a legislative character.

On the other hand, "Rep. by Pop." could never be acceptable to Lower Canada for it was a direct threat to French-Canadian interests. The necessity of finding some alternative led to a renewed interest in the "double majority" principle and the experiment of John Sandfield Macdonald from 1862 to 1864. The principle proved unacceptable in practice, however, because of the difficulty in securing a double majority for any contentious measure. Even John Sandfield Macdonald, the professed champion of the principle, could not resist the temptation in 1863 to carry Upper Canadian separate schools legislation by means of a Lower Canadian majority. With the failure of the "double majority" theory, the only alternative was a proper federal union and this was the solution adopted in 1867.

Numerous factors, lying beyond the scope of this study, but familiar to every historian, determined that Confederation should embrace Nova Scotia and New Brunswick as well as the Canadas. There were also distinctive maritime factors which favoured a federal union, but the predominant federal influence was the dual character of the Canadas. Confederation was an impossibility without the concurrence of French Canada and that concurrence was forthcoming only when guarantees for its institutions, language, laws, and religion had been spelled out in the resolutions that were to form the basis for the British North America Act. If the union of 1841 had failed to fulfil the original expectations, it had, nonetheless, served as a useful experiment in federalism, and had produced both the concept and the experience upon which a larger and more satisfactory union could be built.

NOTES

CHAPTER ONE: THE ROOTS OF UNION

1. Public Archives of Canada (P.A.C.), Q 112, pp. 121 ff., Craig to Liverpool, May 1, 1810.
2. C. D. Yonge, *The Life and Administration of Robert Banks, Second Earl of Liverpool*, I, 312–14, Liverpool to Craig, private, undated.
3. Robert Christie, *History of the Late Province of Lower Canada*, VI, 137.
4. William Ormsby, "The Problem of Canadian Union, 1822–1828," *Canadian Historical Review*, XXXIX (1958), 277–95.
5. Q 337A, pp. 99–100, Bathurst to Maitland, Jan. 13, 1823.
6. *Report from the Select Committee on the Civil Government of Canada* (reprinted at Quebec, 1829), p. 5.
7. P.A.C., Upper Canada Sundries, vol. 57, Robinson to Maitland, July 16, 1822.
8. *Ibid.*, vol. 57, Robinson to Hillier, Aug. 23, 1822.
9. *Ibid.*, vol. 58, Robinson to Hillier, Nov. 11, 1822.
10. Q 165, pp. 10–47, Strachan to Horton [?], June 5, 1824.
11. Q 163–1, pp. 147–59, petition from the Eastern Townships.
12. Q 391, pp. 226–28, "Memorandum on the present political State of the Canadas," enclosed in Head to Glenelg, Oct. 28, 1836.
13. 1 & 2 Wm. IV, c.23.
14. *Journal of the Legislative Assembly of Upper Canada*, 1836–37, p. 130.
15. *Ibid.*, p. 626.
16. *Ibid.*, p. 625. In favour of the address: *Tories:* Boulton, Burwell, Draper, Gowan, Hagerman, Jones, Alexander McDonell, Prince, Robinson, Sherwood, Thomson; *Reformers:* Armstrong, David Duncombe, McIntosh; *undetermined political affiliation:* Alexander Chisholm. Opposed: *Tories:* Bockus, William Chisholm, Kearnes, MacNab; *Reformers:* Gibson, Donald A. McDonell, Morrison, Thorburn, Woodruff; *undetermined political affiliation:* Ferrie, Manahan.
17. *Ibid.*, pp. 620–21, 636.
18. P.A.C., R.G. 7, G 1, vol. 80, Glenelg to Head, no. 170, April 21, 1837.
19. *Journal of the Legislative Assembly of Upper Canada*, 1837, p. 27. In favour of the motion: *Tories:* Bockus, McKay; *Reformers:* Cameron, Charles Duncombe, Gibson, Mathewson, McIntosh, McMicking [McMicken], Moore, Morrison, Norton, Parke, Rolph, Shaver, Thorburn, Wells, Woodruff. Opposed: *Tories:* Aikman, Boulton, Caldwell, William Chisholm, Cornwall, Elliott, Gowan, Hagerman, Jarvis, Kearnes, Marks, Donald McDonell, Alexander McDonell, Merritt, Prince, Richardson, Robinson, Ruttan, Sherwood, Thomson, Wickens; *Reformers:* Armstrong; *Independents:* Dunlop; *undetermined political affiliation:* Alexander Chisholm, Detlor, Ferrie, Manahan.
20. P.A.C., Grey of Howick Papers, pt. I (microfilm), "Epitome of the proposed Canada Act," Jan. 19, 1837.
21. P.A.C., Russell Papers (photostat), Howick to Russell, March 30, 1837.
22. *Ibid.*, Howick to Russell, April 7, 1837.
23. *Appendix to the Journal of the Legislative Assembly of Upper Canada*, 1837–38, p. 266, "Report of the Select Committee to which was Referred the Political State of Upper and Lower Canada," Feb. 8, 1838.
24. Rollo Russell, ed., *The Early Correspondence of Lord John Russell*, II, 213–14, Melbourne to Russell, Dec. 31, 1837.
25. P.R.O., Russell Papers, box 3, Howick to Russell, Jan. 1, 1838. A microfilm copy of documents in the Russell Papers which relate to Canada is available in P.A.C.

26. Grey of Howick Papers, pt. 1, pp. 196–207, memorandum by James Stephen on measures to be adopted with regard to Canada, Dec. 28, 1837.

27. Russell Papers, box 3, Howick to Russell, Jan. 2, 1838.

28. *Ibid.*, memorandum on Canada (Jan. 3, 1838?).

29. Viscount Esher, ed., *The Training of a Sovereign*, pp. 104–5.

30. *Appendix to the Journal of the Legislative Assembly of Upper Canada*, 1837–38, pp. 275–77.

31. *Ibid.*, pp. 257–71.

32. *Journal of the Legislative Assembly of Upper Canada*, 1837–38, pp. 350–53.

33. *Journal of the Legislative Council of Upper Canada*, 1838, app. Z, pp. 69–97, "Report of the Select Committee appointed to enquire into and report upon the State of the Province," Feb. 13, 1838.

34. *Journal of the Legislative Council of Upper Canada*, 1838, p. 96, Feb. 20, 1838.

35. P.A.C., Durham Papers, VI, vol. 1, pp. 209–11, Jan. 3, 1838.

36. *Ibid.*, pp. 319–20, extract of a letter to Robert Gillespie dated Montreal, Feb. 9, 1838.

37. *Ibid.*, pp. 466–67, Strachan to Gillespie, March 2, 1838, enclosed in Gillespie to Durham, April 19, 1838.

38. Ontario Archives (P.A.O.), Strachan Letter Book, 1827–41, p. 20.

39. Durham Papers, VI, vol. 1, p. 418, George Moffatt and William Badgley to Durham, April 5, 1838.

40. R. G. Trotter, "Durham and the Idea of a Federal Union of British North America," *Canadian Historical Association Report*, 1925, pp. 55–63.

41. Durham's copy of Roebuck's plan is in the Durham Papers, VI, vol. 3, pt. 2, pp. 578–646. The original is in the Roebuck Papers (P.A.C.), but some pages are missing. Roebuck published the plan in its entirety in *The Colonies of England* (London, 1849), pp. 195–220.

42. Charles Buller, "Sketch of Lord Durham's Mission to Canada in 1838 [written in 1840]," *Public Archives of Canada Report*, 1923, p. 358.

43. *Supra*, p. 14.

44. Durham Papers, VI, vol. 3, pt. 2, pp. 647–73. This copy of the summary contains extensive pencil comments by John Beverley Robinson.

45. *Ibid.*, VI, vol. 1, pp. 486–92, "Heads of Objections to a Federative Union of British North America."

CHAPTER TWO: LORD DURHAM'S MISSION

1. Durham Papers, VI, vol. 1, pp. 721–40, Markland to Durham, undated.

2. *Ibid.*, pp. 659–68.

3. *Ibid.*, pp. 551–61, Morris to Durham, Dec. 29, 1838.

4. *Ibid.*, p. 746, memorial enclosed in Marks to Durham, July, 1838.

5. *Ibid.*, VI, vol. 2, pp. 263–73.

6. *Ibid.*, VI, vol. 1, pp. 631–38, Buller to Durham, June 21, 1838.

7. *Ibid.*, pp. 784–90.

8. *Ibid.*, pp. 829–36, Moffatt to Colborne, July 13, 1838.

9. *Public Archives of Canada Report*, 1923, pp. 326–28, Baldwin to Durham, Aug. 23, 1838.

10. Durham Papers, VI, vol. 3, pt. 2, pp. 647–73. On July 27, 1838, Robinson returned Sir George Arthur's copy of the summary similarly annotated. See *Arthur Papers*, nos. 271–72.

11. Charles R. Sanderson, ed., *The Arthur Papers*, no. 271.

12. Durham Papers, Lady Durham's Journal, p. 39.

13. Durham Papers, III, vol. 2, pp. 378–89, Harvey to Durham, no. 7 (confidential memorandum), Aug. 16, 1838.

14. P.A.C., Sir John Harvey Papers, vol. 5, 1433–35, Durham to Harvey, Sept. 6, 1838.

15. Charles Buller, "Sketch of Lord Durham's Mission to Canada in 1838 [written in 1840]," *Public Archives of Canada Report*, 1923, p. 358.

16. *P.A.C. Report*, 1923, p. 325, Durham to Glenelg, Aug. 9, 1838.

17. Durham Papers, III, vol. 2, pp. 560–62, Campbell to Durham, Sept. 4, 1838.

18. *Ibid.*, VI, vol. 2, pp. 134–65, Buller to Durham (draft), Sept. 7, 1838.

19. Sanderson, *Arthur Papers*, no. 316.

20. *Ibid.*, no. 333.

21. Durham Papers, VI, vol. 2, pp. 220–21.

22. *Montreal Courier*, Oct. 3, 1838.

23. Durham Papers, III, vol. 2, pp. 815–23, Durham to Arthur, Oct. 9, 1838. This despatch was drafted by Charles Buller, but it could not have been sent without Durham's approval. It should be remembered, however, that Buller continued to support the confederation scheme after Durham had decided upon the necessity of a legislative union of the Canadas.

24. *Quebec Gazette* (by authority), Oct. 9, 1838.

25. *Le Canadien*, Nov. 2, 1838.

26. Sir Francis Bond Head, *The Emigrant*, p. 238, MacNab to Head, March 28, 1846.

27. *Ibid.*, pp. 238–39, Jarvis to Head, March 12, 1846.

28. John Richardson, *Eight Years in Canada*, p. 227, Durham to Richardson, Oct. 2, 1838.

29. Head, *The Emigrant*, pp. 239–40, Hagerman to Head, July 12, 1846.

30. Lloyd C. Saunders, ed., *Lord Melbourne's Papers*, pp. 438–39.

31. Sanderson, *Arthur Papers*, no. 495.

32. Saunders, *Lord Melbourne's Papers*, p. 441, Melbourne to Russell, Dec. 8, 1838.

33. Rollo Russell, ed., *The Earlier Correspondence of Lord John Russell*, II, 221, Russell to Melbourne, Sept. 3, 1838.

34. Saunders, *Lord Melbourne's Papers*, pp. 441–42.

35. *Ibid.*, pp. 443–44, Melbourne to Russell, Dec. 19, 1838.

36. *Ibid.*, p. 444.

37. Sanderson, *Arthur Papers*, no. 555, Robinson to Arthur, Dec. 11, 1838.

38. *Ibid.*, no. 613, Robinson to Arthur, Jan. 2, 1839.

39. Lambton Manuscripts, Ellice to Durham, Dec. 30, 1838. Cited in Chester W. New, *Lord Durham*, p. 488.

40. *Ibid.*, Ellice to Durham, Tuesday evening (Jan. 8, 1839?). Printed in full in New, *Lord Durham*, pp. 488–89.

41. Lord Durham, *Report on the Affairs of British North America*, Sir C. P. Lucas, ed., II, 296.

42. *Ibid.*, II, 70.

43. *Ibid.*, II, 288 ff. The quotations from Lord Durham's Report which follow are taken from the same source, pp. 290–324.

44. Sanderson, *Arthur Papers*, no. 712, Robinson to Arthur, March 25, 1839.

45. Lord Durham, *Report*, II, 311.

46. *Ibid.*, II, 113.

47. *Ibid.*, II, 304–7.

48. Buller, "Sketch," p. 359.

49. *Edinburgh Review*, April 1847, review of Sir Francis Bond Head's *Emigrant*.

50. Lord Durham, *Report*, I, 125.

51. Chester W. New, *Lord Durham*, pp. 467–90.

52. *Ibid.*, p. 490.

53. D. G. Creighton, "The Commercial Class in Canadian Politics, 1792–1840," *Papers and Proceedings of the Canadian Political Science Association*, V (1933), 43–58.

54. This letter is published in full in New, *Lord Durham*, pp. 488–89.

CHAPTER THREE: IN THE WAKE OF THE
DURHAM REPORT

1. P.A.O., Macauley Papers, Feb. 13, 1839.

2. Charles R. Sanderson, ed., *The Arthur Papers*, no. 701, Feb. 23, 1839.

3. *Christian Guardian*, March 20, 1839.

4. *Journal of the Legislative Assembly of Upper Canada*, 1839, pp. 83–84, 100–2.

5. *Christian Guardian*, March 21, 1839.

6. *Ibid.*

7. *Journal of the Legislative Assembly of Upper Canada*, 1839, pp. 83–84.

8. *Ibid.*, p. 84.

9. *Ibid.*

10. *Ibid.*, pp. 100–3.

11. Durham Papers, VI, vol. 3, pp. 262–64.

12. P.A.O., Strachan Letter Book, 1827–41, pp. 69–70, Strachan to unnamed recipient, April 10, 1839.

13. Sanderson, *Arthur Papers*, no. 715, March 30, 1839.

14. Sir John Colborne had seen the Report by March 31, but it apparently did not reach Toronto until April 3 or 4. The *Christian Guardian* published its first account of the Report on April 6.

15. Sanderson, *Arthur Papers*, no. 718.

16. *Ibid.*, no. 726, April 6, 1839.

17. *Ibid.*, no. 734, April 11, 1839.

18. Donald R. Beer, "The Political Career of Sir Allan MacNab," unpublished M.A. thesis, Queen's University, 1963, p. 48.

19. Sanderson, *Arthur Papers*, no. 757, May [?], 1839.

20. Macaulay Papers, April 7, 1839.

21. Gerald M. Craig, *Upper Canada: The Formative Years, 1784–1841*, pp. 268–69.

22. P.A.C., LaFontaine Papers, vol. 1, pp. 207–8, April 12, 1839.

23. *Ibid.*, vol. 1, pp. 209–12, April 30, 1839.

24. Sanderson, *Arthur Papers*, no. 770, May 14, 1839.

25. *Ibid.*, no. 794, June 8, 1839.

26. *Ibid.*, no. 663, Robinson to Arthur, Feb. 19, 1839.

27. *Ibid.*, no. 668, Robinson to Normanby, Feb. 23, 1839.

28. *Ibid.*, no. 663, Feb. 19, 1839.

29. *Ibid.*, no. 698, Robinson to Arthur, March 19, 1839.

30. *Ibid.*, no. 668, Robinson to Normanby, Feb. 23, 1839.

31. *Ibid.*

32. *Ibid.*, no. 679, Robinson to Arthur, March 4, 1839.

33. *Ibid.*, no. 712, March 25, 1839.

34. Grey of Howick Papers, pt. I, "Suggestions for a Scheme for the Future Government of the Canadas," Dec. 21, 1838.

35. Sanderson, *Arthur Papers*, no. 698, March 19, 1839.

36. *Ibid.*

37. Q 266–1, pp. 93–95, Carter to Glenelg, Jan. 26, 1839.

38. Durham Papers, VI, vol. 3, pp. 167–81, Proceedings of the North American Colonial Association, Feb. 25, 1839.

39. *Ibid.*, Howick to Durham, Feb. 7, 1839. Published in the *P.A.C. Report*, 1923, pp. 338–40.

40. Durham Papers, VI, vol. 3, pp. 194–99. "Memorandum on the advantages of a Legislative Union over a Federal Union," unsigned but in Charles Buller's hand (Feb. 1839).

41. *Ibid.*, VI, vol. 3, pp. 152–55, Wakefield to Durham, Feb. 9, 1839.

42. Grey of Howick Papers, pt. I, Howick Journal, March 26, 1839.

43. *Ibid.*, "Heads of a Bill for the better Government of the Provinces of Upper Canada and Lower Canada," March 27, 1839.

44. Russell Papers, box 3, "Memorandum on the Nature of the Union that should be effected in the Canadas," March 28, 1839. This memorandum is published in O. A. Kinchen, *Lord John Russell's Canadian Policy*, app. 5, pp. 207–8, but there are inaccuracies in the text and the document is incorrectly dated as March 2, 1839.

45. Grey of Howick Papers, pt. I, Howick Journal, March 28, 1839.

46. *Ibid.*, "Heads of a Bill for the future Government of the Canadian Provinces," March 29, 1839.

47. *Ibid.*, Howick Journal, March 30, 1839.

48. Lloyd C. Saunders, ed., *Lord Melbourne's Papers*, pp. 444–45, April 2, 1839.

49. Q 268–1, pp. 116 ff., W. Badgley to Normanby, April 12, 1839.

50. Q 266–2, pp. 211–14, Robert Gillespie to Normanby, April 27, 1839.

51. P.A.C., J. B. Robinson Papers (microfilm), pp. 27–28, John Beverley Robinson's Diary, May 4, 1839.

52. Russell Papers, box 3, May 2, 1839.

53. Sanderson, *Arthur Papers*, no. 745, Robinson to Arthur, April 19, 1839.

54. *Hansard*, Third Series, vol. 47, cols. 1254–75, June 3, 1839.

55. *Ibid.*, cols. 1276–82.

56. *Ibid.*, cols. 1282–86.

57. Durham Papers, VI, vol. 3, pp. 361–65, June 4, 1839.

58. *Hansard*, Third Series, vol. 47, col. 1287, June 3, 1839.

59. *Ibid.*, cols. 965–67, June 27, 1839.

60. Paul Knaplund, ed., *Letters from Lord Sydenham to Lord John Russell*, pp. 23–24, June 28, 1839.

61. Q 270, pp. 236–300.

62. Spencer Walpole, *The Life of Lord John Russell*, I, 335.

63. P.A.C., Ellice Papers (microfilm), bundle 59, Aug. 3, 1839.

64. *Ibid.*, bundle 27, Russell to Ellice, Aug. 26, 1839.

65. Russell Papers, box 3, Ellice to Russell, Aug. 29, 1839.

66. Ellice Papers, bundle 48, McGillivray to Ellice, Sept. 5, 1839.

67. C. C. F. Greville, *Greville Memoirs*, II, 222.

68. Sanderson, *Arthur Papers*, no. 824, Arthur to Normanby, July 3, 1839.

69. Q 259–2, pp. 399–401, Colborne to Normanby, July 28, 1839.

70. Knaplund, *Letters*, p. 25, Thomson to Russell, Aug. 20, 1839.

71. P.A.C., R.G. 7, G 5, vol. 27, pp. 2–16, Russell to Thomson, Sept. 7, 1839.

72. *Ibid.*

73. G. Poulett Scrope, *Memoir of the Life of the Right Honourable Charles Lord Sydenham*, pp. 101–2.

74. See J. R. M. Butler, "Notes on the Origin of Lord John Russell's Despatch of October 16, 1839, on the Tenure of Crown Offices in the Colonies," *Cambridge Historical Journal*, II (1928), 248–51, for an explanation of the Australian origin of this change in policy.

75. Q 261, pp. 41–42, Thomson to Stephen (H.M.S. *Pique*, Lat. 48°, Long. 40° 10′), Oct. 3, 1839.

CHAPTER FOUR: PRELUDE TO UNION

1. Charles R. Sanderson, ed., *The Arthur Papers*, no. 910, Arthur to Normanby (draft), ca. Sept. 15, 1839. Apparently Arthur cancelled this despatch on learning of Thomson's appointment for it was never sent.

2. *Le Canadien*, Oct. 25, 1839.

3. Q 261, pp. 93–95, Thomson to Russell, Oct. 31, 1839.

4. *Ibid.*, pp.101–2, Thomson to Russell, Nov. 1, 1839.

5. Sanderson, *Arthur Papers*, nos. 967–68, Arthur to Thomson, Nov. 9, 1839. C.O. 42, vol. 463, pp. 292–95, Arthur to Russell, Nov. 11, 1839.

6. P.A.C., LaFontaine Papers, vol. 1, pp. 232–34, Oct. 9, 1839.

7. *Ibid.*

8. *Ibid.*, vol. 1, pp. 240–42, Nov. 14, 1839.

9. Q 261, pp. 192–96.

10. Macaulay Papers, Macaulay to John Kirby, Nov. 22, 1839.

11. *Ibid.*, memorandum of an interview between Thomson and Arthur, Nov. 24, 1839.

12. Paul Knaplund, ed., *Letters from Lord Sydenham to Lord John Russell*, pp. 35–38, Thomson to Russell, Nov. 25, 1839.

13. Sanderson, *Arthur Papers*, nos. 1000–1001, Arthur to Thomson, Nov. 26, 1839, and Thomson to Arthur, Nov. 27, 1839.

14. *Ibid.*, no. 1003, Nov. 28, 1839.

15. LaFontaine Papers, vol. 1, pp. 243–47, Hincks to LaFontaine, Dec. 4, 1839.

16. Upper Canada Sundries, Merritt to Thomson, Nov. 28, and Nov. 30, 1839.

17. Knaplund, *Letters*, pp. 35–38, Nov. 25, 1839.

18. *Ibid.*

19. *Journal of the Legislative Council of Upper Canada*, 1839–40, pp. 14–32. Thomson's proposals were supported by Wells, Dunn, Baldwin, Adamson, John Macaulay, Sullivan, Fergusson, Radcliffe, McDonald, DeBlaquière, McGillivray, Fraser, Crooks, and Morris. Union on these terms was opposed by Crookshank, Strachan, Allan, McDonell, Elmsley, Vankoughnet, J. S. Macaulay, and Wilson.

20. Knaplund, *Letters*, pp. 38–40, Dec. [18?], 1839.

21. *Ibid.*

22. Nicholas F. Davin, *The Irishman in Canada*, p. 398.

23. Macaulay Papers, John Macaulay to Ann Macaulay, Dec. 17, 1839.

24. *Quebec Gazette*, Dec. 18, 1839, report of the debates in the Legislative Assembly of Upper Canada on Dec. 10, 1839.

25. Sanderson, *Arthur Papers*, no. 1032, Dec. 13, 1839.

26. W. G. Ormsby, "The Civil List Question in the Province of Canada," *Canadian Historical Review*, XXXV, no. 2 (June 1954), 93–118.

27. LaFontaine Papers, vol. 1, pp. 254–56, Dec. 20, 1839.

28. *Quebec Gazette*, Dec. 20, 1839, report of debates on Dec. 12, 1839.

29. Sanderson, *Arthur Papers*, nos. 1031, 1034, 1037, 1039, 1041, Dec. 13–15, 1839.

30. *Journal of the Legislative Assembly of Upper Canada*, 1839–40, p. 58. Robinson's amendment was supported by Boulton, Caldwell, Cartwright, Elliott, Gamble, Hagerman, Jarvis, McCrae, and Murney. In the vote on the original question Cartwright, Gamble, Hagerman, and Murney supported union.

31. *Ibid*. Tories: Aikman, William Chisholm, Draper, Ferrie, Hotham, Hunter, Kearnes, Lewis, Malloch, Marks, McKay; *Reformers*: D. A. McDonell, McMicking, Shaver, Thorburn, Woodruff.

32. G. Poulett Scrope, *Memoir of the Life of the Right Honourable Charles Lord Sydenham*, p. 163, Thomson to unnamed recipient, Dec. 31, 1839.

33. Q 262, pp. 97–98, Dec. 15, 1839.

34. Scrope, *Sydenham*, pp. 148–51.

35. Q 262, pp. 116–17, Dec. 15, 1839.

36. *Ibid.*, pp. 128–128a, Dec. 23, 1839.

37. LaFontaine Papers, vol. 1, pp. 248–53, Dec. 11, 1839.

38. *Ibid.*, vol. 2, pp. 257–59, Jan. 9, 1840.

39. Strachan Letter Book, 1839–43, p. 34, Dec. 19, 1839.

40. Q 270–2, pp. 515–17, Dec. 16, 1839.

41. Knaplund, *Letters*, p. 42, Thomson to Russell, Jan. 18, 1840.

42. John S. Moir, *The Relations of Church and State in Canada West*, pp. 30–32.

43. Scrope, *Sydenham*, pp. 161–62, Dec. 24, 1839.

44. Upper Canada Sundries, Thomson to Hagerman, Jan. 13, 1840. Unfortunately no record of the Governor's original proposals has been found.

45. Sanderson, *Arthur Papers*, nos. 1097, 1099–1103, 1105, 1107–8, exchange of notes between Thomson, Hagerman, and Arthur, Jan. 10–14, 1840.

46. *Journal of the Legislative Assembly of Upper Canada*, 1839–40, p. 174, Jan. 15, 1840. Moderates who supported clergy reserves bill: *Tories*: Burritt, William Chisholm, Draper, Hotham, Hunter, Jarvis, Kearnes, Malloch, Donald McDonell, McKay, McLean, Richardson, Ruttan, Shade, Sherwood, Wickens; *Reformers*: Armstrong, Cook, Mathewson, McCargar, D. A. McDonell, Morris, Shaver; *undetermined political affiliation*: Alexander Chisholm, Detlor, Ferrie, Manahan, McCrae. Burritt, Jarvis, Richardson, Ruttan, Shade, Sherwood, and Armstrong (Reformer) had previously insisted upon the Upper Canadian terms of union. Aikman and Lewis had been converted from their insistence on the terms, but now realigned themselves with the High Tory opposition.

47. Knaplund, *Letters*, pp. 41–44, Thomson to Russell, Jan. 18, 1840.

48. *Ibid.*, pp. 44–46, Jan. 23, 1840.

49. Sanderson, *Arthur Papers*, no. 1134, Arthur to Lord Fitzroy Somerset, Jan. 24, 1840.

50. *Ibid.*, no. 1093, Arthur to Thomson, Jan. 6, 1840.

51. *Ibid.*, no. 1094, Thomson to Arthur, Jan. 7, 1840.

52. Q 270–1, p. 69, Jan. 18, 1840.

53. *Ibid.*, pp. 111 ff., Thomson to Russell, Jan. 22, 1840.

54. Q 262, pp. 141–61, Dec. 24, 1839.

55. Q 270–1, pp. 111 ff., Thomson to Russell, Jan. 22, 1840.

56. *Ibid.*

57. Scrope, *Sydenham*, pp. 171–72, ca. Feb. 13, 1840.

58. *Quebec Gazette*, July 29, 1839.

59. *Ibid.*, Dec. 23, 1839.

60. *Ibid.*

61. *Le Canadien*, Feb. 3, 1840.

62. Q 270–2, pp. 485–88, Thomson to Russell, Feb. 12, 1840.

63. Q 271–1, pp. 27–37, Thomson to Russell, March 9, 1840.
64. John Beverley Robinson, *Canada and the Canada Bill* (London, 1840).
65. Sanderson, *Arthur Papers*, no. 1200, Feb. 27, 1840.
66. P.A.C., J. B. Robinson Papers (microfilm), John Beverley Robinson's Diary, pp. 113–14, April 9, 1840.
67. *Ibid.*, p. 98, March 17, 1840.
68. *Ibid.*, pp. 113–14, April 9, 1840.
69. Knaplund, *Letters*, p. 64, Thomson to Russell, May 6, 1840.
70. *Ibid.*, p. 74, June 27, 1840.
71. *Hansard*, Third Series, vol. 54, cols. 1119–27, May 29, 1840.
72. *Ibid.*, cols. 1129–36, May 29, 1840.
73. *Ibid.*, col. 1151, May 29, 1840.
74. *Ibid.*, vol. 55, cols. 244–46, June 30, 1840.
75. *Ibid.*, cols. 246–47, June 30, 1840.
76. *Ibid.*, cols. 248–52, June 30, 1840.
77. *Ibid.*, cols. 505–6, July 7, 1840.
78. Durham Papers, VI, vol. 3, pp. 485–88, Buller to Durham, July 7, 1840.
79. Sir Francis Bond Head, *The Emigrant*, pp. 197–200.

CHAPTER FIVE: FINAL PREPARATION

1. 3 & 4 Vic., c. 35.
2. Paul Knaplund, ed., *Letters from Lord Sydenham to Lord John Russell*, pp. 85–87, Aug. 28, 1840.
3. Q 273–2, pp. 276–93, Thomson to Russell, Sept. 16, 1840.
4. Q 272–2, pp. 356–60, Thomson to Russell, June 27, 1840.
5. Q 272–1, pp. 144–58, Thomson to Russell, May 22, 1840.
6. Knaplund, *Letters*, pp. 76–79, June 28, 1840.
7. Q 273–2, pp. 304–7, Sydenham to Russell, Sept. 27, 1840.
8. *Ibid.*
9. Knaplund, *Letters*, pp. 88–92, Thomson to Russell, Sept. 16, 1840.
10. G. Poulett Scrope, *Memoir of the Life of the Right Honourable Charles Lord Sydenham*, pp. 198–200, Sept. 18, 1840.
11. Knaplund, *Letters*, pp. 92–96, Sydenham to Russell, Sept. 27, 1840.
12. *Ibid.*
13. *Ibid.*, pp. 96–98, Sydenham to Russell, Oct. 12, 1840.
14. *Ibid.*, pp. 100–3, Sydenham to Russell, Nov. 24, 1840.
15. Adam Shortt, *Lord Sydenham*, p. 280.
16. Scrope, *Sydenham*, pp. 207–9, Nov. 23, 1840.
17. *Ibid.*
18. *Ibid.*, pp. 210–12, Sydenham to unnamed recipient, Dec. [?], 1840.
19. C.O. 42, vol. 477, pp. 120–39, Sydenham to Russell, Jan. 26, 1841.
20. Toronto Public Library, Alfred Sandom Scrap Book, "The Governors of Canada," Sydenham to Sullivan, Oct. 14, 1840. See also C. B. Sissons, *The Life and Letters of Egerton Ryerson*, I, 537–41, 560.
21. *Le Canadien*, May 11, 1840.
22. Strachan Letter Book, 1839–43, p. 58, Strachan to Rev. A. N. Campbell, May 22, 1840.
23. C.O. 42, vol. 470, pp. 455–59, Arthur to Russell, May 27, 1840.
24. LaFontaine Papers, vol. 2, pp. 269–72, May 2, 1840.
25. *Ibid.*, vol. 2, pp. 279–82, June 17, 1840.
26. *Montreal Gazette*, Oct. 6, 1851, speech by LaFontaine at a banquet in his honour.
27. *Le Canadien*, July 6, 1840.
28. LaFontaine Papers, vol. 2, pp. 264–66, Feb. 22, 1840.
29. *Ibid.*, vol. 2, pp. 293–96, Aug. 15, 1840.
30. *Ibid.*, vol. 2, pp. 302–6, Aug. 28, 1840.
31. *Ibid.*, vol. 2, pp. 297–301, Aug. 23, 1840.
32. *Ibid.*, vol. 2, pp. 350–53, Dec. 29, 1840.
33. *Ibid.*, vol. 2, pp. 344–49, Dec. 15, 1840.

34. *Ibid.*, vol. 2, pp. 356–58, Jan. 16, 1841.

35. *Ibid.*, vol. 2, pp. 362–65, Feb. 14, 1841.

36. *Ibid.*, vol. 2, pp. 297–301, Aug. 23, 1840.

37. Jacques Monet, "The Crown and the Politicians, 1839–1848: A Study of the French-Canadian Attitude to the British Connection," unpublished M.A. thesis, University of Toronto, 1961, pp. 62–77.

38. *Le Fantasque*, Oct. 26, 1840.

39. *P.A.C. Report*, 1883, note B, pp. 169–70, Morin to Hincks, May 8, 1841.

40. *Le Canadien*, Nov. 20, 1840.

41. LaFontaine Papers, vol. 2, pp. 330–43, Baldwin to Hincks, Nov. 7, 1840. Enclosed in Hincks to LaFontaine, Nov. 27, 1840.

42. *Ibid.*, Hincks to Baldwin, Nov. 25, 1840. Enclosed in Hincks to LaFontaine, Nov. 27, 1840.

43. Charles R. Sanderson, ed., *The Arthur Papers*, no. 1727, Feb. 7, 1841.

44. *Le Fantasque*, Feb. 11, 1841.

45. Scrope, *Sydenham*, pp. 212–13.

46. *Quebec Gazette*, Feb. 15, 1841.

47. Sanderson, *Arthur Papers*, no. 1739, Feb. 10, 1841.

48. Macaulay Papers, Helen Macaulay to Ann Macaulay, Feb. 10, 1841.

49. Sanderson, *Arthur Papers*, no. 1752, Arthur to Sydenham, Feb. 13, 1841.

50. C.O. 42, vol. 477, pp. 457–61, Sydenham to Russell, Feb. 23, 1841.

51. J. E. Hodgetts, *Pioneer Public Service*.

52. C.O. 42, vol. 480, pp. 72–81, Sydenham to Russell, July 18, 1841.

53. *Ibid.*

54. C.O. 42, vol. 479, pp. 133 ff., Sydenham to Russell, May 22, 1841.

CHAPTER SIX: A THIN VEIL OF SUCCESS

1. LaFontaine Papers, vol. 2, pp. 310–12, R. Adamson to LaFontaine, Sept. 10, 1840.

2. *Quebec Gazette*, Oct. 20, 1840.

3. P.A.C., Neilson Papers, vol. 12, pp. 584–89, Neilson to Sydney Bellingham, Dec. 23, 1840.

4. *Ibid.*

5. C.O. 42, vol. 478, pp. 13–21, Sydenham to Russell, March 6, 1841.

6. Paul Knaplund, ed., *Letters from Lord Sydenham to Lord John Russell*, pp. 118–23, Feb. 24, 1841.

7. Charles R. Sanderson, ed., *The Arthur Papers*, no. 1667, Jan. 20, 1841.

8. *Ibid.*, no. 1783, Sydenham to Arthur, Feb. 27, 1841.

9. *Ibid.*, no. 1820, Sydenham to Baldwin, March 1, 1841.

10. *Ibid.*, no. 1821, Baldwin to Sydenham, March 5, 1841.

11. *Ibid.*, no. 1840, Sydenham to Arthur, March 15, 1841.

12. LaFontaine Papers, vol. 2, pp. 366–67, Feb. 16, 1841.

13. Knaplund, *Letters*, pp. 110–11, Sydenham to Russell, Jan. 29, 1841.

14. Sanderson, *Arthur Papers*, no. 1544, Nov. 1, 1840.

15. *Ibid.*, no. 1550, Sydenham to Arthur, Nov. 3, 1840.

16. *Ibid.*, no. 1794, Sydenham to Arthur, March 1, 1841.

17. R.G. 7, G 14, vol. 6, Thomas Steers to Sydenham, Sept. 9, 1840.

18. *Ibid.*, endorsement on a letter from E. H. Berry to Sydenham, Jan. 1, 1841.

19. G. Poulett Scrope, *Memoir of the Life of the Right Honourable Charles Lord Sydenham*, p. 227.

20. *Le Canadien*, April 2, 1841.

21. Ellice Papers, bundle 3, Gerrard to Ellice, March 25, 1841.

22. C.O. 42, vol. 477, pp. 495–500, Sydenham to Russell, Feb. 25, 1841.

23. Q 272–2, pp. 390–401, Russell to Sydenham, May 3, 1841.

24. Knaplund, *Letters*, pp. 137–40, May 25, 1841.

25. *Ibid.*

26. LaFontaine Papers, vol. 2, pp. 393–98, Hincks to LaFontaine, April 19, 1841.

27. *P.A.C. Report*, 1883, note B, pp. 168–73, Morin to Hincks, May 8, 1841.

28. LaFontaine Papers, vol. 2, pp. 405–9, May 29, 1841.
29. Knaplund, *Letters,* pp. 140–44, June 12, 1841.
30. *Ibid.,* pp. 145–49, June 27, 1841.
31. L. C. Saunders, ed., *Lord Melbourne's Papers,* pp. 448–49, Sydenham to Melbourne, June 27, 1841.
32. *Journal of the Legislative Assembly of the United Province of Canada,* I (1841), 64.
33. Knaplund, *Letters,* pp. 145–49, Sydenham to Russell, June 27, 1841.
34. Scrope, *Sydenham,* pp. 244–45, June 27, 1841.
35. Knaplund, *Letters,* pp. 151–54.
36. Scrope, *Sydenham,* pp. 253–55, Aug. 28, 1841.
37. *Ibid.,* pp. 385–91, "Memorandum on the Paper Currency suggested for Canada by Lord Sydenham."
38. P.A.C., Hill Collection, vol. 4, pp. 1281–82, Johnston to Christie, Sept., 1841.
39. Donald R. Beer, "The Political Career of Sir Allan MacNab, 1839–1849," p. 94.
40. Sanderson, *Arthur Papers,* no. 1925, Arthur to Robinson, Aug. 31, 1841.
41. *Ibid.,* no. 1927, Sept. 1, 1841.
42. P.A.C., Peel Papers (microfilm), Peel to Stanley, Oct. 5, 1841.

CHAPTER SEVEN: TRANSFORMATION

1. P.A.C., Bagot Papers, vol. 7, pp. 16–23, Bagot to Stanley, Jan., 1842.
2. *Ibid.,* vol. 7, pp. 54–60, Feb. 8, 1842.
3. *Ibid.,* vol. 7, pp. 10–13, Bagot to Stanley, Jan. 18, 1842.
4. *Ibid.,* vol. 12, pp. 71–78, Stanley to Bagot, June 3, 1842.
5. *Ibid.,* vol. 7, pp. 28–33, Bagot to Stanley, Jan. 26, 1842.
6. *Ibid.,* vol. 9, pp. 254–56, Bagot to Stanley, May 11, 1842.
7. *Ibid.,* vol. 7, pp. 255–75, June 12, 1842.
8. *Ibid.,* vol. 9, pp. 153–61, Feb. 23, 1842.
9. *Ibid.,* vol. 9, pp. 189–91, March 23, 1842.
10. *Ibid.,* vol. 7, pp. 107–13, March 26, 1842.
11. William G. Ormsby, "The Civil List Question in the Province of Canada," *Canadian Historical Review,* XXXV (1954), 93–118.
12. Bagot Papers, vol. 7, pp. 210–17, Bagot to Stanley, May 28, 1842.
13. *Ibid.,* vol. 12, pp. 49–59, April 1, 1842.
14. *Ibid.,* vol. 12, pp. 110–20, July 4, 1842.
15. *Ibid.,* vol. 8, pp. 18–21, July 28, 1842.
16. *Ibid.,* vol. 10, pp. 211–34, Bagot to Stanley, Sept. 26, 1842.
17. *Ibid.,* vol. 9, pp. 153–61, Bagot to Stanley, Feb. 23, 1842.
18. *Supra,* p. 101.
19. Bagot Papers, vol. 2, pp. 310–17, vol. 3, pp. 354–57, Cartwright to Bagot, May 16 and June 6, 1842.
20. *Ibid.,* vol. 7, pp. 325–37, July 10, 1842.
21. *Ibid.,* vol. 3, pp. 412–27, Harrison to Bagot, July 11, 1842.
22. *Ibid.,* vol. 3, pp. 442–48, July 16, 1842.
23. *Ibid.,* vol. 8, pp. 22–38, July 28, 1842.
24. *Ibid.,* vol. 12, pp. 143–45, Stanley to Peel, Aug. 27, 1842.
25. *Ibid.*
26. *Ibid.,* vol. 8, pp. 22–38, Bagot to Stanley, July 28, 1842.
27. *Ibid.,* vol. 8, pp. 88–96, Sept. 13, 1842.
28. R.G. 7, G 5, vol. 32, pp. 232–37, Nov. 3, 1842.
29. Bagot Papers, vol. 10, pp. 89–91, Bagot to Stanley, Oct. 8, 1842.
30. *Ibid.,* vol. 10, pp. 208–9, Oct. 8, 1842.
31. *Ibid.,* vol. 8, pp. 225–29, Dec. 11, 1842.
32. P.A.C., C.O. 537 (microfilm), vol. 142, pp. 16–24, April 25, 1843.
33. *Ibid.,* pp. 68–75, Metcalfe to Stanley, April 29, 1843.
34. *Ibid.,* pp. 102–8, Metcalfe to Stanley, May 3, 1843.
35. *Ibid.,* pp. 353–54, June 27, 1843.
36. *Ibid.,* pp. 1–14, Metcalfe to Stanley, April 24, 1843.

37. *Ibid.*, pp. 16–24, Metcalfe to Stanley, April 25, 1843.
38. W. G. Ormsby, "The Civil List Question in the Province of Canada," *Canadian Historical Review*, XXXIX (1958), 277–95.
39. C.O. 537, vol. 142, pp. 257–68, Metcalfe to Stanley, May 10, 1843.
40. *Ibid.*, pp. 292–302, May 17, 1843.
41. *Ibid.*
42. *Ibid.*, vol. 141, pp. 5–19, Stanley to Metcalfe, May 29, 1843.
43. *Ibid.*, pp. 59–70, Stanley to Metcalfe, July 3, 1843.
44. *Ibid.*, p. 49, Stanley to Metcalfe, July 3, 1843.
45. *Ibid.*, vol. 142, pp. 368–75, Metcalfe to Stanley, July 19, 1843.
46. *Ibid.*, pp. 376–80, July 21, 1843.
47. *Ibid.*, vol. 141, pp. 101–7, Stanley to Metcalfe, Aug. 31, 1843.
48. *Ibid.*, vol. 142, pp. 355–57, Stanley to Metcalfe, Aug. 18, 1843.
49. *Ibid.*
50. LaFontaine Papers, pp. 4361–85, notes by LaFontaine regarding the question of amnesty.
51. C.O. 537, vol. 142, pp. 428–42, Aug. 7, 1843.
52. *Ibid.*, vol. 141, p. 109, Sept. 3, 1843.
53. *Ibid.*, vol. 143, pp. 4–34, Metcalfe to Stanley, Jan. 26, 1844.
54. *Ibid.*, pp. 196–215, Metcalfe to Stanley, Nov. 23, 1844.
55. *Ibid.*, pp. 325–62, Metcalfe to Stanley, May 13, 1845.
56. *Ibid.*, pp. 240–45, Metcalfe to Stanley, March 13, 1845.
57. *Ibid.*
58. P.A.C., Derby Papers (microfilm), memorandum by Peel, April 25, 1845.
59. R.G. 7, G 5, vol. 34, pp. 412–13, Gladstone to Cathcart, Feb. 3, 1846.
60. 11 & 12 Vic., c. 56.
61. C.O. 537, vol. 142, pp. 347–52, June 25, 1843.
62. J. B. Robinson Papers, vol. 3, March 11, 1844.
63. LaFontaine Papers, vol. 6, pp. 1196–1203, Caron to Draper, Sept. 18, 1845.
64. John William Kaye, *The Life and Correspondence of Charles Lord Metcalfe.*

EPILOGUE

1. *The Annual Register or a View of the History, Politics, and Literature for the year 1791* (London, 1795), pp. 110–11.
2. LaFontaine Papers, vol. 17, pp. 3016–17, Ellice to LaFontaine, March 8, 1860.
3. J. E. Hodgetts, *Pioneer Public Service*, p. 55.
4. *Parliamentary Debates on the Subject of the Confederation of the British North American Provinces* (Quebec, 1865), p. 30.
5. LaFontaine Papers, pp. 5241–42.
6. G. F. G. Stanley, "Act or Pact, Another Look at Confederation," *Canadian Historical Association Report*, 1956, p. 9.

BIBLIOGRAPHY

PRIMARY SOURCES

Unpublished Documents

Public Archives of Canada

Record Group 7, Records of the Governor General's Office

Series G 1, vols. 38–51, 83–110: Despatches from the Colonial Office to the Governor, 1838–45, and the Lieutenant-Governor of Upper Canada, 1838–41.

Series G 5, vols. 17–18, 25–34: Entry books of despatches received from the Colonial Office by the Governor, 1838–45, and the Lieutenant-Governor of Upper Canada, 1838–41.

Series G 12, vols. 28–33, 52–64: Entry books of despatches to the Colonial Office from the Governor, 1838–45, and the Lieutenant-Governor of Upper Canada, 1838–41.

Series G 14, vols. 6–18: Internal correspondence received by the Governor, 1838–45.

Series G 15A, vol. 9: Governor's (Lower Canada) internal letter book, 1830–39.

Series G 16A, vols. 4–6: Lieutenant-Governor's (Upper Canada) internal letter books, 1837–41.

Series G 17A, vols. 1–3: Governor's (Canada) internal letter books, 1839–58.

Upper Canada Sundries, 1838–41: Letters received by the Lieutenant-Governor and his Civil Secretary.

Colonial Office Records

Q Series, vols. 246–77, 404–31: Copies of the despatches from Canada to the Colonial Office transcribed from the originals in the Public Record Office, London. The Q series is virtually a duplicate of C.O. 42 up to 1841 but does not extend beyond that date. Because the series has been calendared it was used in preference to C.O. 42 for the pre-union period, but wherever the wording was vital it was checked against the microfilm of C.O. 42.

C.O. 42, vols. 477–530, 1841–45: Microfilm of original despatches from Canada to the Colonial Office which are now in the custody of the Public Record Office.

C.O. 537, vols. 140–143, 1842–45: Microfilm of confidential correspondence between Lord Stanley and Sir Charles Bagot and Sir Charles Metcalfe.

Bagot Papers
Derby Papers (microfilm)
Durham Papers
Edward Ellice Papers (microfilm)
Grey of Howick Papers, part I (microfilm and photostat)

Hill Papers
LaFontaine Papers (transcript)
Merritt Papers
Sir Allan MacNab Papers (microfilm)
Peel Papers (microfilm)
J. B. Robinson Papers (microfilm)

Ontario Archives

Macaulay Papers
Merritt Papers

Robinson Papers
Strachan Papers

Toronto Public Library
Baldwin Papers

Alfred Sandom Papers

Published Documents, Books, and Pamphlets

Anonymous. *Resolutions at a Meeting of the Friends of the Re-Union of Lower and Upper Canada . . .*, Montreal, 1822.

—— *Petition against Passing a BILL FOR THE UNION OF UPPER AND LOWER CANADA*, Montreal, 1822.

—— *Abstract of a Bill for Uniting the Legislative Councils and Assemblies of the Provinces of Lower Canada and Upper Canada in one Legislature . . .*, London, 1824.

—— *The Colonies and Great Britain must be incorporated and form one universal and indivisible Empire*, London, 1839.

—— *Re-Union: Petition against the Union of Upper and Lower Canada and the signatures thereto*, 1840.

—— *Tracts for the People, No. 1: The Resignation of the Late Ministers*, Toronto, 1844.

—— *Proceedings at the first General Meeting of the Reform Association of Canada . . . Toronto on Monday, 25 March, 1844*, Toronto, 1844.

—— *Address to the People of Canada by the Reform Associations Adopted at a General Meeting held at the Association Rooms, at Toronto, the 16th Day of May, 1844*, Toronto, 1844.

BLISS, HENRY. *An Essay on the Re-Construction of Her Majesty's Government in Canada*, London, 1839.

BONNYCASTLE, SIR R. H. *Canada and the Canadians in 1846*, London, 1846.

[BUCHANAN, ISAAC]. *First Series of Five Letters against the Baldwin Faction by an Advocate of Responsible Government and of the New College Bill*, Toronto, 1844.

BULLER, CHARLES. "Sketch of Lord Durham's Mission to Canada in 1838 [written in 1840]," *Public Archives of Canada Report*, 1923, pp. 341–69.

—— *Responsible Government for the Colonies*, London, 1840. G. M. Wrong, ed., Oxford, 1926.

Canada, Province of. *Journals of the Legislative Assembly*, 1841–45.

—— *Journals of the Legislative Council*, 1841–45.

—— *Statutes*, 1841–45.

—— *Parliamentary Debates on the Subject of the Confederation of the British North American Provinces, 3rd Session, 8th Provincial Assembly of Canada*, Printed by Order of the Legislature, Quebec, 1865.

DURHAM, JOHN LAMBTON, EARL OF. *Report on the Affairs of British North America*, ed. Sir C. P. Lucas, 3 vols., Oxford, 1912.

Great Britain. *Report from the Select Committee on the Civil Government of Canada: Ordered by the House of Commons to be Printed*, Reprinted by Order of the House of Assembly of Lower Canada, Quebec, 1829.

—— *Hansard*, Third Series, vols. 47, 55.

GREVILLE, C. C. F. *The Greville Memoirs, 1814–1860*, Lytton Strachey and Roger Fulford, eds., 7 vols., London, 1938.

[HALIBURTON, T. C.] *The Bubbles of Canada*, London, 1839.

HEAD, SIR F. B. *An Address to the House of Lords against the Bill Before Parliament for the Union of the Canadas*, London, 1840.

—— *Narrative*, London, 1839.

—— *The Emigrant*, London, 1846.

HINCKS, FRANCIS. *Address of the Honourable Francis Hincks to the Reformers of Frontenac*, Toronto, 1844.

—— *The Ministerial Crisis: Mr. D. B. Viger and his Position* (By a Reformer of 1836), Kingston, 1844.

HORTON, R. W. *Exposition and Defence of Earl Bathurst's Administration of Affairs of Canada*, London, 1838.

KAYE, J. W., ed. *Selections from the Papers of Lord Metcalfe*, London, 1855.

KNAPLUND, PAUL, ed. *Letters from Lord Sydenham to Lord Russell*, London, 1931.

Mirror of Parliament of the Province of Canada, Montreal, 1846.

O. T., *Remarks on a Legislative Union of the Provinces of British North America*, Cobourg, 1839.

PAPINEAU, L. J., and J. NEILSON. *Letter from L. J. Papineau and J. Neilson, Esqs., Addressed to His Majesty's Under Secretary of State on the subject of the Proposed Union of the Provinces of Upper and Lower Canada*, London, 1824.

PRESTON, T. R. *Three Years Residence in Canada, 1837–1839*, London, 1840.

RICHARDSON, JOHN. *Eight Years in Canada*, Montreal, 1847.

ROBINSON, J. B., *Remarks on the Proposed Union of the Provinces*, [London], 1839.

—— *Canada and the Canada Bill*, London, 1840.

ROEBUCK, J. A. *Remarks on the Proposed Union of the Canadas* (Published in the Year, 1822), Quebec, 1835.

RUSSELL, ROLLO. *The Earlier Correspondence of Lord John Russell*, 2 vols., London, 1913.

RYERSON, EGERTON. *Some Remarks upon Sir Charles Bagot's Canadian Government*, Kingston, 1843.

—— *The Hon. R. B. Sullivan's Attacks upon Sir Charles Metcalfe Refuted*, Toronto, 1844.

—— *Sir Charles Metcalfe Defended Against the Attacks of His Late Counsellors*, Toronto, 1844.

SANDERSON, C. R., ed. *The Arthur Papers*, 3 vols., Toronto, 1957, 1959.

SAUNDERS, L. C., ed. *Lord Melbourne's Papers*, London, 1889.

[SEWELL, J., and J. B. ROBINSON]. *Plan for a General Legislative Union of the British Provinces in North America*, London, [1823].

[STRACHAN, JOHN]. *Observations on a Bill for Uniting the Legislative Councils and Assemblies of the Provinces of Lower Canada and Upper Canada in one Legislature . . .* , London, 1824.

[STUART, JAMES]. *Remarks on a Plan Intituled "A Plan for a General Legislative Union of the British Provinces in North America,"* London, 1824.

[STUART, JAMES]. *Observations on the Proposed Union of the Provinces of Upper and Lower Canada under one Legislature*, London, 1824.

[STUART, JAMES]. *Letter to His Majesty's Under Secretary of State, respecting a Plan for a General Union of the British Provinces, and on the subject of the proposed Union of the Canadas*, London, 1824.

[SULLIVAN, R. B.]. *"Legion," Letters on Responsible Government*, [Toronto], 1844.

TAYLOR, HENRY. *Considerations on the Past, Present and Future Condition of the Canadas*, Montreal, 1839.

Upper Canada, Province of. *Journals of the Legislative Assembly*, 1836–39.

—— *Journals of the Legislative Council*, 1836–39.

VIGER, D. B. *The Ministerial Crisis*, Kingston, 1844.

[WAKEFIELD, E. G.]. *"A Member of the Provincial Parliament," A View of Sir Charles Metcalfe's Government of Canada*, London, 1844.

WILLSON, JOHN. *Address to the Inhabitants of the District of Gore and Speeches upon the Bill for compensating the losses of sufferers by the late Rebellion, and an extract from a speech upon the Union of the Provinces*, Hamilton, 1840.

NEWSPAPERS

L'Aurore des Canadas, 1840–41
Christian Guardian, 1839
Le Canadien, 1839–45
Le Fantasque, 1839–45
Kingston *Chronicle & Gazette*, 1839–42
Montreal Gazette, 1839–45
Quebec Gazette, 1839–45
Toronto *Patriot*, 1839–45.
Union, 1841 (November 6–26)

SECONDARY SOURCES

BOOKS

BETHUNE, A. N. *Memoir of the Right Reverend John Strachan, D.D.; L.L.D., First Bishop of Toronto*, Toronto, 1870.

BLOOMFIELD, PAUL. *Edward Gibbon Wakefield: Builder of the British Commonwealth*, Toronto, 1961.

BRADSHAW, F. *Self Government in Canada*, London, 1903.

BRUNET, LUDOVIC. *La Province du Canada, histoire politique de 1840 à 1867*. Quebec, 1908.

BRUNET, MICHEL. *Canadians et Canadiens*, Montreal, 1955.

—— *La Présence anglaise et les Canadiens: Etudes sur l'histoire et la pensée des deux Canadas*, Montreal, 1958.

CARELESS, J. M. S. *Brown of the Globe*, vol. I, Toronto, 1959.
——— *The Union of the Canadas, 1841–1857*, Toronto, 1967.
CHRISTIE, ROBERT. *History of the Late Province of Lower Canada*, 6 vols., Montreal, 1866.
CLARK, S. D. *Movements of Political Protest in Canada, 1640–1840*, Toronto, 1959.
CORNELL, P. G. *The Alignment of Political Groups in Canada, 1841–1867*, Toronto, 1962.
COTÉ, J. O., ed. *Political Appointments and Elections in the Province of Canada from 1841–1865*, 2nd ed., Ottawa, 1866.
CRAIG, G. M. *Upper Canada: The Formative Years, 1784–1841*, Toronto, 1963.
CREIGHTON, DONALD. *John A. Macdonald, the Young Politician*, Toronto, 1952.
——— *The Commercial Empire of the St. Lawrence*, Toronto, 1937.
[CROFTON, W. C.]. *A Brief Sketch of the Life of Charles, Baron Metcalfe . . .* , Kingston, 1840.
DAVID, L. O. *L'Union des deux Canadas, 1841–1867*, Montreal, 1898.
DAVIN, N. F. *The Irishman in Canada*, London, 1877.
DeCELLES, A. D. *LaFontaine et son temps*, Montreal, 1912.
——— *Papineau, Cartier*, Makers of Canada Series, rev. ed., Toronto, 1926.
DENT, J. C. *The Last Forty Years*, 2 vols., Toronto, 1881.
DUNHAM, AILEEN. *Political Unrest in Upper Canada, 1815–1836*, London, 1927.
EGERTON, H. E. *Federations and Unions in the British Empire*, Oxford, 1911.
——— and W. L. GRANT. *Canadian Constitutional Development*, Toronto, 1907.
FRENCH, GOLDWIN. *Parsons & Politics: The Role of the Wesleyan Methodists in Upper Canada and the Maritimes from 1780 to 1855*, Toronto, 1962.
GLAZEBROOK, G. P. DeT. *Sir Charles Bagot in Canada*, London, 1929.
GUERIN-LAJOIE, ANTOINE. *Dix Ans au Canada de 1840 à 1850*, Quebec, 1888.
HARROP, A. J. *The Amazing Career of Edward Gibbon Wakefield*, London, 1928.
HINCKS, FRANCIS. *The Political History of Canada between 1840 and 1855*, Montreal, 1877.
——— *Reminiscences of His Public Life*, Montreal, 1884.
HODGETTS, J. E. *Pioneer Public Service*, Toronto, 1955.
KAYE, J. W. *The Life and Correspondence of Charles, Lord Metcalfe . . .* , 2 vols., London, 1854.
KENNEDY, W. P. M. *Documents of the Canadian Constitution*, Toronto, 1930.
——— *The Constitution of Canada*, 2nd ed., Toronto, 1938.
KILBOURN, WILLIAM. *The Firebrand: William Lyon Mackenzie and the Rebellion in Upper Canada*, Toronto, 1956.
KINCHEN, O. A. *Lord John Russell's Canadian Policy*, Lubbock, 1945.
KINGSFORD, W. K. *History of Canada*, vol. X, London, 1898.
LANGSTONE, R. W. *Responsible Government in Canada*, Toronto, 1931.
LEACOCK, STEPHEN, *Mackenzie, Baldwin, LaFontaine, Hincks*, Makers of Canada Series, rev. ed., Toronto, 1926.
LINDSEY, CHARLES. *The Life and Times of William Lyon Mackenzie*, 2 vols., Toronto, 1862.
LONGLEY, R. S. *Sir Francis Hincks*, Toronto, 1943.
MANNING, H. T. *The Revolt of French Canada, 1800–1835: A Chapter in the History of the British Commonwealth*, Toronto, 1962.
MARTIN, CHESTER. *Empire and Commonwealth*, Oxford, 1929.
MERRITT, J. P. *Biography of the Hon. W. H. Merritt*, St. Catharines, 1875.
MOIR, J. S. *Church and State in Canada West: Three Studies in the Relation of Denominationalism and Nationalism*, Toronto, 1959.
MORRELL, W. P. *British Colonial Policy in the Age of Peel and Russell*, Oxford, 1930.
MORRELL, W. P., and K. N. BELL. *Select Documents on British Colonial Policy, 1830–1860*, Oxford, 1925.
MORRISON, J. L. *British Supremacy and Self Government, 1839–1854*, Glasgow, 1919.
NEW, C. W. *Lord Durham*, Oxford, 1929.
ORMSBY, WILLIAM, ed. *Crisis in the Canadas, 1838–1839: The Grey Journals and Letters*, Toronto, 1964.
OUELLET, FERNAND. *Louis Joseph Papineau*, Canadian Historical Association Booklet no. 11, Ottawa, 1960.
ROBINSON, C. W. *The Life of Sir John Beverley Robinson*, Toronto, 1904.
ROEBUCK, J. A. *The Colonies of England*, London, 1849.
RYERSON, EGERTON. *The Story of My Life*, ed. J. George Hodgins, Toronto, 1883.
SCROPE, G. P. *Memoir of the Life of the Right Honourable Charles Lord Sydenham, G.C.B., with a Narrative of His Administration in Canada*, London, 1843.

SHORTT, ADAM. *Lord Sydenham*, Makers of Canada Series, Anniversary Edition, London, 1926.
——and A. G. DOUGHTY, eds. *Canada and Its Provinces*, vol. V, Toronto, 1914.
SISSONS, C. B. *The Life and Letters of Egerton Ryerson*, 2 vols., Toronto, 1937, 1947.
—— *Church and State in Canadian Education*, Toronto, 1959.
THOMPSON, E. J. *The Life of Sir Charles Metcalfe*, London, 1937.
TURCOTTE, L. P. *Le Canada sous l'Union, 1841–1867*, Quebec, 1882.
VAUGEOIS, DENIS. *L'Union des deux Canadas, 1791–1840: nouvelle conquête?*, Trois Rivières, 1962.
WADE, MASON. *The French Canadians, 1760–1945*, Toronto, 1955.
WALLACE, W. S. *The Family Compact*, Chronicles of Canada Series, vol. 24, Toronto, 1915.
WILSON, GEORGE. *The Life of Robert Baldwin*, Toronto, 1933.
YONGE, CHARLES DUKE. *The Life and Administration of Robert Banks, Second Earl of Liverpool*, 3 vols., London, 1868.

ARTICLES

AUDET, F.-J. "L'honorable Louis Joseph Papineau," *Canadian Historical Association Report*, 1929, pp. 47–56.
BAILEY, T. M. "Dundurn and Sir Allan MacNab," *Ontario Historical Society Papers and Records*, XXXVI (1944), 94–104.
BONENFANT, J. C., and J. C. FALARDEAU. "The Cultural and Political Implications of French Canadian Nationalism," *Canadian Historical Association Report*, 1946, pp. 56–73.
BORDEN, SIR ROBERT. "Want of Vision—or What?", *Canadian Historical Review*, IV (1923), 5–11.
BROWN, GEORGE. "The Durham Report and the Upper Canadian Scene," *Canadian Historical Review*, XX (1939), 136–60.
BRUNET, MICHEL. "The British Conquest: Canadian Social Scientists and the Fate of the *Canadiens*," *Canadian Historical Review*, XL (1959), 93–107.
BUTLER, J. R. M. "Notes on the Origin of Lord John Russell's Despatch of Oct. 16 on the tenure of Crown Offices in the Colonies," *Cambridge Historical Journal*, II (1928), 248–51.
CARELESS, J. M. S. "Frontierism, Metropolitanism and Canadian History," *Canadian Historical Review*, XXXV (1954), 1–21.
CRAIG, G. M. "The American Impact on the Upper Canadian Reform Movement Before 1837," *Canadian Historical Review*, XXIX (1948), 333–52.
CREIGHTON, D. G. "The Struggle for Financial Control in Lower Canada, 1818–1831," *Canadian Historical Review*, XII (1931), 120–44.
—— "The Commercial Class in Canadian Politics, 1792–1840," *Papers and Proceedings of the Canadian Political Science Association*, V (1933), 43–58.
—— "The Victorians and the Empire," *Canadian Historical Review*, XIX (1938), 138–53.
DOBIE, EDITH. "The Dismissal of Lord Glenelg," *Canadian Historical Review*, XXIII (1942), 280–85.
EWART, ALISON, and JULIA JARVIS. "The Personnel of the Family Compact," *Canadian Historical Review*, VII (1926), 209–21.
FOX, GRACE. "The Reception of Lord Durham's Report in the English Press," *Canadian Historical Review*, XIV (1933), 276–88.
GLAZEBROOK, G. P. DET. "Representation by the Act of Union," *Canadian Historical Review*, X (1929), 252–56.
JACKSON, ERIC. "The Organization of Upper Canadian Reformers," *Ontario History*, LIII (1961), 95–116.
JENSEN, V. J. "LaFontaine and the Canadian Union," *Canadian Historical Review*, XXV (1944), 6–19.
—— "LaFontaine and 1848 in Canada," *Canadian Historical Association Report*, 1948, pp. 46–54.
KENNEDY, W. P. M. "The Nature of Canadian Federalism," *Canadian Historical Review*, II (1921), 106–25.
KINCHEN, O. A. "The Stephen-Russell Reform in Official Tenure," *Canadian Historical Review*, XXVI (1945), 382–91.
KNAPLUND, PAUL. "Gladstone's Views on British Colonial Policy," *Canadian Historical Review*, IV (1923), 304–15.

—— "Sir James Stephen and British North American Problems," *Canadian Historical Review*, V (1924), 22–41.

—— "The Buller-Peel Correspondence Regarding Canada," *Canadian Historical Review*, VIII (1927), 41–50.

—— "Some Letters of Peel and Stanley on Canadian Problems," *Canadian Historical Review*, XII (1931), 45–54.

—— "Extracts from Gladstone's Private Political Diary Touching Canadian Questions in 1840," *Canadian Historical Review*, XX (1939), 195–98.

—— "James Stephen on Canadian Banking Laws, 1821–1846," *Canadian Historical Review*, XXXI (1950), 177–87.

LABRUERE, M. B. DE. "LaFontaine, Rolph et Papineau: épisodes de 1838 et de 1843," *Canadian Historical Association Report*, 1923, pp. 56–64.

LANCTOT, GUSTAVE. "Deux Appréciations sommaires de la Confédération," *Canadian Historical Association Report*, 1927, pp. 97–102.

LONG, D. E. T. "The Elusive Mr. Ellice," *Canadian Historical Review*, XXIII (1942), 42–57.

LONGLEY, R. S. "Francis Hincks and Canadian Public Finance," *Canadian Historical Association Report*, 1934, pp. 30–39.

—— "Emigration and the Crisis of 1837 in Upper Canada," *Canadian Historical Review*, XVII (1936), 29–40.

LOWER, A. R. M. "Edward Gibbon Wakefield and the Beauharnois Canal," *Canadian Historical Review*, XIII (1932), 37–44.

—— "Two Ways of Life: The Primary Antithesis of Canadian History," *Canadian Historical Association Report*, 1934, pp. 5–18.

—— "Two Ways of Life: The Spirit of Our Institutions," *Canadian Historical Review*, XXVIII (1947), 383–400.

LUCAS, SIR CHARLES. "Want of Vision," *Canadian Historical Review*, III (1922), 343–50.

LYON, E. W. "Proposals to Transfer the French Population of Canada to Louisiana," *Canadian Historical Review*, XVI (1935), 300–9.

MACDONNELL, U. N. "Gibbon Wakefield and Canada Subsequent to the Durham Mission, 1839–1842," *Bulletin of the Departments of History and Political and Economic Science in Queen's University*, no. 49 (1925).

MCDOUGALL, D. J. "Lord John Russell and the Canadian Crisis, 1837–1841," *Canadian Historical Review*, XXII (1941), 369–88.

MACKAY, R. A. "The Political Ideas of William Lyon Mackenzie," *Canadian Journal of Economics and Political Science*, III (1937), 1–22.

MAHEUX, A. H. "Durham et la nationalité canadienne-française," *Canadian Historical Association Report*, 1943, pp. 19–24.

MANNING, HELEN TAFT. "The Civil List of Lower Canada," *Canadian Historical Review*, XXIV (1943), 24–47.

—— "The Colonial Policy of the Whig Ministers, 1830–37," *Canadian Historical Review*, XXXIII (1952), 203–36, 341–68.

MARTIN, CHESTER. "Lord Durham's Report and its Consequences," *Canadian Historical Review*, XX (1939), 178–94.

MARTIN, K. L. P. "The Union Bill of 1822," *Canadian Historical Review*, V (1924), 42–54.

—— "The Influence of the Crown in the Evolution of Responsible Government," *Canadian Historical Review*, III (1922), 334–42.

METCALF, GEORGE. "Draper Conservatism and Responsible Government in the Canadas, 1836–1847," *Canadian Historical Review*, XLII (1961), 300–24.

MOIR, J. S. "Methodism and Higher Education, 1843–1849, a Qualification," *Ontario History* XLIV (1952), 109–28.

MONET, JACQUES, "La Crise Metcalfe and the Montreal Election," *Canadian Historical Review*, XLIV (1963), 1–19.

MORISON, J. L. "Sir Charles Bagot: An Incident in Canadian History," *Bulletin of the Departments of History and Political and Economic Science in Queen's University*, no. 4 (1912).

—— "The Last of the Old Tories," *Canadian Historical Review*, III (1922), 24–36.

MORRISON, H. M. "The Principle of Free Grants in the Land Act of 1841," *Canadian Historical Review*, XIV (1933), 392–407.

NEW, CHESTER. "The Rebellion of 1837 in its Larger Setting," *Canadian Historical Association Report*, 1937, pp. 5–17.

——— "Lord Durham and the British Background of His Report," *Canadian Historical Review*, XX (1939), 119–35.

ORMSBY, W. G. "The Civil List Question in the Province of Canada," *Canadian Historical Review*, XXXV (1954), 93–118.

——— "The Problem of Canadian Union, 1822–1828," *Canadian Historical Review*, XXXIX (1958), 277–95.

OUELLET, FERNAND. "Le Nationalisme canadien-français: de ses origines à l'insurrection de 1837," *Canadian Historical Review*, XLV (1964), 277–92.

PARKER, W. H. "A New Look at Unrest in Lower Canada in the 1830's," *Canadian Historical Review*, XL (1959), 209–17.

PIERCE, D. J., and J. P. PRITCHETT. "The Choice of Kingston as the Capital of Canada, 1839–1841," *Canadian Historical Association Report*, 1929, pp. 57–64.

POTVIN, PASCAL. "Papineau et l'orientation du nationalisme québecois," *Canadian Historical Association Report* (1943), pp. 43–49.

POULIOT, LEON: "Les Evêques du Bas Canada et le projet d'Union, 1840," *Revue d'histoire de l'Amérique française*, VIII (1954), 157–70.

RIDDELL, R. G. "A Study in the Land Policy of the Colonial Office, 1763–1853," *Canadian Historical Review*, XVIII (1937), 385–405.

SAUNDERS, R. E. "What was the Family Compact?" *Ontario History*, XLIX (1957), 165–78.

SAUNDERS, R. M. "History and French Canadian Survival," *Canadian Historical Association Report*, 1943, pp. 25–34.

SISSONS, C. B. "Ryerson and the Election of 1844," *Canadian Historical Review*, XXIII (1942), 157–76.

——— "Letters of 1844 and 1846 from Scobie to Ryerson," *Canadian Historical Review*, XXIX (1948), 393–411.

SMITH, WILLIAM. "Sidelights on the Attempted Union of 1822," *Canadian Historical Review*, II (1921), 38–45.

——— "The Reception of the Durham Report in Canada," *Canadian Historical Association Report*, 1928, pp. 41–54.

SPRAGGE, G. W. "John Strachan's Connexion with Early Proposals for Confederation," *Canadian Historical Review*, XXIII (1942), 363–73.

STANLEY, G. F. G. "Act or Pact? Another Look at Confederation," *Canadian Historical Association Report*, 1956, pp. 1–25.

TALMAN, J. J. "The Position of the Church of England in Upper Canada, 1791–1840," *Canadian Historical Review*. XV (1934), 361–75.

TROTTER, R. G. "An Early Proposal for the Federation of British North America," *Canadian Historical Review*, VI (1925), 142–55.

——— "Durham and the Idea of a Federal Union of British North America," *Canadian Historical Association Report*, 1925, pp. 55–63.

UNDERHILL, F. H. "The Development of Canadian National Political Parties in Canada," *Canadian Historical Review*, XVI (1935), 367–87.

——— "Aspects of Upper Canadian Radicalism," *Canadian Historical Review*, XVI (1935), 46–51.

WADE, MASON. "Some Aspects of the Relations of French Canada with the United States," *Canadian Historical Association Report*, 1944, pp. 16–39.

WALLACE, W. S. "The Growth of Canadian National Feeling," *Canadian Historical Review*, I (1920), 136–65.

——— "The Journalist in Canadian Politics: A Retrospect," *Canadian Historical Review*, XXII (1941), 14–24.

WHITELAW, W. M. "Responsible Government and an Irresponsible Governor," *Canadian Historical Review*, XIII (1932), 364–86.

WRONG, G. M. "Two Races in Canada," *Canadian Historical Association Report*, 1925, pp. 21–27.

THESES

AITCHISON, J. H. "The Development of Local Government in Upper Canada, 1783–1850," unpublished Ph.D. thesis, University of Toronto, 1953.

BEER, DONALD R. "The Political Career of Sir Allan MacNab, 1839–1849," unpublished M.A. thesis, Queen's University, 1963.

BURCHILL, C. S. "The Evolution of the Cabinet from the Executive Council with Special Reference to Upper Canada," unpublished M.A. thesis, Queen's University, 1930.

JENSEN, V. J. "LaFontaine and the Canadian Union," unpublished M.A. thesis, University of Toronto, 1942.

LONG, D. E. T. "Edward Ellice," unpublished Ph.D. thesis, University of Toronto, 1942.

MOIR, J. S. "The Political Ideas of the *Christian Guardian*, 1829–1849," unpublished M.A. thesis University of Toronto, 1949.

MONET, JACQUES. "The Crown and the Politicians, 1839–1848: A Study of the French Canadian Attitude to the British Connection," unpublished M.A. thesis, University of Toronto, 1961.

INDEX

www.ingramcontent.com/pod-product-compliance
Lightning Source LLC
Chambersburg PA
CBHW080557030426
42336CB00019B/3229